IFLA

International Federation of Library Associations and Institutions
Fédération Internationale des Associations de Bibliothécaires et des Bibliothèques
Internationaler Verband der bibliothekarischen Vereine und Institutionen
Международная Федерация Библиотечных Ассоциаций и Учреждений
Federación Internacional de Asociaciones de Bibliotecarios y Bibliotecas

IFLA Publications 84

Library Preservation and Conservation in the '90s

Proceedings of the Satellite Meeting
of the IFLA Section
on Preservation and Conservation,
Budapest, August 15–17, 1995

Edited by
Jean I. Whiffin and John Havermans

K · G · Saur München 1998

IFLA Publications
edited by Carol Henry

Recommended catalogue entry:

Library preservation and conservation in the '90s : proceedings of the satellite meeting of the IFLA Section on Preservation and Conservation, Budapest, August 15 – 17, 1995 / ed. by Jean I. Whiffin and John Havermans. – München : Saur, 1998. 191 p. 21 cm
(IFLA publications : 84)
ISBN 3-598-21809-5

Die Deutsche Bibliothek – CIP-Einheitsaufnahme

Library preservation and conservation in the '90s : proceedings of the satellite meeting of the IFLA Section on Preservation and Conservation, Budapest, August 15 – 17, 1995 / ed. by Jean I. Whiffin and John Havermans. – München : Saur, 1998
(IFLA publications : 84).
ISBN 3-598-21809-5

∞

Printed on acid-free paper
The paper used in this publication meets the minimum requirements of American National Standard for Information Sciences – Permanence of Paper for Printed Library Materials, ANSI Z39.48.1984.

Printed / Bound by Strauss Offsetdruck GmbH, Mörlenbach

ISBN 3-598-21809-5
ISSN 0344-6891 (IFLA Publications)

TABLE OF CONTENTS

SESSION 2:

Preventive Conservation and Disaster Recovery: Preservation of Collections

SESSION 3:

Mass Conservation: Methods and Dilemmas

SESSION 4:

International and Regional Efforts in Preservation and Access: Training for Preservation and Conservation

SESSION 5:

National and Local Activities in Preservation and Training in Central and Eastern Europe

INTRODUCTION

The 61st Council and General Conference of IFLA was held in Istanbul from August 20-26, 1995 with the theme *Libraries of the Future*. The location, the timing and the conference theme were all appropriate to the organization by the IFLA Section on Conservation (as it was then known) of a satellite meeting in Budapest, Hungary, dealing with the theme of library preservation.

Almost ten years earlier in April 1986 an important conference on the preservation and conservation of library materials had been sponsored jointly by IFLA and UNESCO in Vienna with directors and preservation specialist from the national libraries of the world in attendance. That conference was organized to take stock of the situation in preservation and conservation in the mid-80s and to study preservation methods and problems.

The Budapest satellite meeting in 1995, although more modest in scope, had a similar aim of drawing attention to some of the current issues of library Preservation in the 90s with some attempt to outline potential solutions. The 70 participants represented 27 countries on 4 continents. They were librarians, preservation and conservation experts, and scientists concerned with issues related to library preservation and conservation.

The following five themes of the satellite meeting reflected the most important issues of library preservation in the 90s and were organized in such a way as to outline the problems while providing real or potential solutions.

- National libraries as museums of books and living libraries at the same time, resolving contradictions,
- Preventive conservation and disaster recovery--preservation of collections,
- Mass conservation methods and dilemmas,
- International and regional efforts in preservation and access; training for preservation and conservation, and
- National and local activities in preservation and training in Central and Eastern Europe.

The success of the satellite meeting as well as the completion of the present publication are due to the diligent and generous contributions of members of the Standing Committee of the IFLA Section on Conservation, particularly Diane N. Kresh, Galina Kislovskaya, Jean I. Whiffin, Ralph W. Manning (Secretary) and Beatrix Kastaly (Chair) as well as Marie-Thérèse Varlamoff (Director of the IFLA-Preservation and Conservation Core Programme), and John Havermans of the TNO Institute of Industrial Technology who generously volunteered his time. Special thanks are also due to the 29 speakers.

We acknowledge with thanks all of these contributors as well as colleagues at the National Széchényi Library in Budapest whose contributions made the satellite meeting at the National Library both possible and successful.

Beatrix Kastaly

Chair
IFLA Section on Preservation and Conservation

BOOK MUSEUM OR A BIG RESEARCH LIBRARY? THE DILEMMA OF NATIONAL LIBRARIES

Géza POPRÁDY

National Széchényi Library (Hungary)

INTRODUCTION

I shall try to throw light on the question through the example of the National Széchényi Library and its growing problems in recent years. However, I believe that these problems are not confined to Hungary: they are arising in other national libraries too, even if in slightly different forms. The issue is also reflected in the literature. This is why I am pleased to have the opportunity to address this meeting.

THE BASIC PROBLEM

The basic task of the National Széchényi Library (OSZK) is to collect, process and preserve "for all time" all documents of patriotic interest, known as Hungarica. This is the case for other national libraries too. At the same time, the OSZK is also a functioning big research library, the specialised library for Hungarian literary science and Hungarian history studies. The readers use its documents, which inevitably results in deterioration of their state and is thus contrary to the library's museum function of preserving them.

FACTORS ADDING TO THE PROBLEM

1. In 1985 the OSZK moved into a building of its own - it had previously been a "tenant" of the National Museum - and this also meant a five-fold increase in the number of places available for readers. This resulted in an increase in the number of readers and so in the use - and deterioration - of documents. In 1993 we had 25,000 registered readers who made a total of around 170,000 visits to the national library. In 1994 the corresponding figures were 30,000 readers and 200,000 visits, representing quite a rapid growth.

2. In the new building there are 60,000-70,000 volumes on open shelves in the big reading rooms. The resulting lower level of supervision unfortunately tempts many readers to damage the books (underlining, tearing out pages, etc.) and there has also been an increase in attempted thefts.

3. The number of university and college students in Budapest is steadily increasing. The development of the university libraries is not keeping pace with this growth. As a result, growing numbers of university students are using the OSZK. The number of readers has been increasing steadily since 1985 and within this the proportion of university student readers is also growing: in 1993 more than half of the 25,000 registered readers were university students. In

1994, out of the 30,000 registered readers, 16,500 were university students. It would appear that the university students use the OSZK not only out of necessity: it has become chic to read in the national library and we have become a kind of meeting place for university students.

4. There has been a change of attitude in the management of the national library over the last 8-10 years: many of the top managers - including myself - had previously worked in specialised, technical libraries which were characterised by a service-oriented attitude. My predecessor, Gyula Juhász, who was appointed head of the library in 1986, came from "the other side": he had been an historian using the library. Obviously, he too was a proponent of a reader-friendly, service-oriented library.

5. The growth of air pollution has been contributing to the deterioration of the state of paper-based documents. Unfortunately, the air-conditioners in our storage areas are unable to guarantee the optimal parameters.

WHAT COULD THE SOLUTION BE?

Excluding or strictly selecting readers

There is an opinion among librarians, and especially among researchers belonging to the older generation, that the national library should not be reduced to the level of a public library or a student library: they propose the use of the library should be strictly restricted and, in practice, it should be made available only to scientific researchers. For professional reasons, and on principle, I do not regard this solution as acceptable. Professor Máté Kovács, former head of the department of library science, trained library students in the spirit that a library consists of three components: a classified stock of books, librarians and readers. If any of these is lacking, we cannot speak of a library. I regard this concept as one of the foundations of my work as a librarian. The exception to the principle is that the operation of the national library is financed by the central budget, that is, by the taxpayers' money. I therefore consider that we do not have the right to exclude any adult citizen from the library. Any Hungarian citizen over the age of 18 may be a reader of the National Széchényi Library. It may be possible to direct the reader to other libraries with good advice and persuasion, but administrative means must not be used to achieve this.

Acquisition of separate document copies for the purposes of archive storage and service (use)

This solution is logical and self-evident. Indeed, Ranganathan writes of a three-stage national library system: preservation, storage library, service. The National Széchényi Library has been receiving two deposit copies since 1952: one for museum purposes and one for use. This solution, too, can only be partial. In our case the basic contradiction exists for books published before 1952 and for foreign Hungarica (which we are able to acquire in only a single copy): the same copy has to serve the purpose of archive storage and use.

A frequently proposed solution is to forbid readers to bring their own books into the library and use them there

The proponents of this recommendation anticipate that there would be fewer users of the library. This is probably true. In my opinion, however, the ban would also have the result of even more people using the documents of the national library, in place of their own books.

Complex treatment of the tasks of archive storage, providing services, and preservation and conservation

If we wish to carry out both our archive storage and our service tasks and we do not have at our disposal a separate copy of every document - which is naturally not possible - then it is only by drawing on preservation and conservation that we can meet these requirements. Preservation and conservation have a dual task here: (1) to repair and restore any documents that may have been damaged and to preserve the state of those still in a good (acceptable) condition; (2) to make a copy for use of documents existing in only one copy and which are intended for archive storage.

The progress of technology can bring increasing help for both tasks. On the one hand, the possibilities for restoration are advancing and, on the other hand, the technique of transfer to other information carriers is developing with great speed. The original document can now be substituted or transferred to other information carriers in the following ways:

a) **Facsimile** or reprint edition.
   This is an expensive solution and can only be considered if reissue is financially feasible independent of the library.
b) **Electrostatic copying**.
   This technique is not suitable for the copying of complete volumes - even apart from the copyright problems that arise; it is not recommended for the purpose of preservation.
c) **Microfilm**
d) **Optical disc**

These two procedures can offer a real solution for "copying" and substituting for the original document. The use of microfilm is a well-established practice in Hungary. It is our hope that transfer to optical disc will also become a practice in the near future, although the national library does not yet use this procedure. A number of questions can arise in connection with these two procedures:-

The question of sequence: In what order should we make copies? The practice of the National Széchényi Library is that microfilm copies are systematically made of newspapers and materials in the special collections (in the case of newspapers, for example, we first copied all newspapers from the beginnings up to 1945), and, in the case of books, among the books in circulation (in use by readers) we copy those in a condition justifying this.

The question of preserving the original document: That is, whether we have to preserve only the content of the original document or the actual physical document. This question cannot arise in the case of codices and incunabula, but in the case of newspapers it does. It is the position of the OSZK that everything must be preserved in the original form too, including newspapers. Let me give one concrete example to show that this is not simply respect of tradition, or what could be called a conservative attitude. We had to supply a newspaper published in 1944 for a court case in the United States, so that the age of the paper and printing ink could be examined. This was because a lawyer argued that a newspaper article incriminating his client was not original but had been produced at a later date to "create" evidence. Naturally, the newspaper was shown to be original. But it would not have been possible to prove this on the basis of only film or optical disc.

The question of readers' habits: I presume it is not only in Budapest that readers are not happy if they ask for an old newspaper to read and instead they receive a film and are sent to the microfilm reading room. It is true that they are gradually becoming accustomed to this solution which they find less pleasant (we have acquired considerable experience in the past 40-50 years in becoming accustomed to more unpleasant things) and there are now fewer complaints because of this. But there are always people who would like to get special treatment, on the grounds of health reasons or by referring to librarians they know. We do not yet have experience with readers in the field of optical disc.

Making copies: Naturally, copies cannot be made of documents withdrawn from use by readers; copies may only be made from the material on the new information carriers.

Stricter control in the library: The question of stricter control of readers belongs in the general problem of the preservation of holdings and the provision of services. This is a delicate question because it is difficult to find the borderline where the reader feels that the supervision and control is in his interest too (since the library's documents are being preserved for him too) and does not regard it as harassment. Unfavourable experiences led us to install cameras in the reading rooms in the course of 1994 so that we are better able to prevent damage to books by readers.

SUMMING UP

I am afraid that I have not succeeded in finding the sole ideal solution; probably such a solution does not exist. Nevertheless, I am pleased to have had the opportunity to speak about the question.

BIBLIOGRAPHY

Antonsson, Birgit. "National Libraries", *Librarianship and Information Work Worldwide,* 1993.

Häkli, Esko. "Helsinki University Library", *Alexandria*, 2 (1), 1990.

Jauslin, Jean-Frédéric. "The Swiss National Library", *Alexandria,* 4 (3), 1992.

Line, Maurice B. "Do we need National Libraries, and if so What Sort?", *Alexandria*, 2 (2), 1990.

Line, Maurice B. *National Library and Information Needs: Alternative Means of Fulfilment, with Special Reference to the Role of National Libraries.* (PGI-89/WS/9) Paris: General Information Programme and UNISIST, UNESCO, 1989.

Ranganathan, S.R. "System of National Central Libraries", *Herald of Library Science,* 11 (3), 1972.

Smethurst, J. Michael. "The British Library: A Response to a Set of Questions put by the Organisers of the WESS Seminar", *Collection Management*, 15 (1/2), 1992.

CHRONICLE OF A DISAPPEARING FUTURE: CONSERVATION AND PRESERVATION IN THE ROYAL LIBRARY OF BELGIUM

Wim DE VOS

Bibliothèque Royale Albert 1er (Belgium)

In this paper, I should like to present a few problems with which the Royal Library of Belgium is presently dealing. When the Royal Library was created in 1837, the government considered it as a place of conservation of printed books, but also of manuscripts, maps, drawings, *etc.*, produced in Belgium or in the countries that had been brought together in the Belgian State. The aim was to build a collection as complete as possible, but, and this little sentence is important for my paper, the official text in the *Moniteur belge* foresaw that selection would be inevitable: the head librarian was supposed to propose to the government a list of important books which were not present in the Royal Library, so that they could be bought.

In the following decades, different head librarians dealt with the problem of which books had to be bought: works concerning philosophy or history, works about natural sciences, voluminous works or works with few pages. Had the public to receive what it asked for or did librarians have the right or the duty to make them read things they were not actually looking for? All these questions, which one finds in the annual reports of our library in the nineteenth century, prove that the collection of the Royal Library, which in many domains is an important one, is partly the result of arbitrariness. Even when an important library or specialized library does concentrate on some domains of science, the collection will always be the result, partly at least, of arbitrary choices.

In 1837, the optimistic young Belgian State created its national, its royal library. At the same time, chemists and paper manufacturers were creating something else. In the first decades of the nineteenth century, they decided to substitute wood paper for rag paper. I have been looking over the programme of this conference and concluded that other speakers, more specialized than I, will deal with this nineteenth century innovation. All I want to say is that, at that moment, a virtual catastrophe was born. At the end of the century, only a few persons realized that the real catastrophe had begun. We had to wait until the seventies of this century in the United States, and the eighties in Europe, for alarming reactions, for a kind of civilized panic, which brought together many librarians at the IFLA meeting in Vienna in 1986. Acidification, acid paper, acidified paper, need for deacidification, all these terms became very current in conversation among librarians in a few years' time. However, outside the small world of libraries, until now, few people seem to be aware of the problem, and even less really to worry about it. This allows us to formulate a question, which will also be important for the conclusions I would like to draw: does society really care about conservation in general, and about the conservation of the written word in particular?

But, before asking a few questions about possible aims of conservation, let me invite you on a virtual journey to Brussels. Our journey is also a journey into the past. I will try to expound what has been done so far about conservation in our library, not because I am particularly proud of it, but because I like telling you the truth, because I should like to be informed about the real situation in your libraries, a situation which could be less rosy than declarations of intentions lead us to suppose.

Like every library, the Royal Library of Belgium passed through a period in which real knowledge about conservation physics or conservation chemistry did not exist. Pages were repaired - one called this restoration - with cheap adhesive tape. Covers that came off were re-attached to the book block with a kind of fluid white adhesive, stored in enormous white buckets. Sometimes, covers of the seventeenth or eighteenth century were thrown away and replaced by new ones, preferably of a stiff blue cardboard. Let us not incriminate our predecessors; let us just conclude these things happened almost everywhere. Since then, the history of the book and its binding has become the subject of scientific research. Bookbinding of old, let us say hand-made, books became more an art than a profession. We all know the basic rules of this art: one should respect and conserve as much as possible the original state of each work. As the director of the conservation department in the National Library of the Czech Republic told me, you should restore an old book, you should not make a facsimile of a mediaeval book. The Royal Library of Belgium does not have its own bookbinding or restoration workshop: these activities are contracted out to private restorators or bookbinders. The respect of the general principles is the first criterion in choosing a restorator or a bookbinder for the old or precious books. The price comes second. However, in each important library, millions of books, journals or newspapers are conserved which at the moment seem of little value, but which, in the future, can be unique sources of information for the following generations.

Until a few years ago, for the bookbinding of "banal" books, the Royal Library could spend about 25 million Belgian francs, which is almost one million dollars. Today, this budget has fallen to 12 million Belgian francs. Concerning ordinary preservation bookbinding, a few decisions had to be taken.

First of all, newspapers from abroad were only bought in their microform version, which appeared to be cheaper than buying the paper version and binding it. For the Belgian papers, which the Royal Library obtains through legal deposit, we continue binding, but, for newspapers with various editions each day (regional editions, or morning, noon and afternoon editions), we only bind one version: the others are conserved in the book stocks, in packets.

For the scientific journals, we can operate in a more selective way. Everything need not be bound to make conservation possible; every year of each journal need not be a separate volume. We should bear in mind different criteria: the solidity of the original cover of each journal issue, its number of pages, the actual importance of the journal (which determines the frequency of consultation and the rapidity of deterioration), the language (journals in languages which are not currently read by our readers, such as texts in non-Roman alphabets, will not receive preferential treatment).

Another general rule is that monographs will not be bound any more. However, the criteria mentioned for the journals can be taken into account: a dictionary published as a paperback, present in the reference library and often consulted by readers or staff, will receive a solid binding as soon as possible.

Nevertheless, the percentage of our budget spent each year on ordinary bookbinding is much higher than in most university libraries. This is a consequence of our legal role as a conservation library: a judicious bookbinding is the most elementary preservation measure that can be taken in order to avoid conservation being compromised from the beginning.

In the field of preservation, deacidification of books printed on wood paper seems to be by far the most discussed topic of the last year. Our head librarian asked me in January 1994 to start reading about all these techniques. With the help of my brother, a chemist, I read a lot of excellent studies about them, some written by librarians or other scientists I will have the pleasure of meeting here in Budapest. But this did not bring me to a solution.

I read the already historical overviews of different techniques, some of them working only partially, others containing chlorofluorocarbons (CFC) which damage the ozone layer, others modifying the colour of the white pages into yellow or brown, others creating other destructive processes, others attacking the printer's ink, *etc.* The diethylzinc (DEZ) method, developed by the Library of Congress, seemed to convince everybody at the beginning of the nineties. But a study by Astrid-Christiane Brandt of the Bibliothèque Nationale de France concluded that this technique causes a photochemical degradation of the paper.[1] Furthermore, this technique seemed to be quite explosive. According to persistent rumours, in the test phase of this method a collection of dummies was destroyed by the fire after an explosion. I do not know whether this is true. The Library of Congress and AKZO Chemicals opened a deacidification unit in Houston, Texas, which closed some years ago. Originally, it seemed desirable to install a deacidification unit for the DEZ method in Europe, at first in Germany, afterwards in The Netherlands. Mr. Pattavina, responsible for AKZO Europe, working in The Netherlands, told me this unit was never opened, because of lack of interest on the part of libraries. Why are we not interested any more in this deacidification unit? Is the price to be paid too high? Did the doubts about the efficiency of the system decide libraries not to adopt it? I should like to know the answer, but the report of the Bellagio Conference, organized in 1993 by the Commission on Preservation and Access, during which the European Commission on Preservation and Access was founded, concluded that all the existing systems for deacidification needed to be improved.[2] A report of the same year, published by the Dutch Coördinatiepunt Nationaal Conserveringsbeleid (CNC), a collaboration between the Dutch Royal Library and Royal Archives, concluded that "there is no single method pre-eminently suitable for mass conservation".[3] Like other studies, this text emphasizes the fact that deacidification techniques stop the deterioration process, but do not reinforce the paper. A library is not a museum. Why spend money to deacidify our brittle books, when, after new manipulation by the inevitable readers, the pages will continue to be destroyed? Last year, a very interesting conference in Delft, organized by Dr John Havermans from TNO Papier en Karton, put forward that all the deacidification systems, tested in a project financed partly by DGX and DGXII of the European Commission, were stopped by their owners and needed urgent new developments.

At the moment, the Royal Library of Belgium sees two reasons for optimism in the field of deacidification. The German procedure developed by the Deutsche Bibliothek and the Battelle firm did not entirely convince the experts of the above-mentioned CNC. In Belgium, some book conservators are enthusiastic about the Bookkeeper system, especially for manual deacidification of single pieces. The Royal Library will ship some books overseas for a test, but I have not yet found time to do this.

Anyway, if we can still believe that the price of deacidification per item varies between 5 and 10 dollars[4], the Royal Library cannot afford massive treatment of its brittle books. Studies by the Institut Royal du Patrimoine Artistique put forward that, in our collections, 70% of the books acquired since 1800 - this means two million books or almost half our collection - are brittle or are getting brittle.[5] Total cost of the deacidification operation (without reinforcement of the pages!): 10 to 20 million dollars. We do not have this money. And I became even more doubtful about deacidification in the month of May, when two leading persons of the Bibliothèque Nationale de France told our head librarian and me that the various techniques do stop a deterioration process, but cause still worse destruction of the paper at its molecular level.

At the moment, we cannot appeal to deacidification for mass preservation. So, as the CNC in The Hague advised us to do, we go on microfilming our brittle items. At the moment, microfilming is the official preservation measure of our institution. Our actual films are of a quality which guarantees three to five centuries of conservation. At the moment, the Royal Library is working on two projects in the field of microfilming. The first has nothing to do with brittle books, but should not be forgotten. For a few years, a special budget from the Minister of Scientific Policy has allowed us to microfilm systematically all our precious manuscripts, so that the originals only have to leave the book stocks in very exceptional cases, even though students do not easily accept this obligation to work with a microfilm, and not with a prestigious mediaeval manuscript. The other project is much more problematic, and even when the items to be filmed are much more recent, the project itself already has a long history.

In the sixties, the bad condition of the collections of newspapers brought together representatives of the most important libraries in Belgium. The purpose was to assemble complete collections of newspapers with the newspapers conserved in these libraries. A mother-film, from which different positive films were going to be taken, had to be made. The principles were good, the will even better, the chosen method seemed alright, and there were certainly no financial problems. And yet the project was a failure. Now, thirty years later, when we analyze the reasons for this failure, we always come to the same conclusion: this global, national approach was not flexible enough to allow an easy running of things.

In 1990, the Royal Library of Belgium started a new microfilming project. But, at that time, all cultural institutions had financial difficulties. Thanks to a subvention of 7 million Belgian francs (about 230,000 dollars) from the National Lottery (a very important Maecenas in Belgium), the Library had been able to buy cameras and to hire some people to make films. To be sure not to make the same mistakes as in the past, the chosen approach was of a very modest kind.

The Royal Library still worked together with other libraries, but in a more limited way: we tried to exchange some newspapers with the Parliament Library, or with the liberal and socialist archives, two scientific institutions for historical research. The Royal Library made films of their newspapers, leaving them a copy, or it made a positive of their negative master copies. Other ways of co-operation were also taken into consideration: if local authorities want to acquire for their own libraries the microfilm of a newspaper they do not possess in its entirety and the Royal Library owns an almost complete collection of this newspaper, they can send some staff members to film

themselves the entire collection, using the cameras of the Royal Library. They can keep a positive of the film but have to leave the master film in the Royal Library.
Thanks to efforts during several years, the Library was able to compile a small catalogue of microfilms of newspapers existing in Belgian libraries: this modest brochure just wants to simplify and promote co-operation.

Yet the budgetary problems became more and more serious, while the newspapers continued deteriorating at an even quicker rate. The subvention of the National Lottery that started the whole project expired last year. The Royal Library could only re-engage one single person on its own funding. The main problem is that subventions of the National Lottery have to be employed for infrastructure, not for paying staff members. I wonder whether in other countries this problem also exists: in the case of microfilming - impossible without sufficient staff - it causes many problems.

In January 1994, Mr. Frans Van Wijnsberghe, director of the Newspapers and Journals section in the Royal Library, took the initiative of bringing together, for the first time for thirty years, persons from Belgian institutions possessing important collections of newspapers, to attempt restarting a new common project.

These persons agreed with a first preparatory step. Since ignorance of the collections of other libraries remains one of the most important obstacles for eventual co-operation, the various institutions agreed to try to enter their various newspapers, particularly their historical collections, into the catalogue-network which links most of the libraries. When this catalogue is made, the next step, a rational co-operation in microfilming, can be considered. But, one-and-a-half years after this new beginning, this collective catalogue does not yet exist. The Royal Library is one of those responsible for this lack of success: it does not have the staff to enter in the computer its thousands and thousands of newspaper titles; and problems with the conversion from one automation system to another seem to make it impossible to catalogue newspapers in the necessary format.

Here I have to speak about EROMM, the European Register of Microform Masters. The official intention of the Belgian libraries is to send their newspaper microfilms data, which will be entered in their collective catalogue, to EROMM. The Royal Library will assume the role of go-between. But, as I said, at the moment our newspapers have not been catalogued in the computer. And still another problem exists: to allow exchanges, EROMM has developed a very specific UNIMARC format for microfilms. The last meeting of the Steering Committee, on April 28 in The Hague, dealt with very detailed cataloguing problems. It is obvious to me that, with its actual human resources, the Royal Library will never be able to respect all these rules. And I hereby ask the big brothers in the European library field not to forget their little sisters: at the moment, EROMM is not yet operational. If I am well informed, a real exchange of microfilms (free of charge or not) is not yet taking place between the partners. In the future, if the microfilm cataloguing format becomes too complicated, small libraries could be afraid of joining the EROMM libraries. I hope this register, which could be extremely useful, will not be the victim of its own perfectionism.

The Royal Library of Belgium became a somewhat hesitant partner of EROMM after having been a partner in the MICROLIB project, financed mainly by the European Commission (DGXIII), the German "Land" Niedersächsen and the Dutch library automation group PICA. The third MICROLIB conference was organized in Brussels, in September 1994. The theme of the conference was: "Between microforms and digitizing: which way to the future?". In the discussions, it appeared that you cannot invest all the little money you have in one technique.

But, on the other hand, it seemed entirely clear that, at this moment, the cost of digitizing a book is much higher than the cost of microfilming it. According to the delegate of the Sercu firm, involved in both domains, microfilming is ten times cheaper than digitizing: the problem in digitizing is that, after the OCR (Optical Character Recognition) phase, one has to go back to an ICR (Intelligent Character Recognition) programme, in order to introduce a little structure in the scanned texts, indispensable if readers have to consult them. The conference participants visited the firm Xerox Engineering Systems. It was obvious that their docuplex software is merely an office management programme. For millions of books, it seemed to be too elementary. The main argument of most librarians in favour of microfilming was that it seemed to be a necessary intermediate step before digitizing. So, anyway, our actual microfilming efforts should not be useless.

As far as I know, no library already uses scanning for systematic and massive preservation aims. But, for a few months, adherents of an immediate digitizing made me doubt about these MICROLIB conclusions. Digitizing should be much less expensive than I thought. The microfilm is not a useful intermediate process before scanning: scanning a microfilm should even be more difficult than scanning a paper version of a text. This debate is a good example of the difficult situation in which librarians can find themselves. I am not a specialist in computers or image recognition. I am not a specialist in microfilming. I only know that both techniques cost a lot. With my head librarian and my colleagues, I want to make a good choice for a collection we are proud of and we love. But each choice we make is condemned by a part of the so-called specialists. I believe that, for this kind of situation, dictionaries contain the words "desperate" and "frustration".

As I already told you, we are not a rich library. We lack human resources, and we also lack money. But I believe these two main problems exist in all libraries over the world. We cannot start massive preservation campaigns. However, what we try to do is sensitization. We try to explain, not only to readers, researchers and other scientists, but to everyone, what is happening with our library collection.

A few years ago, the Royal Library, together with the Institut Royal du Patrimoine Artistique, organized an exhibition concerning book deterioration and restoration. The exhibition covered all kinds of book material, from all periods. In February and March 1995, we had another exhibition about book deterioration, concentrated this time on the books printed after 1840. We showed the contrast between the conservation state of a manuscript, a printed book from the sixteenth century, and a book published in 1940. We juxtaposed two volumes of the same newspaper, one cataloguing newspapers of 1830, the other being newspapers of 1880. This exhibition was opened at our yearly Open House day, which attracted more than 3,000 persons. Five or six newspapers published an important article on it. Regional radio and TV spoke about it in their news flashes and, in the following weeks, in their cultural programmes. On the evening of our Open House day, 700,000 people who watched the television news of the national Dutch-speaking broadcasting centre learned about the conservation catastrophe. Our head librarian and I published a booklet, printed in 1,000 copies, about the history of paper and the causes of the actual paper disease. All 1,000 copies, which were available for 50 BEF (1.70 dollars) have been sold. A few weeks ago, we printed it again[6]. But did all these activities change anything?

In order to prevent the problem for the next generations of books, one could publish them on acid-free paper, permanent paper as it is sometimes called. According to its aim of sensitization, on March 17, 1995, the Royal Library organized a conference on permanent paper. One of the speakers was Mr. Walckiers, of the European Foundation for Library Cooperation, an organization which is working hard to make known the existence and availability of permanent paper. We invited specialists in paper manufacture, representatives of book and newspaper publishers, printers, and a Dutch archivist, specialist in norms for permanent paper. The conclusion of this conference was that acid-free paper cannot be used for newspapers: all kinds of papers are getting more and more expensive; all newspapers are losing readers and advertising funds because of the growth of audio-visual media. Printing a few copies of each edition on permanent paper is technically impossible, because of the strength of the rotary press, producing thousands of copies immediately after having started the printing process. For newspapers, it seems clear that electronic media, CD-ROM, online databases, even floppies, will be the conservation supports of the future. For books, this is not so evident. Books can be printed on acid-free paper, and they will cost only a little more. Strictly speaking, the price of permanent paper should not be higher than the price of "normal", *i.e.* acid paper. All depends on the demand: when libraries, publishers, printers, ask for acid-free paper, the paper factories will consider it a current product that does not have to be separately ordered; when it will no more constitute a separate, small and annoying stock, its price will go down automatically. The results of our conference will be published in the month of September, by Editions Grama, a publisher working in Paris and Brussels, who has started a literary series containing re-editions of novels published in the first decades of the twentieth century. The aim of this campaign was to sensitize participants, especially printers and publishers, to the problem. But two categories of people almost did not show up at our conference: indeed, printers and publishers.

But is our current offset paper really acid? Many tests prove that this current paper, especially when produced in Germany or in the Scandinavian countries, is almost always pH-neutral. So, according to some chemists, there is no real difference between this kind of paper and others, sold as "acid-free" and five times as expensive. Moreover, according to some chemists, chemistry is not yet capable of making a complete analysis of all substances present in a sheet of paper. Furthermore, some paper factories are reported to cheat: during the production they should add a substance which covers up the acidity of the paper - a practice I am tempted to compare with the abuse of drugs by certain sportsmen. The Royal Library tries to participate in an honest debate, but cannot be sure that every participant is playing an honest game.

CONCLUSION

The Royal Library, with modest means, has undertaken a lot of efforts in the conservation and preservation field. We are making efforts to save a collection, constituted in an arbitrary way, for following generations. The ancestors of these following generations, the society of today, does not really seem to care about this. So why should we care about it? Suppose that, in 1850, the head librarian decided to buy a book by Mr. Dupont, and not to buy a book by Mr. Ducart. The book by Mr. Ducart does not exist any more, so is it so important to save a book, which can be a stupid publication, by an unknown Mr. Dupont? I think it is. Maybe Mr. Dupont was more intelligent than we can understand; maybe his work will be important one day for the history of sciences. Maybe the head librarian of 1850 has taken a subjective but very wise decision. Maybe Mr. Dupont is warning society against some hidden dangers. Maybe he is explaining ideologies we should be afraid of. Maybe the book contains a joke, unknown nowadays, which will make millions of people laugh in the coming generations. I think our duty is to work for the preservation of our complete collection. But, on the other hand, we do not have to be desperate when items arrive at the point of no return without having been microfilmed or scanned. We cannot do miracles. That is why we do not have to feel ashamed. Maybe society has other priorities (medical or environmental research, social programmes, school financing, etc.) than the saving of unknown books. This is a fact libraries have to accept. We all are glad when medicine is making progress. But let us hope the results of this innovative research will be published on permanent paper.

REFERENCES

1. Brandt, Astrid-Christiane. *La Désacidification de Masse du Papier.* Paris: Bibliothèque Nationale, 1992, p. 21.

2. Commission on Preservation and Access. *Preserving the Intellectual Heritage. A Report of the Bellagio Conference, June 7-10, 1993.* Washington, D.C.: October 1993, p. 19.

3. Coördinatiepunt Nationaal Conserveringsbeleid. *The Future of our Paper Past. Final Report of the National Preservation Office of the Netherlands (CNC) on the Mass Conservation Trial Programme.* (CNC Publications, 5) The Hague: CNC, 1993, pp. 4-7.

4. This seemed to be the average cost in 1993.

5. Liénardy, Anne and Philippe Van Damme. *Papier en Péril. Papier in Gevaar.* Brussels: Institut Royal du Patrimoine Artistique, 1994, pp. 27-28, 53-54.

6. Cockshaw, Pierre and Wim De Vos. *Petite Histoire du Papier et de son Impossible (?) Conservation.* Brussels: Bibliothèque Royale de Belgique, 1995.

PERMANENT PAPER: MYTH OR REALITY, DREAM OR NECESSITY?

Marc WALCKIERS

European Foundation for Library Cooperation (Belgium)

INTRODUCTION

Since the end of the last century, several American librarians have been intrigued by the sight of books produced in the last few decades being in an inferior state to older ones, but it was only just before 1980 that the cause and the magnitude of this major cultural disaster were understood by the majority of North American librarians.

THE CAUSE

In order to meet the growing demands for paper in the larger European countries in the middle of industrialization, European chemists launched, about 1840, the production of paper from wood, which quickly took over the rags used since the invention of paper but which no longer met the demand and had become more and more expensive.

But, until recently, nobody realised that:

- the cellulose fibre of wood is less strong and smaller (up to ten times smaller) and therefore much less resistant than that of textiles;
- wood consists of 25% lignin, which is an acid which stiffens, weakens and destroys the cellulose fibres of paper;
- alum, which for the past 150 years has been the principal component of paper paste made from wood, transforms itself eventually into sulphuric acid on contact with damp, which contributes further to the brittleness and destruction of cellulose fibres of paper;
- heat, the chlorine used to bleach the paper, and the pollution from cities, further destroy cellulose fibres.

This is how paper produced in the last 150 years from wood is a victim of a real but imperceptible phenomenon, that of auto-destruction resulting in a slow but irremediable combustion of its components with oxygen and ambient humidity.

The phenomenon has been known for a long time by the chemists in the paper industry, as has the method of producing lasting paper such as paper for share certificates or State documents, of which the composition has been well-ordered for over a century!

THE MAGNITUDE OF THE DISASTER

American librarians rapidly measured the magnitude of the disaster: a quarter of the 305 million volumes of North American libraries, *i.e.*, 78 million volumes, have become brittle and are about to fall to dust, whereas a large part of the remainder will inevitably suffer the same fate if nothing is done to save them.

In Europe, the library authorities have established more recently that the situation is also dramatic:

- 40 out of 152 million volumes in German research libraries need urgent treatment if they are not to disappear;
- the library experts from 13 European countries who met in The Hague in December 1991 also concluded that 25% of the written heritage is no longer in a fit state to be read, nor will it survive much longer, and that a large part of the remainder of publications from the last 150 years will suffer the same fate in the medium term if nothing is done to save them.

The situation of our affluent society and, in particular, the information world, is plainly that of being virtually deprived of the original texts from our greatest scholars and poets of the last 150 years, texts which risk not being known in future except for sparse snatches and quotes, as is the case with literary and scientific texts from antiquity which were lost in the fires of the famous library of Alexandria.

PREVENTION: PERMANENT PAPER

In the face of this alarming discovery, American library authorities are merited with rapidly controlling the cause of the problem. Since the beginning of the 1980s, they have managed to:

- draw attention to the subject through the media, and convince numerous authors to demand from their publishers that they print their books on acid-free paper;
- create since 1984 a national standard for "permanent paper";
- persuade the majority of American publishers to use permanent paper for all publications destined to last;
- get a resolution adopted by the Association of American Publishers to this effect;
- get Congress and the majority of States to pass a vote demanding the printing of official documents on permanent paper.

In barely five or six years, the battle for permanent paper was won in the U.S.A.; since 1989 practically all American publishers of works of lasting interest print them only on permanent paper.

THE TREATMENT OF BRITTLE BOOKS

What remains is, of course, the preservation of publications which have become brittle over the past 150 years.

The first method is by microfilming, which is the most current. An alternative and more recent method is by digitization through scanning and transfer to optical discs. But both methods mostly entail the destruction of the originals, as they cannot withstand the inevitable handling. The only method which preserves the original document is the mass deacidification by various chemical processes.

However:-

- deacidified books remain fragile;
- deacidified paper is often browned and the colours and binding often deteriorate;
- the chemical processes used are dangerous: grave risk of explosion, threats to the ozone layer, and the greenhouse effect.

Nevertheless, despite considerable federal and private funding and a remarkable coordination drive at North American level, experts agree that a maximum third of the threatened writings can be saved.

IN EUROPE

In Europe, the authorities of the largest libraries have gradually been made aware of the problem of brittle books identified and treated with the greatest effect and publicized by their American colleagues. Furthermore, an international meeting was organised in 1987 in Vienna on this subject.

But, in Europe, efforts have been concentrated on microfilming, digitization and deacidification, prevention through printing on permanent paper not having played a part in efficient campaigns. In particular, the following should be noted:-

- the process of deacidification of acid books developed by Battelle in Frankfurt and ready to treat 400,000 books a year for the price of DM13 per book in Leipzig, but without being able to avoid the inconveniences quoted above;
- the European Register of Microform Masters - which has the great merit of existing to avoid double usage - only registered in 1993 (after 5 years) 50,000 publications ...

That is to say that the methods used are very insufficient, while hundreds of thousands of books are under threat in European libraries ... It must be said that, in Europe, public funds destined for preservation are negligible and private funds virtually non-existent.

Therefore, while European libraries only deserve minimal credit for their preservation efforts for brittle books, they generally do not appear concerned to halt the printing of new books on paper containing acid (in continental Europe at least!). This situation is, moreover, more absurd as the adoption of permanent paper by publishers would not cost anything. In addition, in not making any effort to halt the production of new books still printed on acid paper, library authorities are giving their financing bodies an excellent reason not to pour their funds into a bottomless pit!

This is actually the paradox:-

- approximately a billion books from the past 150 years are threatened with extinction very shortly in European libraries, which will result in the irremediable loss of a large part of our cultural heritage;
- the means put into practice to save them in Europe are ridiculous;
- the library authorities have not yet taken the initiative of an efficient campaign to halt the printing of books on paper containing acid in continental Europe, whilst acid-free and permanent book paper is widely available.

THE EUROPEAN FOUNDATION FOR LIBRARY COOPERATION (EFLC)

To get out of this impasse, EFLC proposed in 1992 the publication of a *European Directory of Acid-Free and Permanent Book Paper* to be distributed widely and free of cost within the book sector in Europe, which was carried out in1993 with the support of the European Commission.

In 1994, this *Directory* was re-edited and 10,000 copies distributed throughout the book sector in Europe, thanks to contributions from paper manufacturers who were mentioned in it. In this *Directory* are to be found technical descriptions of 100 different types of permanent book papers with the names and addresses of the 23 manufacturers in 10 European countries.

Effectively, for more than 15 years, the paper industry has spontaneously initiated a reconversion of its production lines in acid environment to production lines in neutral environment at a price completely competitive, thanks to the low cost of calcium carbonate being used in paste in a neutral environment.

Moreover, after a process entailing several years and involving 20-odd countries, the International Organization for Standardization officially published in March 1994 an international standard for permanent paper.

Finally, the main European scientific publishers, aware of the demands of American libraries, did not have difficulty in printing their publications on permanent paper in Europe and have never complained about the quality or the price.

Permanent paper is therefore a reality which is completely plain and concrete.

THE PRICES

Nothing fluctuates more than the price of paper, not only with time, but also for the same type of paper at any given time according to the quantity ordered, the desired substance, the intermediary chosen, *etc.*

In fact, with the production of large quantities, the prices of permanent paper and acid paper hardly differ (5% maximum according to PRAS, 1990, but mostly around 1%) and are therefore negligible for the author.

Furthermore, the production in a neutral environment continues to grow naturally, especially in Scandinavia, to the extent that certain publishers, having selected a paper for purely aesthetic reasons or having left free choice to their printer, realised that their books were being printed on permanent paper without their prior knowledge.

However, there remains the question of finding a means to increase the demand: each printer or other supplier will react favourably to an isolated demand for small quantities of acid-free paper or other little-used paper and will not hesitate to increase his price, both to amortise his costs and the resulting complications of stocking a new product and to discourage the client.

Likewise, the publisher who is above all a business man is not usually interested in the negligible purchasing power of European libraries or in the problems of auto-destruction of brittle books published 50 or 100 years ago. He will most frequently only regard the problematic of acid versus permanent paper as a moral constraint which can only cause complications and supplementary expense ...

It is therefore indispensable to:

- widen the demand by a media campaign on a sufficiently large scale, *i.e.*, a supranational scale in Europe;
- emphasize amongst authors and publishers the threat of acid paper for the survival of our cultural heritage over the coming centuries and the moral obligation of producers and distributors to respect the moral rights of authors to be read by future generations;
- initialise the demand through wide appeals for quotations for the supply of large quantities of book paper, and preferably for collective appeals, or those co-ordinated by groups of public or private publishers;
- expand the requests for quotations to producers or wholesalers in neighbouring countries producing or consuming acid-free book paper.

CHECKING THE COMPLIANCE WITH THE PERMANENT PAPER STANDARD

Checking the acidity of paper is very easy: it suffices to use a felt-tip pen whose colour varies according to the degree of acidity.

Furthermore, manufacturers distribute widely their technical specifications and their papers. Considering the enormous quantities of paper emanating from each production chain, it should be absolutely exceptional that a manufacturer takes the risk of discrediting himself and of discrediting his production by deceiving distributors and consumers concerning the quality of his product.

On the other hand, a supplier confronted with the wish of a client not particularly *au fait* with technical peculiarities of paper may risk being less scrupulous.

Various measures allow the improvement of the visibility and credibility of permanent paper:-

- the use of the permanent paper logo on technical papers or packaging, as a watermark in the paper, or by printing it in a suitable place on printed books;
- the use of the expertise of an independent laboratory to confirm complete compliance with the permanent paper standard when ordering large quantities.

CONCLUSION

I hope that I have managed to present succinctly:

- the discovery and the magnitude of the cultural disaster which brittle books present;
- the lack of means to remedy this situation in Europe;
- the imperative need to promote the use of permanent paper amongst European publishers to avoid aggravating the disaster, and to demonstrate that the evil can be easily avoided for new books.

THE SPANISH REGISTER OF REPRODUCTIONS

Francisca HERNÁNDEZ and Xavier AGENJO

National Library of Spain

The growing expansion of microfilming and digitization procedures in Spanish libraries is giving rise to great progress in the use and availability of preservation resources in Spain.[1] However, this growth has not occurred within a general framework of cooperative use of the existing resources, and has not therefore involved optimizing them. In order to explain this situation and to subsequently put forward a solution, we must briefly mention the development of Spanish libraries in the last ten years.[2]

The present position of Spanish libraries shows several peculiarities, mostly caused by the way in which the technological modernization of the libraries has been carried out, and by the actual development of the offer of computer technology in the Spanish market.

The automation of Spanish libraries began with great enthusiasm during the second half of the 1980s in a non-generalized way, since comparably a large part of the financial resources was used for the necessary renovation and expansion of the existing libraries and the creation of new ones: construction of new buildings or remodeling of existing ones, renewal of collections, increase in the number of librarians, etc. The above has resulted in a radical change in the Spanish libraries' panorama with regard to the number of libraries, their ability to deal with the users, the diversification of services, etc. It has also been a result of the initiatives undertaken, in a different way, by all the public administrations involved in library development: Ministry of Culture, Universities, Autonomous Communities and Local Administration.

From this initial state, automation has basically consisted of the computerization of the most urgent library processes such as cataloguing, acquisitions or loan. For whomever it is useful, it should be said that, due to a lack of planned management in the development of the computerization of the Spanish library system, this process has depended to a large extent on the existing offer of information technology in the national market. One of the characteristics of the latter (and that which has had the most influence in subsequent development) has been the lack of standardization. For several years the Spanish market has been a secondary market for the sale of library management systems which are not adapted to Spanish needs, or even obsolete in other countries. Undoubtedly, planning at national level of the automation of libraries would have reduced these problems, and, in fact, at the end of the 1980s and at the beginning of the 1990s, this panorama began to change with the development of an automation plan for Public Libraries influenced by the computerization of the National Library[3] in the Spanish library environment.

In the same way, the experience acquired by Spanish librarians during these years has called for a decided change towards standardization in the computer technology market.

We must take into account that the introduction of the IBERMARC[4] format is still not generalized, which is delaying the construction of union catalogues, and, as a result, the setting-up of cooperative access to information and documents programmes.[5] The decisive influence which bibliographic control and the exchange of information have over the information preserved is one of the greatest points of interest to be mentioned within the framework of this meeting.

As can be understood in this situation, the introduction of reproduction technology of bibliographic materials to be preserved, whether it be microfilming or digitization, has gone behind the above-mentioned changes, in such a way that, when Spanish libraries have been able to finance preservation programmes, the market has spectacularly developed image management systems to which it is possible to gain access both locally and remotely.[6] In fact, the controversy between microfilming and digitization has not even taken place at a national level, as only a few centers (amongst them the large libraries and national archives) have been able to develop microfilming programmes, which is why there are no large collections of microfilm except in these centers.[7]

In recent years there has not even been a national microfilming plan for newspapers.[8] However, the individual intervention of librarians has to a large extent limited the problems of duplication. The technological change which has occurred in Spain has been so sudden and so quick that we have practically gone from nothing to digitization.[9] This very quick technological change has the advantage that we do not need to make a great effort, and we are still talking on a national level, to create and develop digitization programmes or to reconvert the collection of microfilms to a digital format, which is why more and more institutions will join in this process.

It is not a question of discussing herein the advantages and disadvantages of one type of technology or another, rather the way in which we must deal with cooperation between Spanish libraries at a national level in order to share the resources to be used to preserve information. The obstacles are not attributable in any way to technology, but to the bibliographic tools available for existing reproductions or those underway, and to the habits acquired in handling the reproduction programmes of holdings which show a lack of coordination and information.

If there is one field of library work which has remained apart from cooperative efforts it must undoubtedly be the non-existence of a national catalogue of microforms, or reproductions, and in a parallel way of a national microfilming plan. It is hoped that this point will be solved with the creation of a Spanish Register of Reproductions (RER) which, like the European Register of Microform Masters (EROMM), provides detailed information on copies which are being preserved.

In the same way the RER has to be the nucleus around which the development of a true national reproductions plan revolves, including both microfilming and digitization programmes of photographic reproductions, and extendible to all existing bibliographic materials reproduced in Spanish libraries. At present the design of the Memoria Hispánica project has been started, which will have to gather together the digitization of the fundamental works of Spanish culture.

For this purpose, and along the basic guidelines put forward by UNESCO in its Memory of the World programme, it firstly involves establishing what is the extent, condition and degree of distribution of what we can call the national collection of reproductions.

The aim of the proposal for the setting-up of a Spanish Register of Reproductions, which the National Library is carrying out, is to install a bibliographic control mechanism of reproductions which will make it possible to share the available resources and means a real tool for access to documents.[10]

It therefore involves knowing exactly the environment in which we move, concerning which there is a great lack of knowledge. For this purpose a questionnaire [11] has been prepared which will extract the following information[12]:-

1. Extent of the national collection of reproductions:-
   - Number of reproductions, since at a national level the extent of the collection of reproductions is not known.
   - Type of existing reproductions.

2. Technical and human resources available:-
   - In order to set up the centers or libraries with human and technical resources available to carry out reproductions and their capacity to deal with other libraries in their environment.

3. Availability of reproductions, although there are no permanent laboratories.

4. Extent to which commercial microfilming services are used.

5. Knowledge of work procedures, *i.e.*, degree of prior treatment of the documentation, the existence or non-existence of specifications for microfilming, to establish the degree of standardization of the processes and to assess the quality of the reproductions which are being carried out.

6. Degree of conformity with the international standards on microfilming.

7. Extent to which the collections are integrated to establish basic exchange nuclei.

8. Existence of printed or automated catalogues or bibliographic references of reproductions for the control of reproductions at a national level, including the level of bibliographic description and the relationship established between bibliographic and holdings information.

9. Storage conditions.

10. Short- or medium-term holdings reproduction programmes and the extent to which they are continued, including cooperative programmes.

11. Level of exchange of reproductions and possibilities envisaged of access for existing reproductions.

The setting-up of the ex-novo RER also forces us to ask ourselves what the degree of standardization is in the exchange of bibliographic information, in particular in the exchange of holdings records, and what are the bibliographic tools available for all types of bibliographic materials upon which to establish the RER.

Since 1986 we have had the Union Catalogue of Patrimonio Bibliográfico, a database with 162,150 bibliographic records, and 265,210 holdings all over Spain, which would cover the identification of monographs prior to 1830. Serials are described in the Union Catalogue of Serials database (100,000 bibliographic records and 340,000 holdings), and with respect to modern monographs, the National Library's database, ARIADNA, will offer more than one million bibliographic descriptions once the reconversion of its General Index of Prints is complete. In the same way, ARIADNA can serve as a basic source for obtaining bibliographic records for monographs after 1984, sound and videotape recordings.

We discover therefore that, more than bibliographic descriptions, it is a question of defining the method of obtaining information on holdings (information which to our way of thinking must be completely separate from bibliographic information) since it allows a greater flexibility at the time of information exchange. Owing to the foregoing, the RER would form a type of subgroup and at the same time an extension of the union catalogues already in existence in Spain.

For the record of reproductions we have opted for using the MARC holdings format[13], which would mean the preparation of guidelines for its application. This will entail checking the use of specific fields in order for information on digital reproductions (as detailed as those which can be coded in field 007 of physical description) to be included, in such a way that the level of resolution used, the coding scheme, the exchange of images format, the type of compression and the storage support can be indicated.

Finally, and strongly linked to the Union Catalogue of Serials[14], is the Directory of Spanish Libraries[15], a database which can be extended with general information on the cooperative or non-cooperative programmes of reproductions which are being carried out by Spanish libraries.

REFERENCES

1. It is necessary to add to the already known digitization programme of the Archivo de Indias other great projects such as those of the National Library (*cf.* note 4) or that of the library of the Universidad Complutense of Madrid. This year this particular library started an interesting digitization project called DIOSCÓRIDES in order to create an electronic library with 13,000 works of biomedical interest printed from the 15th to the 18th centuries. *Proyecto Dioscórides*. Aurora Miguel Alonso, directora del Proyecto, Pilar Moreno García, coordinadora técnica y J. Carlos Regidor, Servicios Informáticos. Madrid: Universidad Complutense, 1995.

2. Various studies have been published in conjunction on the position of libraries in Spain, especially those promoted by the European Union; however, they draw considerable blanks. Cf. *Estado actual de la aplicación de las nuevas tecnologías de la información en las biobliotecas y su impacto sobre el funcionamiento bibliotecario, puesta al día: LIB-2/13 update (Spain)*. Por Purificación Moscoso, Yolanda Ríos García; coordinación, Miguel Jiménez. Madrid: Fesabid, 1992. ISBN 84-604-2167-8.

Progress in that field could be followed also in ELAG's reports. The last one describes on pages 137-144 the Spanish scenario: *Library Services in an electronic environment: 18th Library Systems Seminar, Budapest 27-29 April 1994.* Editor, Màrta Sipor. Budapest: National Széchényi Library, 1994. ISBN 963-200-345-4.

3. One of the most important effects of the computerization process of the National Library has been the thorough incorporation of international bibliographic standards on the exchange of information.
Cf. Agenjo, Xavier. " La Biblioteca Nacional y la normativa internacional para el intercambio de información bibliográfica", *Boletín de la ANABAD*, ISSN 0210-0614, 39: 3/4 (July/Dec. 1989), pp. 519-526.

4. *Formato IBERMARC para registros bibliográficos*. 5th ed. Madrid: Biblioteca Nacional, 1996. ISBN 84-88699-19-0.

5. Agenjo, Xavier. *Normas vigentes: presente y perspectivas de los proyectos SR e ILL. Seminario sobre redes de Comunicación Interbibliotecarias*. Madrid: Ministerio de Cultura; FUNDEBI; Junta de Comunidades de Castilla-La Mancha, 1994, pp. 51-56.

6. Cf. Agenjo, Xavier and Francisca Hernández. "The Digitization of Library Materials in the National Library of Spain", *LIBER Quarterly*, 4 (1994), pp. 144-153. The corrected and very extended Spanish version of this paper at the LIBER Annual General Conference in 1994 can be read in the *Boletín de la ANABAD*, ISSN 0210-4164, 45:3 (Julio/Sept. 1995), pp. 77-94.

7. "El Servicio Nacional de Microfilm", *Anejos del Boletín de la Dirección General de Archivos y Bibliotecas*, 17, 31, 33, 42, 48, 50 and 60.

8. Girón, Alicia. *La prensa en peligro. Hemeroteca Municipal de Madrid: 75 aniversario.* Edición literaria y selección ilustraciones, Carlos Dorado Fernández. Madrid: Ayuntamiento de Madrid, 1995. ISBN 84-7812-280-X, pp. 73-77.

9. In fact the digitalization process of the Archivo de Indias, which is a very well-known project internationally, and regarding which there is a considerable bibliography, suddenly appeared on the Spanish scene. The event of the Indian Archive has exerted a still not sufficiently valued influence over both Spanish libraries and the information technology market *Computerization project for the Archivo General de Indias*. Coordination, Rafael Blázquez odoy. Madrid: Dirección General de Bellas Artes y Archivos, 1990.

10. It is clear that, within the present preservation and access philosophy, Spain is hoping to simultaneously solve and obtain feedback on two of its fundamental problems; one is the preservation of its documents, and the other (and of no less importance) is the supply of documents. It should be pointed out that at the same time the RER project is being started up, we are beginning to see the results of CNAD (National Access to Document Centre) which is dependent on the National Library, located in Alcalá de Henares 35 km. from Madrid, and which at present has about 7 million bibliographic units.

It is already possible to use an electronic mail address for interlibrary loan: <ill@bne.es>, and to use ARIADNA's OPAC postbox to make all types of requests. Before the end of the year a group of formatted screens (according to ISO 10160/1 standards) will be available as another of OPAC's options.

11. The addressees of this questionnaire are approximately 8,800 libraries registered in the Directory of Spanish Libraries database, which will hugely facilitate all types of mailing tasks, as well as data feedback.

12. There is a copy of the above-mentioned questionnaire as an appendix to this paper.

13. *Formato IBERMARC para registros de fondos y localizaciones.* Madrid: Biblioteca Nacional. It is interesting to mention that the ARIADNA database, whose analysis of the structure of information is based on the IBERMARC format, has incorporated a field of fixed longitude and coded positions, tagged as 009, in the holdings and locations handling subsystem, in which information is included on the different types of possible reproductions. This information has also been proposed for the draft of the UNIMARC format of holdings and locations, which the writers of this paper have prepared within their work in the Section on Information Technology of IFLA and which is at present in the discussion phase in the *Permanent UNIMARC Committee.*

14. Accessible via Internet, at the address <ariadna@bne.es> and <http://www.bne.es>. Cf. Agenjo, Xavier and Belén Altuna. "El directorio español de bibliotecas: un proyecto X.500 en marcha", *UDT Information Bulletin,* ISSN 1021-3333, 21 (Spring 1993), pp. 1-3. *Directorio de Bibliotecas Españolas.* [Computer file] Madrid: Biblioteca Nacional, 1996.

DIGITAL LIBRARIES: A NEW APPROACH TO PRESERVATION FOR A BROADENED ACCESS

Yannick MAIGNIEN

Bibliothèque Nationale de France

FRAMEWORK

1. **Quantitative aims**
2. **Scientific goals**
3. **Broadening access to the public**
4. **Electronic format**
5. **Intermediary carriers**
6. **Approach from a librarianship viewpoint**
7. **Relationship between broadened sophisticated access and preservation**
8. **Preservation "New Deal"**
9. **New responsibilities in serving information**

One of the main projects of the new Bibliothèque Nationale de France (BNF) is to give access to an electronic and digital collection of printed books, pictures and audiovisual materials, but also to new multimedia. As a matter of fact, the 1993 law on the legal deposit of electronic documents and software requires the legal deposit of multimedia.

First, I will present the main requirements of this digitization programme. Then, I will try to point out some of the theoretical issues arising from digitization.

The digitization programme has to take into account the following requirements:-

QUANTITATIVE AIMS

About 100,000 volumes (30 million pages) are to be scanned and stored on a computer server. All these materials will be accessible from the local network inside the Library as soon as it opens in 1997, and later on through remote access networks.

Afterwards, we plan to increase this by about 25,000 documents a year, in order to cover about 300,000 documents in the next eight years. Moreover, 300,000 pictures and 3,000 ancient recordings - amounting to 1,000 hours of listening - should be digitized by 1997.

SCIENTIFIC GOALS

The digitization programme began in 1989. It is based on the concept of an encyclopaedic collection covering all areas of the Humanities and Sciences: science and history of science, literature, history, philosophy, ethnology, economics, law, politics, all subjects taken from both monographs and periodicals.

Most of the books to be digitized are in French and European languages, about 28% from the 18th century, 21% from the 19th, 16% from the 20th, 14% from the 16th, 9% from the 17th, and about 13% from the Middle Ages and Antiquity.

The programme has selected rare books and also books that are very often asked for but no longer available. This selection represents a major added value. But 100,000 books is a very small figure compared to the 10 million documents that belong to the Library. Nevertheless they represent an interesting sample of the most important and rare books of the holdings. Our goal is that scholars get access to complete collections and corpora thanks to a lexical research automated system.

BROADENING ACCESS TO THE PUBLIC

The aim of the project is to give access to the digital library within the Library and to make it accessible to other libraries as well as to private users.

This digitized collection will be accessible both from the "scholar level" (ground floor) and from the "public level" (top floor) through sophisticated tools which already exist as prototypes of computer- assisted reading stations. Readers will be able to read, but also to underline, annotate, cut and paste, restructure, digitized texts, which will considerably improve searching and working methods.

The integrated computerized information system will be extended to new services. As C. Lynch says: "New services such as document requesting and document delivery, printing on demand of electronic information, electronic publishing, current awareness (selective dissemination of information) and access to fee-for-service information services and resources, are being developed in response to the growing demand."[1]

ELECTRONIC FORMAT

Studies indicate that a graphic format (bit map) is the most cost-effective option for a library, and that it respects the bibliophilic appearance of a document. This is the reason why documents are scanned with a 300 dpi resolution, using the group IV mode of compression, in TIFF standard. Statistics on digitized collections give an average of 2,4 Mgs (Megabytes) for a 300 page book, which implies that our server will need a minimum capacity of 2 Tbs (Terabytes) by 1997.

The Bibliothèque Nationale de France also plans the digitization of mode text holdings: about 10% of all digitized holdings will come from mode text data bases, mostly from the Frantex collection of the CNRS (National Centre for Scientific Research) - about 4,000 books of French Literature.

One important stage of the digitizing programme consists in making technical choices and testing the main working hypothesis on real samples, tailored to the nature of documents.

INTERMEDIARY CARRIERS

Microforms are the best intermediary carriers between primary documents that need to be carefully reproduced as analogic copies, and digitization which needs semi-industrial scanning from this photographic image. Nevertheless, the production of microform with the sole aim of digitizing increases cost rates considerably.

That is the reason why the Bibliothèque Nationale de France has chosen to digitize two types of documents:-

- Book sheets, which represent 40% of the corpus, mainly coming from recently published or antiquarian works.
- Microforms, which represent 60% of the collection, mainly coming from the duplication service of the library, others having been bought from specialized publishers.

  In the future, it will be possible to store digital images directly with CCD cameras which will provide good analogic microform whenever necessary. What is even more important, it will allow electronic storage control, cataloguing, reference enrichment or indexing of all documents in a new chain of bibliographic treatment.

APPROACH FROM A LIBRARIANSHIP VIEWPOINT

Moreover, the digitization of documents entails a completely new approach with regard to library management.

To sum up, four main objectives are pursued through digitization:-

- reduction of pressure on collections;
- facilitation of access to all documents;
- provision of high-level services to readers;
- provision of the contents of documents by means of a network rather than by a mere catalogue.

Of course, digitization is part of preservation policies, as it produces copies, entails mass storage and broadens communication to the public. To a certain extent, it goes beyond that which has already been made possible with analogic microform.

RELATIONSHIP BETWEEN BROADENED SOPHISTICATED ACCESS AND PRESERVATION

The next step will be devoted to the preparation of the computer-assisted system for research, retrieving techniques and standards, and thus go beyond the OPAC (On-Line Public Access Catalogue). Items of bibliographic information will be collected and entered in order to add increasing value to the references for library users and the whole community of scholars and searchers.

It is a sophisticated project, as it implies describing very different categories of publishing structure information, such as author and title, in a standardized language (SGML or Text Encoding Initiative), but also enriched references like tables of contents and indexes that are added and entered, or thanks to a special documentary layer, included in the digital architecture of the information system.

This is necessary to improve interchange but also to share and use resources within networks.

A digital document is not the mere copy of a printed one.

Through the CARE (Computer-Assisted Reading Environment) workstation, readers can use both logical and physical structures from primary documents, so as to compose their own digital corpus, where their own text and data can be added. Original documents are saved, but readers can change DTD (Document Type Definition) thanks to the optical character recognition system and thus create new documents, from a physical and logical viewpoint. They can also duplicate, mail or print them. The preservation of the intellectual integrity of original documents could be one of the responsibilities for national libraries.

The possibility of using the logical structure (as it is coded in a standardized language) allows a lot of possibilities for consulting, searching and retrieving through very different kinds of documents, which explains why the digital space is no longer like the printed one.

With the HTML (HyperText Markup Language) it will be possible to make one's way among remote libraries without being worried with identifying the library that houses the needed documents. As a matter of fact, it is the definition of a virtual library.

So this meta-information, hypertext link network architecture, will have to be preserved in addition to primary documents.

PRESERVATION "NEW DEAL"

Is there a direct relationship between easier and broadened access and better preservation?

A better and more clever way to improve access to documents fits in with preservation requirements as it allows answering the demand wittingly and takes pressure off original books.

To a certain extent, dissociating conservation from access (to copies) solves the problem of the conservation of the most precious materials.

But the characteristics of virtual and digital libraries raise other issues linked to memory. Today's publishing world is growing at an increasing speed, with more and more physical carriers but many non-material ones too. Today, the legal deposit is growing by nearly two million documents per year.

A recent American study pointed out that the collections of research libraries are doubled every other twelve years. Such a rate and speed imply that spatial, physical and, above all, economic constraints are to be taken into account.

Digitized collections meet intellectual and economical requirements in the short term.

Are we not compelled to separate the mission that consists in storing documents from the mission that consists in giving access to them? Is it not necessary to make a distinction between the huge mass of documents that are very rarely consulted and the other ones that have to be communicated often and rapidly? These could be digitized on request. Rare and precious documents could be inserted into a digitized collection, created according to intellectual and functional criteria.

Libraries and the legal deposit have to meet a new challenge: classical preservation policies have to be reconsidered because of exponential and on-line publishing. How to keep all these materials?

How to retrieve relevant pieces of information? Which criteria will help select among what has to be preserved forever, and what can be left aside?
Libraries need a new theoretical and conceptual approach to preservation: hosting and retrieving methods, which will become a new way to get access to live information, will be more and more included in new preservation activities.

These issues are not only and mainly technical. In the future, more clear-sightedness will be needed to solve the issues arising from the social and cultural use of virtual information.

The digitization of printed documents together with the computerization of the publishing chain lead to a paradoxical situation. A floppy disc is given by an author to a publisher, who lays out and structures the document with generalized marks and languages tags, so as to modify eventually the printing and allow interchange formats. Printing machines are operated by computers. But paper-based documents are now scanned, so all this interchange of information is lost. It is an utter nonsense which could be avoided by a closer co-operation between publishers and printers and by saving available mode text.

This explains why the BNF tried to negotiate in order to preserve documents that have already been produced in mode text with tapes laid out and given by printers, but failed. However, the National Centre for Scientific Research agreed to co-operate with the Treasures of the French Language (Trésor de la Langue Française) that are partly electronically composed.

Several reasons account for this reluctance to co-operate; the lack of standardized machines, old habits, and, above all, the fear of losing the legal control over this important step in issuing documents.

An official decision might be taken regarding the preservation of university theses issued on paper or on computerized media, at least as far as tables of contents, abstracts, indexes or bibliographies are concerned.

NEW RESPONSIBILITIES IN SERVING INFORMATION

The genuine nature of computerized documents is to disseminate and run information. This has become obvious with scholarly periodicals whether they are issued as computerized media, as printed documents, or both. Scholarly periodicals are often cut and tailored according to the reader's profile, thus it seems difficult to identify a document in its complete original form.

A World Wide Web is responsible for its own documents but it also holds shared ones served or modified by other members on the network. A W3 server in the Internet network is fully responsible, as a publisher, to serve, modify, forbid access to, or delete documents previously hosted. If no copy of each step is made, whole parts of this knowledge will disappear. In a recent paper published in *Bulletin des Bibliothèques de France*[2] , Hervé le Crosnier calls for cautiousness: How to save updating data brought by everyone on the Net? Who can tell what belongs to whom?

New institutional and legal rules are to be set up for the new electronic age.

One has to bear in mind that the very first duty of a library is to organize knowledge. It is an encyclopaedic task, a kind of "Ars Memoria" run through organization and cataloguing, which goes beyond mere safeguarding. It entails a power of *consignatio*, which means putting together in an external place, in order to retrieve efficiently what we have forgotten or what would have been destroyed.

In his preliminary discourse of the *Encyclopaedia,* D'Alembert stressed that if the Ancients had had the idea of writing an Encyclopaedia gathering all their knowledge, and provided it had been the only document saved from the fire in Alexandria, we would have been consoled for the loss of all the other manuscripts.

How to organize a dynamic preservation policy?

One of the problems raised by the digital era concerns the uncertainties about the location of original documents.

This is due to the circulation of information. Information has become a fluid: it is not a paper-based document made of ink and composed in the old way any longer. The real nature of digitized documents comes in the form of e-mail, new networks, traffic ... It is like economics, where wealth cannot be touched and seen since electronic money has overwhelmed the worldwide financial bubble.

Jacques Derrida, a French philosopher, has developed his viewpoint on memory in the electronic age versus the printing age in a recent book titled *Mal d'Archive*[3] , which could be translated as "Archive's evil" or "disease", but also as "yearning for Archive". He compares the electronic media to an archival earthquake:-

> *"L'archive, comme impression, écriture, prothèse ou technique hypomnèsique en général, ce n'est pas seulement le lieu de stockage et de conservation d'un contenu archivable passé qui existerait de toute façon, tel que, sans elle, on croit encore qu'il fut ou qu'il aura été. Non, la structure technique de l'archive archivante détermine aussi la structure du contenu archivable dans son surgissement même et dans son rapport à l'avenir. L'archivation produit autant qu'elle enregistre l'évènement. C'est aussi notre expérience politique des média dits d'information."...... "Mais cela ne doit pas nous fermer les yeux sur le bouleversement sans limite de la technique archivale en cours. Cela doit surtout rappeler que la dite technique archivale ne détermine plus, et ne l'aura jamais fait, le seul moment de l'enregistrement archivable."...... "On ne vit plus de la même façon ce qui s'archive de la même façon."* [4 5]

I included this long quotation to stress that electronic Archive and conservation cannot be considered according to the long tradition of printing, but must be reconsidered according to the new conditions set by the network.

We have pinpointed the dangers that threaten electronic publication, what Derrida calls the new "anarchivic" and "archiviolithic" disruption, and the new responsibilities to deal with it. Digital documents are virtual, precarious, and they sometimes saturate networks. Copyrights and conditions of access have to be redefined among authors, the public, libraries and publishers.
"It is a real challenge for the future." Derrida says. "Archives have always been regarded as tokens, and as any tokens, tokens for the future."

So, in the near future, we will have to elaborate new rules to conserve and preserve digital information on social and legal bases.

REFERENCES

1. Pitkin, Gary M., ed. *The Evolution of Library Automation.* (Supplements to Computers in Libraries, 44) Westport, CT: Meckler, 1991.

2. Le Crosnier, Hervé. "Bibliothèque Virtuelle", *Bulletin des Bibliothèques de France*, 1995 (2).

3. Derrida, Jacques. *Mal d'Archive.* Paris: Galilee, 1995.

4. Ibid., pp. 35-37

5. Translation of the extracts:-

"The archive, defined as printing, writing, prosthesis or more generally hypomnesic techniques (i.e. memorandum, or mnemotechnic help), is not only the storage and preservation place of a passed archivable content, which would exist in any case, such as, without it, we still believe that this passed content really was or will have been. No, the technical structure of archiving archive also determines the structure of the archivable content, in its sudden appearance and with its relation to the future. The archiving activity creates an event, as well as it records it. This is also our political experience of so-called information media." ......"This must not close our eyes on the unlimited disruption of the current archival techniques. Above all, we must remember that the so-called archival technique no longer determines, and will never have done so, the only moment of the recording of the storage, but determines the very implementation of the archival event."...... "We no longer live in the same way which is not archived (recorded) in the same way."

PRESERVATION PROGRAM MANAGEMENT

Diane Nester KRESH

Library of Congress (USA)

INTRODUCTION

After some reflection, I've decided that my proposed title, Preservation Planning for the 21st Century, sounded too futuristic and suggested an emphasis on technology and the impact it will have on libraries, archives, museums, and so forth. Instead, I am going to describe preservation program management at the Library of Congress, with an emphasis on our development and use of a planning process.

From my perspective, preservation program management is a balancing act -- which is part of what makes it so challenging. Too often, program management is construed as continuous conflict resolution. To me, however, conflict suggests clashes and struggles, winners and losers, either/or; while balance implies integrating, respecting differences, having it all.

Preservation program management is ultimately about choice, the type of preservation response we choose to employ: to treat or not to treat, to provide a partial treatment or a full treatment, to discard or keep. These decisions will have lasting consequences. They must not be made arbitrarily and they must be based on a solid foundation of principles and facts.

At LC we know we can't save it all. And if we can't save it all, What, then, are our choices? When I came to the Library's Preservation Directorate I was immediately confronted with this challenge, which was further complicated by the Library's vigorous pursuit of initiatives to increase the availability of its collections, which also meant increasing the preservation burden.
From my perspective, it was clear that our preservation program had to change. Our traditional approach (preservation on demand one step at a time) was just not going to fit the bill anymore, for several reasons. First, resources were reduced and prospects for filling key vacant positions were nil. Second, the nature of the Library's collections was changing. Third, managers and staff throughout the preservation program expressed concern about the direction of the program, and wondered where they and the Directorate fit in the magnetic and electronic world.
In addition, feedback from curators and custodians suggested that the preservation program wasn't meeting their needs. Consequently, we wondered if we should have a more flexible program, if we should expand our services, and if we should seek greater influence over Library operations and programs.

I initiated our planning process to address these and other issues. The whole effort took about 18 months: we began in Spring 1993 and submitted a reorganization plan to Library management in January 1995.

I want to emphasize at the outset that just because we completed a planning process does not mean that we now have a ten-year preservation plan carved in stone. What we do have is a dynamic preservation plan that we intend to revisit constantly over the next 10 years. As the balance (there's that word again) of our collections shifts from paper-based to non paper-based materials, the challenge will be to adapt techniques and practices we know and have been developing -- in some cases -- for centuries, to materials about which we know little.

Our planning process revealed a number of weaknesses in the program. For example, we found that we:

- were not being responsive to the preservation needs of all of the Library's collections;
- lacked a mechanism for identifying preservation priorities Library-wide; and
- did not have a prominent enough influence over top management decision-making.

THE LIBRARY

So, How did we conduct this comprehensive self-examination? What did we do with the information gathered? and Where are we going with it? Those three questions form the core of what I will discuss today. But first, for those of you who aren't familiar with it, a little about the Library of Congress itself. The Library of Congress has been called many things, Congress's Library, the Nation's library, the Multi-Media Encyclopedia (Daniel Boorstin) -- and given the number of tourists who visit the Library each year it sometimes seems to have been recast as a theme park.

A quick recitation of some of our golden oldies reveals the depth and breadth of the collections: the contents of Lincoln's pockets the night he was assassinated; Thomas Jefferson's drawing of a macaroni machine; the records of the NAACP; photographs of migrant workers; episodes from "*I love Lucy*;" Pierre L'Enfant's plan for Washington, D.C.; the Washington Haggadah and the Gutenberg Bible; and even the lyrics to A Hole in the Bucket (a folk-song I sing with my seven-year old son Matthew). All of that and much much more (at last count 100 million+ items) in a variety of formats and materials including leather, vellum, palm leaves, papyrus, paper, nitrate film, CD ROM, vinyl discs, and magnetic tape.

THE PRESERVATION DIRECTORATE

The preservation program is administered by the Director for Preservation (me), who is responsible for planning, coordinating, and directing all activities of the Preservation Directorate. The Directorate is currently organized into five program areas. One of these is the Binding Office, responsible for library binding, repair, and housing.

A second area is the Conservation Office, which provides the most appropriate preventive and phased preservation measures and treats rare, at risk, and intrinsically valuable book and paper collection materials.

The Preservation Microfilming Office is responsible for converting library materials (mostly brittle books) to microfilm or other conversion medium.

A fourth area is the Research and Testing Office, which initiates research and establishes preservation specifications for materials used to treat and house the collections.

Last comes the National Preservation Program Office, an outreach and information clearinghouse that provides preservation reference and consultation services, and training in care and handling to staff Library-wide.

THE PLANNING PROCESS

Over a period of several months beginning in the Spring of 1993, the managers of the various elements of the preservation program began meeting to consider how to begin a comprehensive planning process. Many planning processes at the Library had come and gone and a great deal of cynicism surrounded them because most often the fruits of such labors filled large, impressive-looking volumes and then landed, with a thud, on dusty shelves, never to be looked at again. So we preservation managers agreed on some ground rules in framing the planning activity. For example, we agreed that:

- the process would not drag on interminably;
- staff at all levels of the preservation program would be involved;
- we would develop both short-term and long-term goals;
- we would implement recommendations as we went along to demonstrate commitment to change.

Having set the ground rules, we next tackled the task of developing the construct by which we would collect the data. We decided on an approach that would address the complexities of our organization, would involve the staff, and would reinforce our connectedness and commitment to both the customers we serve and to the preservation community as a whole. In brief, the approach called for open discussion with the customers we serve through analysis conducted by study teams, and through convening large-summit meetings, and action-oriented focus groups.

Both tangible and intangible outcomes of the planning process were expected. The primary tangible products were recommendations and a strategic plan about the Directorate's philosophy, mission, and goals; and proposals for restructuring the preservation program. On the intangible side, the planning process was expected to serve as a vehicle for meeting four specific goals:

1. melding the Directorate's five program areas into a fully integrated team;
2. paving the way for further integrating the preservation program with other programs in the Library;
3. coaching the staff to deal more effectively with change; and
4. building relationships among the staff -- in short, getting everyone on the same team.

With these goals and objectives in mind, the formal planning process was initiated in September 1993 at a Directorate-wide staff meeting -- the first in the history of the organization. Shortly thereafter, six study teams were formed.
All but one team leader were non-management staff and were not necessarily expert at the outset in their designated area of study. Team Members were drawn from all levels of the organization to ensure that a variety of viewpoints was solicited.

The study teams worked in the following six areas:

1. Administration, Communication, Automation, and Budget;
2. Physical Plant and Environmental Monitoring;
3. Physical Treatment;

4. Reformatting;
5. Research and Testing; and
6. Staff Training and Development, and Preservation Outreach.

To get the planning process off to a good start, an organizational development consultant came in to work with the teams, both collectively and individually. She provided information and practice about facilitation skills, how to function as a team, and how to make meetings productive.
To foster openness and to provide opportunities to hear from our customers, two information-gathering strategies were employed that were new to the Directorate: large Summit meetings and small Focus Sessions. In all, three summits were held, two for Library staff and one for members of the national preservation community.

The first summit focused on the collections and was attended by representatives from the custodial units. In a frank brainstorming session that discussed the effectiveness and responsiveness of the preservation program, several common themes emerged.

These included:

- a desire for staff and patron training in the handling of collections items;
- concern about better emergency preparedness for the collections;
- interest in decentralizing preservation activities, *e.g.*, housing, to the custodial level; and
- need to assess the Library's collections at both the collection and single item levels to determine preservation needs.

In this *first* session, preservation made no attempt to respond to what was being expressed by managers and curators. We simply listened, collected the information, prepared an action document, and circulated it for comment.

The *second* Summit was a follow-up to the first and was Preservation's turn to "talk back." Preliminary responses were presented, as were short-term goals and proposed actions.
The purpose of Preservation Summit III was to seek counsel on the role of LC in the national preservation program from many leaders in the field, including preservation administrators, preservation researchers and scientists, archivists, conservators, and representatives of national professional organizations. Five break-out groups discussed specific topics and advanced recommendations that were summarized into a report and shared on the Internet.

As I stated earlier, we also convened six Focus Sessions for Library curators and managers. These small sessions were used to generate action agendas and focused on environmental conditions, staff and patron education and training, selection for preservation, and physical treatment.

The study teams completed their deliberations in April 1994 and submitted their final reports and recommendations by the middle of May. The management team met off-site to discuss these documents and to arrive at a plan of action that would bring the Directorate to its goals by the most efficient and effective route.

From this retreat came management consensus about an organizational structure that would support the mission of the Directorate, which is to provide preservation support for the Library's permanent research collections. Also discussed were a short-term action plan of projects to be completed by the end of FY94, and a synthesis of recommendations to be incorporated into a long-term plan.

In keeping with the inclusive approach that had been taken from the outset, these materials were presented to the staff in a second Directorate-wide meeting held in June of 1994.

Following lively discussion, the staff were invited to submit their comments on the report and organization plan so they could be taken into consideration as the final report was being written. The twelve action projects were initiated immediately. Six of them I will describe in some detail as, collectively, they represent a significant shift in our philosophy. Based on the needs of our collections, we are consciously moving away from single-item treatment and toward preservation intervention at the collections level.

1. Development and implementation of a policy on selection for preservation. An important outcome of the planning process was a consensus that greater coordination was needed among divisions in Preservation. Further, we acknowledged that before we could create preservation strategies, we needed to establish a baseline of preservation needs for each collection area. As a first step, we combined into one plan the annual proposals for preservation reformatting, conservation treatment, and the purchase of phased supplies. We also expanded the number of divisions whose collections could receive services.

2. Development of a collections care program. This program was proposed in order to provide in-house repair to collection items for the reading rooms. The goals were three-fold:
    - To get materials back in circulation as soon as possible;
    - To save unique bindings; and
    - To provide options -- such as constructing protective enclosures -- where binding is inappropriate or costly.

   Plans were also developed for the operation of the Office's newly acquired automated box-making machine, a piece of equipment that can churn out folding boxes (CMI boxes) at the rate of 200+ per day. With this level of productivity, the Library can readily provide stable housing for some of its poorly produced and fragile collection items, items that formerly were merely identified for preservation but left in circulation. This joint endeavor has brought staff from Conservation together with staff from the Binding Office, as part of a long-term effort to link the staffs of these two related -- and previously disconnected -- areas.

3. Development of a blueprint for Environmental Monitoring. Several steps were taken in the Directorate's on-going program to ensure the continued preservation and security of the Library's collections including its Top Treasures. For example, we contracted to house both drafts of the Gettysburg Address in custom-sized, air-tight document containers purged with Argon. In consideration of the general storage needs of the treasures, an environmentally controlled room was installed in the Conservation Office. Steps are also underway to lower the temperature and Relative Humidity in all collections storage areas, to conduct regular monitoring of collections areas, and to schedule regular meetings with the facilities staff charged with ensuring that fluctuations in temperature and relative humidity are addressed.

4. Emergency preparedness. When I first arrived in the Directorate, one of the Senior Paper Conservators approached me about emergency preparedness and the need to do more than simply recover material after an incident occurred. In response, I challenged her to identify the top three action items that would get the emergency preparedness program off the ground. Needless to say, she came up with the three actions and one year later, every custodial area is equipped with a React Pak of emergency response supplies (including rubber boots), we have established a 24-hour call system, and we have recruited and trained a team of "volunteers." This preparedness paid off when one of our buildings flooded early one Sunday morning a couple of weeks ago. Although the worst flood in several years, the good news is that nothing was lost and our response system, while certainly in need of some fine-tuning, worked.

5. Development of a plan to diversify the Conservation Office. Lack of diversity in the field of conservation has become a matter of increasing discussion in recent times. In response to this identified need, the Library of Congress, the National Gallery of Art, the National Museum of American History, and the National Archives and Records Administration agreed to develop a joint program. The goal is to increase diversity in the field of conservation by recruiting minority individuals, by providing mentored learning opportunities in conservation specialties where diversity is currently limited, and by providing job placement assistance when training is complete.

6. Technological advances -- Deacidification program. As you may know, the Library has spent considerable time on research to develop a mass deacidification process. The initial deacidification agent, diethyl zinc (DEZ) -- a gas-phase process -- had proven to be promising. For the past few years, research efforts have been directed toward eliminating process-related problems such as post-treatment odor. Akzo Chemicals withdrew from the deacidification business in April 1994 after the research and development effort had succeeded in resolving problems with the DEZ process.

Following an extensive evaluation, the Library concluded that the Bookkeeper process -- a non-aqueous liquid process -- holds great promise for treating its collections. Over the next two years, further work will be devoted to refining that process and to encouraging the development of other deacidification technologies.

This effort will include using the Bookkeeper process in a pilot project that will deacidify 70,000 books from the Library's collections. The pilot will begin later this year. National Digital Library. We are involving ourselves in this project because we feel strongly that preservation has an important role to play in the digitization of collections. At present we are in the process of defining the exact nature of that role. We are also engaged in research pertaining to the preservation aspects of digitizing various collection materials. For paper-based materials we are looking at issues surrounding image capture, with emphasis on bitonal, gray scale, and color materials. We are also assessing preservation requirements for the digital transfer of audio, motion picture, and film collections. An important project completed this Spring was the digitizing of four notebooks belonging to the American Poet Walt Whitman and a paper butterfly ring he liked to wear. Conservation played a key role in this project.

CONCLUSION

The planning process revitalized an organization that is now better equipped to be responsive, timely, and cost-effective in its operations.

Through the addition of staff and contractors versed in digital technology and audio and moving image preservation, and through the use of new automated technologies and approaches that allow us to serve more collections needs, the preservation program:

1. Is now balanced, addressing the preservation needs of all of the Library's holdings, not just those that are paper-based;

2. Is preventive, emphasizing activities that slow the rate of deterioration; and

3. Is proactive, building operational partnerships with its internal constituents, and with national and international institutions and professional associations.

4. The continuing challenge for a preservation administrator facing such an array of materials in such vast quantities is to use the best methods available, to bite off a chunk at a time, and to plan, not panic. Through sensible choices, cooperative planning and sharing of information, appropriate uses of technology, and full participation by staff at all levels willing to flex in new directions, it is possible to beat back the slow fires not with "one size fits all" solutions but with ingenuity and commitment to periodic self-examination to ensure that the best and most appropriate measures and practices are being applied.

Footnote:

I always feel that when I am speaking to a group like this one, I am speaking to the already initiated and don't need to dwell on why preservation is important. But I came across a quotation that, for me anyway, sums up why we do what we do: "The past is only the present become invisible and mute; and because it is invisible and mute, its memoried glances and its murmurs are infinitely precious. We are tomorrow's past." The quote is by Mary Webb, otherwise known as Mrs. Henry Bertram Law. And in case you have never heard of her, the reason for that may be explained by the English essayist and poet Joseph Addison who said, "I consider time as an immense ocean, in which many noble authors are entirely swallowed up." Let's not let any more Mary Webbs get swallowed up.

COLLECTION AND PRESERVATION OF LOCAL HISTORY IN NEW JERSEY

George W. COOKE

Oradell Public Library (USA)

INTRODUCTION

New Jersey is one of the smallest states of the United States. It is only one-fifth the size of Hungary, but we have a population of over 7 million people of many different nationalities. New Jersey was a major colony of the Netherlands in the 1620s and of Great Britain from 1664 until 1776. Located on the Atlantic Ocean, near New York City and Philadelphia, it was a battleground in the eighteenth century for the British and Colonial armies. New Jersey is a rich and fertile land and because of its productive farms it is called "The Garden State". New Jersey has more than 100 different ethnic groups. These people from a hundred different countries have learned how to co-operate and live together in harmony. We have many different kinds of local history organizations and I want to describe a few of them.

New Jersey has no central control of historical collections or of historical organizations. Some records are maintained by the State Archives, some by the State Library, some by county governments, others by municipal governments, but a great many of the most interesting collections are owned and maintained by private groups.

AMERICAN HUNGARIAN FOUNDATION

The American Hungarian Foundation, located in the city of New Brunswick, is one of hundreds of organizations in the. state of New Jersey that collect local history materials. A large part of the population of New Brunswick is of Hungarian origin, and New Brunswick has entered into a special "sister city" relationship with the Hungarian city of Debrecen. Some of our New Jersey citizens of Hungarian origin arrived after the Revolution of 1848-49, and many others have come over since, especially after the Hungarian Uprising of 1956. Many of the Hungarians who came to the United States to earn their fortunes later returned to Hungary. The American Hungarian Foundation collects local history materials on the Hungarians, such as American Hungarian newspapers, and holds many unique publications and papers of Hungarian Americans. The Foundation provides cultural and academic programs and trade fairs, and publishes a newsletter.

The Hungarian Heritage Museum is also housed in the large modern Foundation building. The Museum provides exhibits of a wide range of art, textiles, ceramics and the like, often with the assistance of curators from the Hungarian National Museum. The air-conditioned research library contains 40,000 volumes covering every aspect of Hungarian culture and it is growing through gifts and bequests. As books are catalogued, the catalogue records are integrated into the electronic database of the major research libraries, known as RLIN (Research Library Information Network). The library's holdings of Hungarian language newspapers are available on microfilm. The Foundation does not yet have a conservator or conservation workshop, but that is considered a possibility for the future. The collection includes personal papers, letters and journals. It also has some earlier Latin works such as the History of Hungary by Janos Thuroczy, from 1488, and a history of Hungary by Antonio Bonfini from 1581. The Sermons of Michael of Hungary from 1480 is the earliest work in the library. With its large modern facilities and growing collections, the American Hungarian Foundation is an example of an outstanding and well-maintained local history collection.

OTHER ETHNIC AND RELIGIOUS ORGANIZATIONS

Many of the early immigrants to New Jersey were deeply religious. They came to the New World to establish communities where their own beliefs and traditions and languages would be tolerated and respected. These immigrants did not desire a strong central government. They wanted to be free to establish their own lifestyles without the interference and control of any provincial or federal government. These settlers looked to their churches and synagogues for preservation of vital records. Birth, marriage, and death records were useful in the wilderness to the institutions of religion and these records are found in many local sites throughout New Jersey. Many types of pastoral reports, journals and other personal records were also preserved by religious institutions, which in time established archives to house these large collections. At the present time, local churches and synagogues are still engaged in collecting and preserving vital records for their communities. They publish newsletters and newspapers. They collect photographs, works of art, oral histories, videotapes, and sound recordings. In many cases, these local records are also transmitted to central archives belonging to the religious organizations. These privately owned archives are some of the finest in the state and they employ certified archivists who use the latest preservation techniques. They are not dependent upon politicians for their continued existence. Many of them are endowed and have their own sources of income.

OLD PARAMUS REFORMED CHURCH AND SCHOOLHOUSE MUSEUM

The Old Paramus Reformed Church was founded by Dutch Calvinists in 1725. It was governed by the church in Amsterdam and the language spoken was Dutch, although the residents were then British subjects. This church is of particular interest because it was located in a battle zone. It sometimes served as George Washington's headquarters in 1778 and 1780. The historical society owns a letter from George Washington. British and American troops fought battles at this site and buried their dead in the churchyard. Journals and church records and papers are owned by the church. The early Dutch churches also built schoolhouses for the education of their children. The pastor of this church organized the Paramus Historical and Preservation Society. Its members assist in the preservation of the church, the cemetery, and the adjacent Schoolhouse Museum built in 1872. The museum is filled with books and artefacts from the eighteenth and nineteenth centuries. Unfortunately, it is not well organized and has no temperature or humidity controls and the storage conditions are poor. A part-time archivist is now cataloguing the materials and some conservation treatments have been completed. The Reformed Church has a central archive in New Brunswick.

UNITED METHODIST ARCHIVES

The Methodist Church is a Protestant denomination with millions of members in the United States, Europe, and Asia. The Methodists founded some 70 universities in the United States, including Vanderbilt, Syracuse, and even UCLA. The Archives and History Center of The United Methodist

Church at Drew University in Madison, New Jersey houses a large collection of books, documents, photographs, and slides. It collects and maintains records for New Jersey Methodists and for world-wide Methodist activities. The Archives building is temperature and humidity controlled and has a sophisticated security system. The archivists plan to replace their halon gas fire suppression for something less damaging to the environment. The large underground vaults provide 180,000 cubic feet of storage space on two floors.

The Methodist library is housed on the second floor of the building. The library specializes in material from northern New Jersey and holds 80,000 volumes. It has collections of materials about women and about ethnic minorities. Newspaper collections have been microfilmed. This archive no longer uses its fumigation system because of concern over carcinogenic effects. It has 1,000 feet of personal papers and 12,000 cubic feet of documents in archival boxes. The collection includes many regional Methodist newspapers and periodicals from around the world but it has special collections on northern New Jersey. In the archives I saw boxes of Hungarian conference journals from 1918 to 1939. This Archive is beautifully designed inside and out. Detailed finding aids have been printed and are also available on the Archive's internal computer network.

The Archive provides a scanner and a Polaroid photograph machine. The staff includes two full-time archivists, two part-time, three students and a project archivist.

JEWISH ARCHIVES

There are five Jewish historical societies in New Jersey and they have divided the 21 counties of the state into five collecting regions. The Jewish Historical Society of Metrowest in Whippany collects material from seven counties in the north-west part of the state. It is located in a fine new building with well-maintained climate-controlled archives. This Jewish archive is managed by a certified archivist who also teaches seminars on preservation. The society's holdings include records of Jewish charities, clubs, and many other organizations, as well as family records, diaries, and photographs. It has microfilmed all the regional Jewish weekly newspapers published since 1921. This Society provides a training program for oral historians and has a collection of oral history audiotapes. It has produced a subject guide to its holdings on computer disks which are available for home use or in the Archive.

NEW JERSEY CATHOLIC HISTORICAL RECORDS COMMISSION ARCHIVES

Seton Hall in South Orange has just built a new library, and the lower level houses the New Jersey Catholic Historical Records Commission Archives and a conservation studio. The Archives collects and preserves Roman Catholic records for churches in the Archdiocese of Newark. It also holds many family papers and has a collection of newspapers. It has a conservation laboratory and a part-time paper conservator.

PUBLIC LIBRARIES

Although you might expect our public libraries to collect a great deal of local history, the fact is that very few of them do. They lack the staff, the space, and the enthusiasm to record the history of their own communities. Public libraries need funding for archives and for professional staff, but most of all they need directors who are enthusiastic about local history. Even without money, libraries can use volunteers to collect local history materials in imaginative projects. A few public libraries are models for others to follow. One of these inspiring libraries is the joint Free Public Library of Morristown and Morris Township. The first circulating library in Morristown was established in 1792. It was followed by a series of library organizations which culminated in the present library. This library is an outstanding example of how public libraries can collect and preserve local history. The local history research collection consists of 22,000 titles. It includes documents from the 1740s, unpublished manuscripts of family histories, and large collections of genealogical materials and immigration records tracing the arrival of the Irish, Italians, Germans, and other ethnic groups. The library also holds 1,000 historic maps from the 1840s to 1860s covering all New Jersey counties. The photograph and postcard collection consists of more than 10,000 items. The library owns a microfiche collection of thousands of local history materials and many local newspapers on microfilm. Local church records, town records, immigration records, New Jersey Federal Census, and many others are to be found in this library. The Morristown library also maintains a conservation laboratory, something very unusual in a medium-sized public library. The unusual local history service provided by the Morristown library has encouraged donations, gifts, and bequests to further their work. It also benefits from a private foundation that raises money for its needs. If anyone doubts the value of local history to a community, they need to study the example of the Morristown library.

LOCAL HISTORICAL SOCIETIES

New Jersey has about 500 independent historical societies. These local historical societies have been formed to collect and preserve local history, usually the history of a single town. Local history societies have saved many historic buildings from demolition. They have also rescued collections of family papers from the trash. Often these local history societies are very small groups of volunteers. They vary greatly from enthusiastic active groups to inactive or marginal groups which may exist in name only. In recent years, historical societies have had a tendency to devote their efforts to the restoration and preservation of historic homes and buildings. The paper records of earlier decades seem to be of less interest to historical societies today than they once were. Historic homes and artifacts and dramatic re-enactments of historic events attract larger numbers of crowds than do manuscripts and rare books.

Nevertheless, these programs do encourage interest in local history and in preserving historic materials. Some individual mansions are maintained by local historical groups organized around the preservation of a single building. Often these historic buildings also house collections of family letters and journals, as well as commercial correspondence. Enormous changes are taking place in New Jersey now that information about proper methods of preservation is filtering down to small repositories.

Almost every local curator has heard of acid paper and archival storage boxes, something they knew nothing about until recently. Many of the history societies are affiliated with the American Association for State and Local History, which has as its mission educating local volunteers in preservation methods. This association has 5,000 members.

GARRETSON FARM

The Garretson Farm in Fair Lawn is a historic Dutch farmhouse built in 1719 by Peter Garretson, and six generations of his family lived in it. It was scheduled for demolition in 1950, but it was saved at the last moment by a handful of volunteers who went from door to door in the community collecting money to buy the farm before the real estate developers could destroy it.

The house is the repository for the Garretson family papers. The Garretsons owned a huge tract of land comprising thousands of acres which they worked with slaves and indentured servants.

The Garretson family also operated an iron forge which was used by the colonists during the Revolutionary War.

VAN VOORHEES-QUAKENBUSH-ZABRISKIE HOUSE

This historic home houses family papers, local maps and business records, letters and poetry written by its residents. It is maintained by the Wyckoff Historical Society and is typical of the many historic sites in New Jersey that preserve family papers in the house where they were written.

THE HERMITAGE

'The Hermitage in Ho-Ho-Kus was owned by four generations of the Rosencranz family, who were textile mill owners. Famous national leaders such as George Washington, Alexander Hamilton, and Aaron Burr attended parties in this house in colonial days. The Rosencranz family saved every piece of paper that ever passed through their hands, so that today their business and family papers are a valuable resource for researchers. This magnificent mansion was abandoned and about to be destroyed by real estate speculators when local residents demanded that it be saved and campaigned long and hard for the money to rescue it. It has now been designated a national historic site.

BERGEN COUNTY HISTORICAL ASSOCIATION

The Steuben house was built before 1700. It was seized by the Americans from its owner, John Zabriskie, who made the mistake of supporting the British during the Revolutionary War. The house was a gift to the Prussian Baron Friederich von Steuben in gratitude for his help in training the Revolutionary army. The Bergen County Historical Society is a private organization which maintains this house and two others. The Society also owns a large collection of manuscripts from 1700 to the present. These documents are housed in special rooms set aside for them in the public library in Hackensack. The collection includes business records, church and cemetery records, local government records from the early 1700s to 1862, local histories and research notes, and a great many miscellaneous papers.

The Bergen County Historical Society sponsors many festivals and historic re-enactments of colonial history. Many of the historical societies in New Jersey also seem to devote most of their energies to their historic houses and antique furniture and costume parties. The public events draw large crowds and serve to spark an interest in local history in children and adults from surrounding communities. Often their collections of books and documents are in need of conservation, cataloging, and finding aids. The Bergen County Historical Society is currently co-operating with a local publisher to produce many reprints of county histories and collections of documents detailing the antislavery movement in the county, and the social, political and religious life of local residents.

Many of the collections of the local historical groups have a great need for improved preservation and conservation programs. Most of them lack the money for such programs, and the current state and federal governments are rapidly eliminating grant funds. Our historical societies will survive the current government budget cuts because they will go on doing what they have been doing for a hundred years. They will continue to raise money privately and carry on their work. This is the great advantage we have in private ownership of historic sites. Often these various historical groups work in isolation from each other and sometimes their volunteer workers damage or destroy manuscripts through lack of proper training or by poor storage conditions. However, major preservation initiatives of the past few years have begun to encourage greater co-operation and better communication amongst the various organizations devoted to collecting historical materials. This is a very positive step towards introducing better methods of collecting historical materials and of preserving them. Librarians and archivists trained in preservation methods are gradually bringing preservation information to the 500 small historical societies in New Jersey.

INDUSTRIAL AND BUSINESS ARCHIVES

Many business records are preserved in local history collections around the state. Scores of local collections have letters, account books, receipts, bills of sale, letters of credit, and the like. These business records are useful in reconstructing the life of residents in earlier times. One unusual type of business involved the buying and selling of African slaves in New Jersey. Records of slave sales are preserved in many local archives.

THE EDISON ARCHIVES

The largest and best-known archive of business records in New Jersey is the Edison Archives, which holds 4.5 million items relating to the work of our great inventor, Thomas Edison. This archive is now operated by the National Park Service. It holds patents, drawings, business correspondence, and descriptions of manufacturing processes as well as examples of Edison phonographs, motion pictures, the electric light bulb, and many technical papers.

WHEATON VILLAGE

The manufacture of glass was once a major industry in southern New Jersey, but it is now a thing of the past. Wheaton Village is a restored glass factory in Millville. The Wheaton Historical Association has collected many nineteenth-century business records and books relating to the glass industry. This is a unique collection and the research library is growing rapidly as collections of papers and drawings of glass manufacturing techniques are donated. The glass factory in Wheaton Village is still in operation, but in place of scientific glassware it now provides a school for glass artists and a gallery filled with modern glass sculptures. The Glass Museum displays hundreds of pressed glass objects for home use, as well as examples of early medicine bottles.

NEW JERSEY NEWSPAPER PROJECT

A large number of regional newspapers have been published in New Jersey since 1800. A recent federal grant permitted the New Jersey State Archives to identify and microfilm as many local newspapers as possible. More than 500 New Jersey newspapers in various languages were microfilmed in this monumental project and this great local history information was saved for researchers.

GUIDED AUTOBIOGRAPHY

In my own work in the public library, I have been teaching classes of elders to write their autobiographies as a way of preserving recent local history. This is a very fruitful and inexpensive way to collect local history and I hope to see this method employed by many other public libraries.

CONCLUSION

The many types of local history organizations in New Jersey have made it possible to collect materials in good times and in bad, with or without government support. And this activity will continue into the future.

ACKNOWLEDGEMENTS

I wish to acknowledge the many archivists who gave me private tours and information about their collections. Thanks to Professor August Molnar of the Hungarian Foundation, Mary Murrin of the New Jersey Historical Commission, Dale Paterson of the Methodist Archives, Susan Gulick and her wonderful staff at the Morristown Public Library, Susan Swartzburg of Rutgers University, Benita Grant of Rutgers, Robert Griffin of the Bergen County Historical Society, Edna Spoorn of the Garretson Farm, George Tselos of the Edison Archives, Gary Suretzky of the Monmouth County Library Archives, Ron Axelrod of the Jewish Historical Society of Central Jersey, Joseph A. Setanni of the Jewish Historical Society of MetroWest, Edward Van Duzer of the Paramus Historical Society, and Robert Stewart of the Asbury Park Public library.

REFERENCES

1. Cohen, David Steven. *New Jersey Ethnic History.. A Bibliography.* Complied by Steven Cohen. Trenton: The Commission, 1986.

2. Cooke, George W. "Building Local History Collections Through Guided Autobiography," *Ameilcan libraides.* October 1994, pp. 825-828.

3. "Drew University Library--Preservation in Practice," *Conservation Administration News,* No. 50 (1992), p. 4.

4. "New Jersey History Resources in Bergen County" A Report to the State librarian. Advisory Committee on Preservation. Unpublished. Midland Park. December 15, 1992.

5. "Ralph Ocker: A Personal Profile," *New Library Scene* (in press).

6. "Susan Swartzburg--Preservation Advocate," *Conservation Administration News,* No. 56 (1994), p. 6.

7. Cunningham, Barbara, ed. *The New Jersey Ethnic Experience.* Union City: William H. Wise, 1977.

8. Jones, Daniel P. "Titles Microfilmed by the New Jersey Newspaper Project" Bureau of Archives & Records Management. Division of Archives & Records Management, Department of State. Photocopied.

9. Princeton University. *Information About the Rare Book, Manuscript, and Special Collections in the Princeton University Library*. October 1987. Mimeographed.

10. Murrin, Mary. New Jersey Historical Commission. *New Jersey Historical Manuscripts: A guide to Collections in the State.* Trenton: New Jersey Historical Commission, Trenton, 1987.

11. Quigley, Mary Alice. *Historical Organizations in New Jersey.' A Directory.* Compiled by Mary Alice Quigley, Judith A. Fullerton and Diane E. Kauffman, League of Historical Societies of New Jersey, New Jersey Historical Commission, 1983.

12. New Jersey State Archives. *New Jersey Laws and Regulations Concerning Local Public Records and Guidelines for Their Custody in Public libraries and Non-Governmental Institutions.* Trenton: New Jersey State Archives, 1993.

13. New Jersey State Library. *Planning the Future of the Past: The Recommendations of the New Jersey State library Advisory Committee and the State Library Response.* New Jersey State Library: Trenton, 1995.

14. Swartzburg, Susan. *Preserving* Library Materials: *A Manual.* 2d ed. Metuchen: Scarecrow Press, 1995.

BIOLOGICAL CONTROL OF BOOK STORAGES IN THE RUSSIAN ACADEMY OF SCIENCES LIBRARY (BAN)

Valeriya I. KOBYAKOVA and Olga SKVORTSOVA

Library of the Russian Academy of Sciences (Russia)

Books and other documents in libraries and archives are being damaged by biological agents. For the storage in the North-West Region of Russia (St. Petersburg), the microscopical fungi are the most dangerous. In Russia the problem of biological control is very current as the result of many different factors. Huge volumes of old books and manuscripts are concentrated in storage rooms without air- conditioning.

The microbiological situation is one of the main parameters of environment hygiene. Increased level of spores and bacteria can cause allergy and infection of people.[1,2] Therefore, this problem is of great importance for book preservation as well as for the health of personnel and readers.

For the collections of the Library of the Russian Academy of Sciences (BAN), the biological control is extremely important due to the consequences of the fire in 1988. The collection with total volume 8.1 million objects treated by fumigation is under continuous monitoring.

Systematic research on the micro-climate and sanitary-hygienic conditions of the collections storage is carried on. Microbiological contamination of air, dusty books and damaged documents is investigated. However, the problem of the maximum allowed contamination for air and surfaces in libraries has been almost completely neglected in Russia. There are few data in the literature on the sanitary-hygienic condition of library and archive storage rooms.[3,4,5] According to the results of Dr Yuliya Nyuksha [3], the contamination level at the Russian National Library is about 800-1500 microorganisms per m^3, which comprises 1/3 of bacteria and 2/3 of fungi spores. This value depends on the type and condition of the building and storage rooms.

In 1994, 28 storage rooms in BAN with different climate condition were investigated. The temperature in these storage rooms varied from 18°C to 22.5°C, and the relative humidity from 32% to 86%. The microflora of air and books surfaces were taken into account both qualitative and quantitative. Air samples were taken using sedimentation on Petri dishes, surface samples - by bacterial seals. The microflora population was calculated per volume or per square unit. The pure cultures of microorganisms were separated and identified. All data were treated using a computer.

All storage rooms were divided into the following 5 groups:-

1. storage with normal storage conditions,
2. storage in emergency,
3. storage with faulty heating and plumbing system,
4. storage which suffered the fire,
5. storage with the increased dust content.

In *Figure 1*, we present our data in CFU (colony forming units) of microorganisms in the air for all these cases. The average data are about 750 CFU/m³, including 400-450 for fungi and 300-350 for bacteria in the acute emergency group (flood, faulty plumbing). This figure can be as high as 1650-1700. In faulty storage, these values are just slightly lower than the allowed level. The worst Figure is observed when the dust content is increased - the air contents 3500-4000 CFU/m³. The analysis of surface contamination by living fungi spores for these cases revealed that maximum contamination of 15000 CFU/m³ is observed for the documents in storage after the fire. The average level for normal storage is 4500 CFU/m³ (see *Figure 2*).

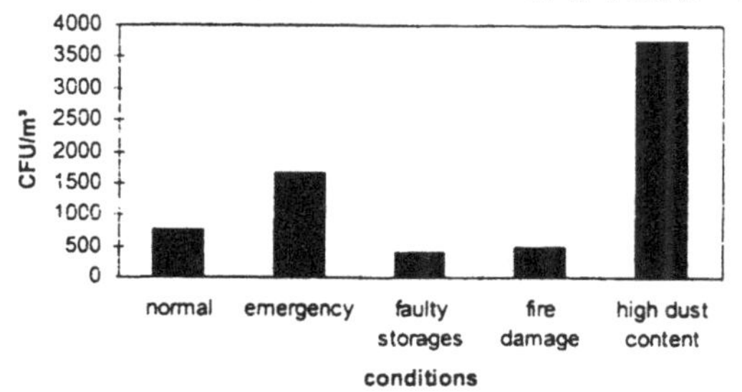

Figure 1 Concentration of micro-organisms in the storage air.

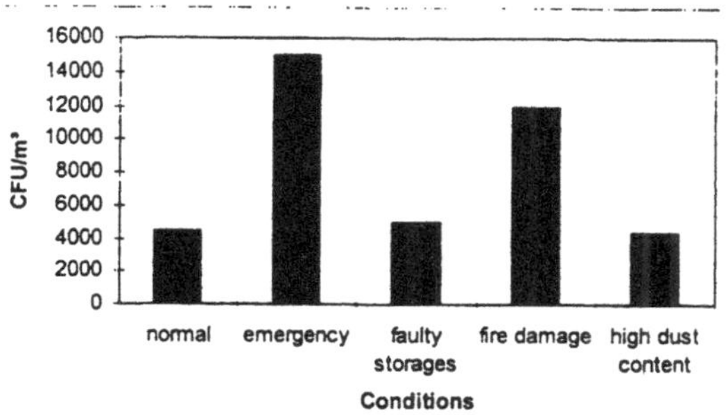

Figure 2 Concentration of fungi on the book surfaces.

The structure of contamination by microorganisms on the surfaces of documents is presented in *Figure 3*. It is the following: fungi - 65%, bacteria - 23.4%, actinomycetes - 6%, yeasts - 5% (average data). For some storages, especially for storage just after the emergency, this structure can be different. For example, for the books from the Baer Collection (foreign editions of the 17th to 18th centuries) which suffered the fire, the relationship between fungi and bacteria is different. The percentage of bacteria in this case increased (fungi comprised 61%, bacteria 37%, actinomycetes and yeasts 1%).

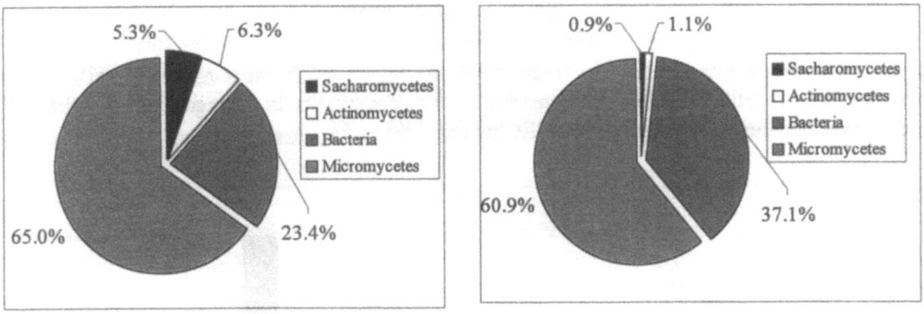

Figure 3 The structure of contamination by micro-organisms on the document surfaces. Left the collection in normal conditions, and right the collection after fire.

The distribution of the contaminated sites in storage is equal as a rule. After an emergency the contaminated sites tend to have some localization.
For example, in storage of the pre-Revolutionary Collection of the Agricultural Library (the map of microbiological investigation is presented in *Figure 4*), the most contaminated site is located near the place of the flood in the ceiling.

The most irregular is the distribution of biodamage in one of the storage of the modern Russian National Collection. The map of its investigation is presented in *Figure 5*.

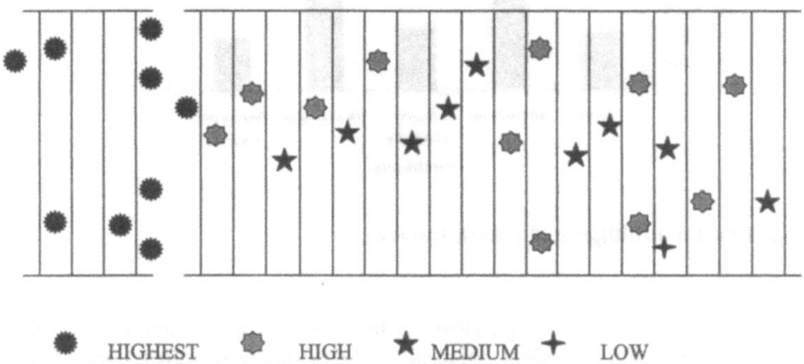

Figure 4 The map of microbiological investigation of one of the Russian National Collection Storages, suffered the fire in 1988.

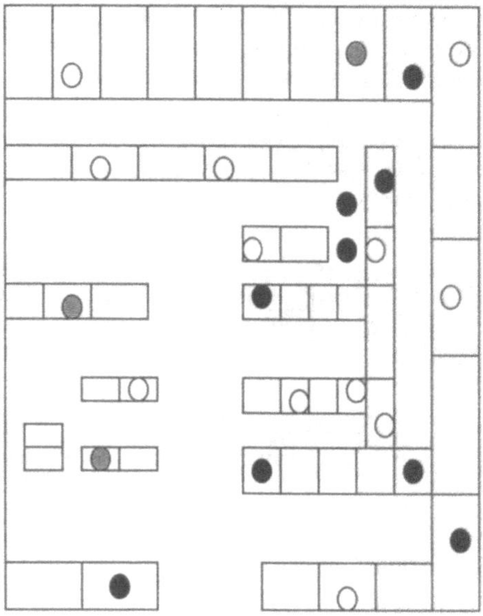

Figure 5 The map of microbiological investigation of the storage damaged by water in the agricultural library. A black circle represents a high level, a grey circle a medium level, and an open a low level of book surface contamination.

Thus, as a result of our research, we have got the data on air and surfaces contamination and their changes due to different environmentally dangerous situations for the BAN.

Considering features of our library, the problem of preservation funds requires a non-traditional approach. This problem can be solved only by the complex investigation of the subjects in question by different biological and physico-chemical methods. Special attention should be given to bio-monitoring and control of the mycological state in book storages to ensure book preservation and a safe environment for personnel and readers. For this purpose the programme of environmental and biological monitoring was developed in our library.[6]

Bio-monitoring will allow us to obtain data characterizing the state of documents in storage as follows:-

- level of contamination by micro-organisms;
- speed of the process of biodeterioration;
- structure of contamination by micro-organisms;
- books that are suffering active process of biodeterioration and need isolation and disinfection;
- quality of disinfection treatments;
- degree of protection for books in containers from biodeterioration and a destructive environment.

The programme of biomonitoring accounts for the features of our book storages and the necessity for quick results. Biomonitoring requires sensitive, selective, express and simple methods of control. It initiated the search for new methods of diagnostics of biodeterioration.

The idea of biomonitoring is to place specially prepared test-samples into the books. After some intervals these test-samples are extracted and analysed for active microflora using traditional microbiological methods and an express method of respiration analysis by gas-liquid chromatography.

Considering the results of these experiments, a 4-level scale of the possible degree of biodestruction was developed (*Table 1*). The conclusion on the degree of biological activity and on the probability of biodestruction of the objects in question can be done using the data on carbon dioxide production by microflora after19-20 and 43-44 hours of cultivation.

This advanced method of diagnostics of biodeterioration has the following advantages. It allows:-

- detection of the process of biodestruction in the very early stage, when visual observation cannot detect it;
- obtaining a quantitative measure of this process to introduce into library experience an objective method of evaluation of preservation funds.

***Table 1* The scale for estimation of the probability of documents bio-deterioration**

Carbon dioxide concentration %(volume) after cultivation 19-20 hours	43-44 hours	The stage of fungi growth	The probability of biodeterioration, marks
0.03 - 0.05	0.03 - 0.05	absent	Extremely low
0.06 - 0.11	0.06 - 1.10	begin	low
0.12 - 0.40	1.11 - 2.50	distinguished	high
> 0.41	> 2.51	well noted	certain

All the monitoring data are placed in the special monitoring chart to form the computer data base. This programme of biomonitoring is applied to the Baer Collection, the Library of Peter the Great, and others.

The approach developed and experience acquired under our monitoring programme can be used in other libraries and archives. It is of special interest for smaller institutions, which have no department of conservation. According to this programme, we worked together with the library of Voronzov Palace, Alupka in Ukraine, and two libraries in Trier, Germany.

REFERENCES

1. Staib, F. "Deteriorating Material as a Possible Source of Fungi Pathogenic to Man: Aspergillus fumigatus as an Example". *Biodeterioration; The Proceedings of the Fourth International Biodeterioration Symposium.* London: Pitman Pub. Ltd. for the Biodeterioration Society, 1980, pp. 341-343.

2. Nyuksha, Yuliya P. *Biodeterioration of Paper and Books.* St. Petersburg: Library of the Russian Academy of Sciences, 1994.

3. Nyuksha, Yuliya P. "Problems of Air Hygienic State in Book Storages", *Opit raboty Gosudarstvennoj Publichnoj Bibioteki imeni M.E. Saltikova-Tchedrina,* 9 (1954), pp. 3-15.

4. Gallo, F. "Contenuto Mikrobio dell' Aria e Infezioni Secondarie dei Libri", *Bollettino dell' Istituto Centrale per la Patologia del Libro,* 23 (1/2) 1964, pp. 1-8.

5. Kowalik, R. and Y. Sadurska. "Mikroflora nisczaca papier, spore i piezecie woskowe, wystepyjaca w powietrzu magazinow archivalnych", *Acta microbiol.,* 5 (2) 1956, pp. 277-284.

6. Nyuksha, Yuliya P., L.G. Levashova, V.I. Kobyakova and Yu. V. Pokrovskaya. "Storage in Containers: Biological Features", *Papers of the 3rd Annual Meeting on the Problems of Preventive Conservation and Storage of the Cultural Inheritance.* "Storages of Artifacts in Small Hermetic Volumes". St. Petersburg: Russian State Museum, 1994, pp. 51-55.

MAINTENANCE OF AIR-CONDITIONING EQUIPMENT: IMPERATIVE STEP AGAINST DISASTERS

Ramón SÁNCHEZ-CHAPELLÍN

National Library of Venezuela

INTRODUCTION

Some of the disasters and accidents occurring in our libraries and archives are due to lack of maintenance of the equipment used to control the environment, or to unnoticed carelessness. Thus, sometimes, a dehumidifier with a damaged floating device becomes full of water, overflowing and creating a source of humidity. A fan with a rusty wire or a wire wrongly connected could provoke a fire. And an air-conditioning system without filters or with old filters can cause the obstruction in the tubes that evacuate the condensed water.

In the tropics, sharp climatic changes are common. After a sun-shiny morning we can easily have a stormy afternoon. These climatic changes transform the environment, and the mechanisms used to control the environmental conditions in most of the cases do not fulfil our needs.

Another factor affecting the creation of the best environment is the lack of space in the deposits. This can compel us to jeopardise security of the collections, since we have to locate them at places such as the upper part close to the lights, or near the floor, and, sometimes, at shelves under pipes that apparently do not present any risk.

This paper describes an accident in the photographs deposit in the National Library of Venezuela, and the way it was solved.

ACCIDENT DESCRIPTION

After a long rainy night, the custodian of the collection noticed the accident when he arrived the next morning at the photographs deposit. Immediately the Conservation Centre and the Maintenance Office of the institution were informed. The air-conditioning system did not have any filter, and, given time, dust entered into the system provoking the obstruction of the tubes. The tray of the air- conditioning unit which accumulates the condensed water overflowed and the water started to fall down to the false ceiling. This ceiling - made out of an absorbent material - softened, and part of it collapsed over the shelves that held the collection. After the collapse of the ceiling, the water fell down directly over the shelves.

Due to lack of space in the deposit and the fact that the unit of the air-conditioning was somewhat hidden by the ceiling, four shelves were located under this unit, whose evacuation system had never failed since its setting-up in 1980.

The collection was kept in corrugated polypropylene boxes, which decreased the damage to the bibliographic material, because of the impermeability of the polypropylene. The individual enclosures within the boxes are made out of paper, and this served as a buffer when the humidity increased. The group of damaged negatives, which were temporarily removed from the boxes, consists of seventy-two envelopes which contain five hundred contemporary photograph negatives and the contact copies of them, adhered to the envelopes. Part of this material already showed some damage. This group represents less than 1% of the collection on the four shelves located under the control unit of the air-conditioning.

RECOVERY OF THE MATERIAL: TREATMENT APPLIED

Under the guidance of a conservator, and with the backing of the Maintenance Office and the personnel of the Photograph Division, the material which had been harmed was recovered.

Every single box was checked in order to observe the condition of the collection. The boxes splashed in the accident were dried with cloths and were placed on other shelves.

The wet material was immediately sent to the Conservation Centre whose headquarters are located in the same building. Apart from the paper laboratory, the photograph laboratory was also used. Here, the negatives were removed from the paper envelopes, were immersed in water for three minutes and then in a Kodak Photo-Flo 200 solution for thirty seconds - so that water could be dried out without leaving a stain. After that, they were hung with clips on strings to be air dried.

The envelopes, with the contact copies, were air dried placed over blotting paper.

Thanks to the immediate action taken, the negatives, envelopes and contact prints, did not suffer evident damage.

STABILIZATION OF THE DEPOSIT

Together with the aforementioned actions, we started the stabilisation of the deposit. The air-conditioning was set out in order to avoid a greater water condensation and to evacuate the water tracts. The collapsed ceiling was cleaned, and the four shelves that were located under the control unit of the air-conditioning system were relocated in the deposit. The shelves near the zone of the accident were covered temporarily with plastic sheeting so that the water could not reach any box within them.

Additional fans and dehumidifiers were set in the deposit to eliminate the accumulated humidity and to create an air flow to try to remove any focus of stagnant humidity.

After covering the shelves, we started to evacuate the condensed water and to eliminate any material that caused the obstruction of the pipes. This procedure took a few hours, and when the relative humidity was measured, we observed it had reached acceptable levels.

CONCLUSION

Always, every experience leads us to knowledge and makes us take steps to avoid the same mistakes.

This accident taught us the following:-

1. The security of the collections must not be jeopardised because of a lack of space. We must never locate shelves and collections under control units of the air-conditioning or pipes and similar facilities that present this type of risk.

2. The importance of creating and fulfilling a maintenance plan for the equipment used to control the environmental conditions.

3. The importance of taking additional measures in case of sharp climatic changes.

4. The importance of an immediate response to avoid major damages.

5. The necessity of creating a disaster plan.

6. The additional advantages given by polypropylene as a conservation material.

FREEZE-DRYING OF WATER-DAMAGED PAPER MATERIALS: A REPORT ON PRACTICAL DISASTER RECOVERY

Peter SCHWERDT

Battelle Ingenieurtechnik GmbH (Germany)

INTRODUCTION

Earthquakes. Floods. Fires. Tornadoes. These are just a few of the natural - or man-made - disasters that can harm cultural properties. But to affect or even destroy, for example, cultural objects made of paper, it does not need a big catastrophe.

The less exciting dangers arise from leaking water pipes, heating and air- conditioning systems, failing sprinklers, minor rainstorms or broken effluent ducts. Water damages from various sources are the most common hazards to papers, books, archives and documents. Fortunately water-damaged valuable or unique materials will not necessarily be lost. Water - theoretically - can be removed by different drying processes.

In my lecture I will talk about strategies and methods to save water-damaged materials. It is addressed to library and archives staff as well as to conservators and restorators, but also to everybody dealing with private or public paper-based collections. Battelle's experience in drying paper materials results from our Paper Deacidification Method where drying plays a major role in the process.

HOW BATTELLE GOT INVOLVED

In summer 1993, a failure of the sprinkler system occurred at the Frankfurt University Library. Fortunately only some 1,200 books in the basement were wetted by water draining from above. The early-morning leakage was detected very soon. It was good fortune that somebody knew what to do then. The books were rescued very quickly by arriving library staff and deep-frozen in the freezers of the university mensa nearby.

Then Battelle was asked to help with drying the books in Battelle's large vacuum chambers.

We first tried our special microwave/vacuum drying process developed for the paper deacidification process. This technique has proved to work well with papers of normal humidity. With these wet and frozen books, the microwave drying did not give good results. For this reason we chose a conventional freeze-drying method to save the University Library material. After reconditioning and pressing, the books returned to the shelves almost without visible effects.

EFFECTS OF WATER DAMAGE TO PAPERS

Wet paper materials are damaged by several factors:-

- it is an excellent medium for mould growth
- the physical strength of the pages is almost lost
- the volume and weight of soaked papers can be doubled
- bindings may be destroyed by expansion and weight of wet books
- labels may fall off, stamp colours may run
- in archives, inks and colours may bleed out and disappear
- coated papers may become fused together
- metal parts, especially in archives and office files, become rusty.

SALVAGE OPERATIONS FOR WATER-DAMAGED COLLECTIONS

The attack and growth of mould is the most severe danger to wetted papers because it can result in complete contamination and loss of the collections. In warm, humid weather, mould-growth will appear within 48 hours! For this reason, every effort should be made to reduce the humidity and temperature and to vent the rooms. The wet materials must be kept as cool as possible by every means and be provided with good air circulation until they can be evacuated and stabilised.

As mould may develop only on the outer edges of the bindings, the books should be kept closed and tight together. In no case should books be separated, opened and dried with a fan or by heating the room! For the same reasons, the common equipment for drying wet walls or floors is absolutely unsuitable to dry wet paper collections. It should not even be operated in rooms containing wet papers.

The most generally accepted method of stabilising water-damaged library and archival materials before they are dried is by freezing and storing at low temperatures. This buys time in which the next steps can be planned and organised. Freezing of wet papers provides safe storage for an indefinite period of time, preserving the physical condition in which they are found and preventing further deterioration by water and mould.

Before freezing, it may seem tempting to wash away accumulated mud and dirt, particularly from a river flood. This should never be attempted by untrained persons nor should time be taken for this purpose if any delay in packing and freezing the complete materials would result.

The materials should be packed as packages with a thickness of 5 to 15 cm. They have to be separated from each other by water-resistant layers like plastic bags, freezer paper or silicone paper. This prevents them from sticking and freezing together. As packing containers, corrugated board boxes or plastic crates can be used. It must be considered that cardboard boxes would lose their stability when getting wet. In any case, packing damaged documents must be closely supervised.

If the materials are to be frozen, prior arrangements should have been made to ship the packed materials immediately to freezing facilities. Although seldom known, there are commercial freezing and storage capacities available in many cities.

The size and formation of ice crystals inside the paper is governed by the rate and temperature of freezing. Blast or shock freezing used for certain types of foodstuffs is designed to freeze quickly in a few hours, often at temperatures below -50°C. Although small crystals cause less additional increase of thickness, no evidence was found of any damage to cellulosic materials caused solely by the action of freezing. Once frozen, the cold temperature conditions should be maintained at about -18°C.

FREEZE-DRYING

Learning from the big floods like 1966 in Florence, there is generally better information about the mechanisms for drying cellulosic materials and about the technologies being developed for this purpose.

The use of vacuum chambers for freeze-drying large quantities of books and paper records has become an acceptable, almost common, approach. Freeze-drying uses the sublimation of frozen water, that is, water removal by transition directly from ice to vapour, without liquid water occurring. This avoids most of the problems related to expansion, sticking and wicking of water-sensitive and soluble media.

Freeze-drying is carried out in chambers where the already frozen material is kept in a vacuum below 6 mbar (abs). This is the physical condition for the sublimation of (pure) water where no liquid water exists. In case of really dirty or salty water or wet materials, the sublimation pressure is somewhat lower. The drying process can be accelerated by careful heating to intensify the formation of water vapour.
The drying process has to make sure that all the books' composite materials have a water content of less than 7%. This must be absolutely guaranteed to avoid the risk of post-drying mould development.

Mould-infected material, if dried completely under freeze-drying conditions, can be safely controlled for a short period of time. The spores remain quite dormant if stored in an air-conditioned environment at low temperature and low humidity. However, the materials must not be returned to the library until the mould contamination is treated. The treatment with ethylene oxide remains the most effective method against mould attack, especially when caused by river water. The use of ETO, however, has become an increasingly controversial subject because this chemical is carcinogenic. An alternative is the sterilisation by gamma-rays. A disadvantage of exposure to radiation in some cases is the certain loss of physical strength.

BATTELLE'S EXPERIENCE

Since we started with drying books of the Frankfurt University Library two years ago, our facility was used quite frequently. Water-damaged materials were sent from offices, industrial companies, museums and municipal archives. Summarised, there were about 3,000 books, 250 m of archival files, and 60,000 documents.

We helped with the assessment of the damage, the planning for salvage, the negotiations with the insurance companies. With our experts, we organised the recovery team for removal and packing on site, transport, freezing and storage, drying, reconditioning, cleaning, pressing and shipment back to the shelves. Often we found little awareness of the urgency for action in the case of water damage to paper materials. Sometimes, wet collections were left for days and weeks before they were finally stabilised by freezing.

DISASTER PREPAREDNESS PLANNING

It is obvious that a well-organised plan can greatly reduce the costs of salvage and restoration as well as the proportion of outright losses. It will also help to lessen the emotional and stressful impact on library staff in any case of emergency. But still only a few institutions seem to be prepared.

Any disaster recovery should be designed "to save the maximum amount of material with minimum amounts of restoration".

But, most importantly, remember that the time to plan for an emergency is ***now***, before a disaster requires immediate action!

Contact Battelle for further information and assistance in establishing a disaster plan.

ENVIRONMENTAL RESEARCH IN THE LIBRARY OF THE RUSSIAN ACADEMY OF SCIENCES

Svetlana V. USPENSKAYA and Valeriya I. KOBYAKOVA

Library of the Russian Academy of Sciences

INTRODUCTION

This report describes the results of scientific and practical work in our Library on collections monitoring and environmental research of the collection after the fire in 1988, as an inherent part of preventive conservation.

The problem of articles of culture being affected by air contaminated by industry in large cities recently became a point of special interest. The city of St. Petersburg is no exception, and our Library, which is in the historical centre of the city, like many other museums and cultural institutions, is affected by a destructive environment [1]. The problem of environmental research and monitoring in the Library of the Russian Academy of Sciences (BAN) has gained special importance after the fire in 1988. Over 3.6 million volumes are known to be damaged by high temperature and humidity as the result of the fire. To prevent large-scale mould infection of books, newspapers and other materials stored in the Library, total disinfection of documents and storage was carried out, and this treatment on that scale has no analogy in library history in the world. Approximately 8.1 million books and newspaper files were treated, as well as storage with a total volume of over 44 thousand m^3. As a result, concentration of fungi spores in air was lowered in storage by 15-75 times, and contamination of air by bacteria became lower than natural contamination in other libraries of the city by 3-4 times. The method of disinfection that was developed, patented and used in the Library allowed in the state of emergency, on the one hand, preserving library storage and, on the other hand, cleaning up an environment contagious for the library personnel and readers[2]. Yet, at present, eight years after the fire, the following negative environmental factors cannot be excluded:-

- possible desorption of formaldehyde from documents, bookcases, walls;
- desorption of volatile compounds from building materials used in repair work;
- contamination of the storage environment as the result of desorption of degradation products from carbonized books.

Considering all these factors, our environmental research should be developed in two main directions:-

1. Influence of the microclimate on documents preservation.
2. Influence of the environment on the health of personnel and readers.

Leading specialists in St. Petersburg and Russia were called upon to solve these problems. The Institute of Toxicology of the Ministry of Health Protection investigated air environment and microflora conditions in our Library in 1991 at the Library's request. The Russian National Library and the Central City Library V.V. Mayakovskii were chosen as control objects.[3] In this study, the air of book storages and work rooms was analyzed for the following parameters:-

- contamination by formaldehyde;
- contamination by other volatile organic compounds, namely acetone, benzene, toluene, ethylbenzene, meta-, orto- and paraxyloles;
- carbon oxides;
- nitrogen oxides;
- sulphur dioxide;
- mercury and lead;
- dust;

  and also:
- contamination by bacteria and by mould, and fungi spores.

All measurements were carried out by standard techniques and such methods as gas-liquid chromatography and spectrophotometry were employed. Measurements of formaldehyde were made by several methods including Drager sorption indicator tubes and individual indicator tickets which were kindly supplied by the Getty Conservation Institute. Formaldehyde concentrations were measured also by the American method by individual indicator tickets based on passive sorption. Such measurements were made in four book storages with eight hours of exposition. Final analysis was made by the Getty Conservation Institute, yet all concentrations were low, two orders of magnitude lower than U.S. limits.

The concentration of dust in the air was also measured, but the chemical nature of the dust was not investigated.

New environmentally ecological dangerous factors appear after the disaster.[4] We pay attention to the following:-

- explanation of the spectrum of air pollutants, residual concentrations of disinfectants; volatile products of thermodestruction of paper and other materials;
- higher level of dust production;
- objects of storage pollution by toxic substances, formed during the disaster;
- new associations of microorganisms formation.

The results of investigations of two damaged collections are presented in this report: The Baer Collection and The Modern National Collection.

Different methods of stabilisation were used to recover damaged collections. Books of the 18th to 19th centuries were dried in the BAN using the conventional drying method. Freezing at –18°C was used as a first measure to conserve the National Collection (modern publications).

Books of this collection were treated for two years and at present they have returned to the storage.

Expertise by the Institute of Paper Industry proved that the longevity of modern paper decreased considerably as the result of destructive factors.[5] The sanitary-hygienic state of these documents also requires attention.

Bindings and text-blocks of many books were considerably deformed, the paper was thermodestructed and polluted by a black-brown thin coating of dirt and soot.

To decide whether readers may have access to these collections, these pollutants should be completely investigated. We decided to carry out complete research including chemical, structural and mycological analysis.

CHEMICAL COMPOSITION OF THE THIN COATING OF POLLUTANTS

The problem was to identify the chemical nature of organic substances in order to determine the toxicity of the thin coating of pollutants.

The analytical experiments were made to identify the chemical composition of the thin coating of pollutants on books thermodestructed by fire. The technique of gas chromatography/mass spectrometry was used.

The film sample of thin coating of pollutants was treated by hexane and acetone concentrated and analysed on GS/MS Finigan System INCOS 50 with NBS Data library using 42000 mass spectra of organic compounds to identify the chemical nature of substances. The most intensive peaks on the chromatograms are due to different phthalates and carboxylic ethers, carbonic acids and their ethers, highest alcohols, heavy hydrocarbons, polyaromatic compounds (PAC) and polychlorobiphenyls (PCBs). We do not give the whole list of chemicals identified: their total amount is about 50. We give only those that are the most toxic. (See *Table 1*)

Table 1 Identified toxic compounds in dust and thin coating on polluted margins of books

Polyaromatic Hydrocarbons (PAH)	Polychlorobiphenyls (PCB)
9-phenanthrene carboxaldehyde	2,2',6-trichoro- 1,1'-biphenyl
Phenanthrene	2,4,6-trichoro- 1,1'-biphenyl
1-methyl-anthracene	2,2',5-trichoro- 1,1'-biphenyl
2-methyl-anthracene	2,3,5-trichoro- 1,1'-biphenyl
1-phenyl-naphtalene	tetrachloro- 1,1'-biphenyl
3,6-dimethyl-phenanthrene	2,3,3',4'-tetrachoro- 1,1'-biphenyl
Pyrene	2,2',3,5'-tetrachoro- 1,1'-biphenyl
2,3,5-trimethyl-phenanthrene	
2,4,5,7-tetramethyl-phenanthrene	
2,5-dimethyl-phenanthrene	
Fluoranthene	
1,2,3,4,4A,9,10,10A-octahydro-1,1A,4A-trimethyl-7(1-methyl)- phenanthrene	
1,2,3,4,4A,9,10A-octahydro-1-1A-dimethyl 1-phenanthrenecarbocyclic acid	
benzo[a]pyrene	

INVESTIGATION OF THE STRUCTURE OF THIN COATING OF POLLUTANTS

The main part of thin coating of pollutants is found on the edges of the sheet. Thin coating of pollutant is an amorphous mass with crystal inclusions, the farther from the edge, the lower the thickness and quantity of the coating of pollutants. The surface of the fibre is covered by the unbroken polymer film with biological structures. At the distance of more than 0.6 cm from the edge, the fibre surface is clean, without thin coating of pollutants.

MICROBIOLOGICAL ANALYSIS

Using the method of luminescent microscopy, we established that the main part of thin coating of pollutants consists of non-luminescent matter. Separate spores and impregnation of green and yellow-green colour was observed with luminescence maximum at 520 - 540 nm when irradiation with wavelength 365 nm was used for excitation. One may suppose that the luminescence is caused by fungi spores and parts of the mycelium. Microbiological analysis of samples from book edges and book bindings revealed live micro-organisms and bacteria. Fungi flora is represented by genera Stemphilium, Monilia, Penicillium, Aspergillus. Biological structure was revealed also by electron microscopy pictures.

THE ANALYSIS OF DUST

In the dust sample from storages of the Modern National Collection, polychlorinated biphenyls (PCB), polyaromatic hydrocarbons (PAH), phthalates and aliphatic acids were identified and PCBs were quantitatively determined. The amount of PCBs in the sample was 118-1000 mg/kg. In the dust sample from the Baer Collection, almost the same compounds were identified. The total content of PCB was determined as 306 mg/kg. In the dust samples from storage of the manuscript collection, no PCB and PAH were found. [6 7]

THE TOXICITY OF CHEMICAL IDENTIFIED

Polyaromatic hydrocarbons identified (*e.g.*, anthracene, phenanthrene, pyrene, benzo[a]pyrene) may appear after high temperature combustion of organic material as a result of incomplete burning.

All PAH have carcinogenic toxicity with benzo[a]pyrene as a leader.

Polychlorinated biphenyls also may appear after incomplete burning of plastics and paints, containing aromatic compounds and chlorine. All kinds of PCB comprise about 129 isomers with 1,1-1', 2', 3' pentachlorobiphenyl as the most toxic. Its toxicity is only two orders less than the toxicity of the most toxic organic compound 2, 3, 7, 8 - tetrachlorodibenzoparadioxene.

The facts that we studied and the problems concerned with them are important not only because our Library suffered the most destructive fire in the history of culture. In recent times, fires in private and public libraries have become more frequent as a result of accidents, natural disasters and vandalism. The foundation of the programme of rehabilitation is an ethical imperative - to rescue and preserve the cultural inheritance. We suppose that environmental problems should be taken into account together with the historical, ethical and money problems in organizing work to rescue cultural inheritance in emergency situations.

REFERENCES

1. Druzik, C.M., D.C. Stulik and F. Preusser. "Carbonyl and Carboxylic Acid Pollutants in the Museum Environments". *American Chemical Society. Division of Environmental Chemistry. Preprints 198th National Meeting*, Miami, FL, 1989.

2. Shchekotihin, E.A. "Disinfection of Large Book Storages of the Library of the Russian Academy of Science. Suffered the Flood as a Result of Fire Extinguishing". In: *The Problems of Preservation of Books Collections*, Leningrad, 1988, pp. 57-77.

3. Havrilenko, K.C. "Sanitary and Hygienic Evaluation of the Air Environment and the Microflora Condition at the Library of the Russian Academy of Science. Suffered the Fire in 14-15 February, 1988". *Report of the St. Petersburg Institute of Toxicology, Russian Ministry of Health Protection*, 1992.

4. Kobyakova, V.I., O.V. Skvortsova and S.V. Uspenskaya. "Environmentally Dangerous Factors at the Libraries Storages". *Papers of the Scientific and Practical Conference "Criteria for the Safe Environment"*, St. Petersburg, 1994, pp. 53-54.

5. Ryabchenko, S.V. "Research Survey of the Collection Storage Conditions at the Library of the Russian Academy of Science. Suffered the Fire in 1988". *Report of the St. Petersburg Technological Institute of Paper Industry*, 1990.

6. Levashova, L.G., S.V. Uspenskaya, V.I. Kobyakova and Yu.A. Ignatiev. "Research of Indoor Pollutants in Storages of Cultural Inheritance using Chromatography and Mass Spectroscopy". *The International Symposium "Chromatography and Mass Spectrometry in Environmental Analysis": Abstracts* (ISCMS'94) will be held on October 3 to 7, 1994 at the Conference Centre Hotel "St. Petersburg", St. Petersburg, Russia, p. 197.

7. Levashova, L.G., S.V. Uspenskaya, V.I. Kobyakova and Yu. A. Ignatiev. "Outdoor and Indoor Sources of Air Pollutants in the Storages of Cultural Inheritance". *Scientific and Regulatory Aspects of Air Quality Management "Air'95" June 7-9 1995*. Edited by Ju. I. Musijchuk, E.P. Vishnevsky, St. Petersburg, 1995, p.75.

THE BATTELLE MASS DEACIDIFICATION PROCESS: ESTABLISHMENT AT DIE DEUTSCHE BIBLIOTHEK IN LEIPZIG AND FUTURE APPLICATIONS

Ulrich BEHRENS

Battelle Ingenieurtechnik GmbH (Germany)

INTRODUCTION

The mission of libraries and archives traditionally is to preserve written knowledge and cultural treasures, to collect present-day information and to disseminate it for future needs. However, most libraries in the world are facing a rapidly growing problem that has already reached threatening dimensions. Almost all collections of books, newspapers and documents printed or written since the mid 19th century are deteriorating in the library stacks.

The lack of paper permanence is due to the sulphuric acids in industrially produced papers. The traces of acid lead to a decomposition of the cellulosic fibres and thus to a loss of paper strength within 50 to 100 years, which is accelerated under insufficient storage conditions.

In order to preserve books and papers in their original form, methods for chemical preservation have been developed in several countries since the mid sixties. The different procedures have in common that the acid content in the paper is neutralised and an alkaline buffer of pH 7.5 to 8.5 is deposited. They differ with respect to the alkaline substances and the solvents used (magnesium or zinc compounds, gas phase or liquid phase). All are working as batch processes and only small pilot plants existed.

In Germany, the demand for mass preservation technologies to save deteriorating books and papers is a topical item in library policies. With support by the German Federal Ministry for Research and Technology, the Deutsche Bibliothek and Battelle in 1987 started a research programme aimed at the implementation of mass deacidification in Germany.

One of the highlights of this programme was the commissioning of the world-wide first mass deacidification plant - the Deutsche Bücherei in Leipzig in June 1994.

The plant was designed and constructed by Battelle. With its projected annual capacity of 400,000 books, it represents the largest mass deacidification facility in the world. In addition, Battelle has a smaller unit in operation at its facilities in Frankfurt. This unit currently has contracts from 20 German libraries and/or archives and is actively treating books with this unit while it develops its plans to establish a second commercial facility in Germany.

A new promising deacidification process to prevent acidic papers from deterioration, which has been developed by Battelle, is used in these facilities. This liquid-phase impregnation process works with a new neutralisation agent containing magnesium-titanium-ethylate which deacidify the paper and supply an alkaline buffer of magnesium carbonate. A new non-polluting, non-toxic silicon-organic solvent replaces the environmentally harmful CFCs used by former processes. Due to the excellent compatibility with most common materials, the process can be applied to both library and archival collections.

The process includes three steps: pre-drying, impregnation and post-drying. The Battelle concept provides, for different applications, two efficient vacuum-drying processes, one with microwave heating, the other with conventional heating. The plants have a closed solvent cycle and an automatic process control. Thus, the paper deacidification process is non-polluting, easy to operate, very fast and allows large annual capacities.

MARKET ASSESSMENT

The total number of books in scientific libraries in Germany is amounting to nearly 200 million volumes. About 90% were printed on acid-containing paper. According to our systematic inquiries, in most cases libraries are eager to start preservation in order to prevent further deterioration. Most libraries are interested in a deacidification service and not in the purchase and operation of a deacidification plant like Leipzig.

This is the reason why Battelle developed the plan to establish restoration centres in Germany and later elsewhere. The first centre should be built at Battelle's site in Eschborn, a suburb of Frankfurt. In the first phase, this restoration centre will have a capacity of 60 tonnes per year, respectably 120,000 volumes. The plant is now under construction. Its start-up is scheduled for April 1996. In this centre, library and archive material can be treated as service processes.

Our prices are based on treatment boxes and graduated according to the quantities ordered. There are three box sizes which correspond to the book formats octavo, quarto and folio with a volume of half of a shelf metre.

MASS DEACIDIFICATION OF BOOKS AND ARCHIVAL MATERIALS

The basic idea of Battelle's mass deacidification method is to subject books and archival documents to a chemical neutralisation treatment and hence to render the acids in the paper innocuous. It is done by a liquid-phase treatment, using non-aqueous, organic solvents. Because of environmental effects (air pollution) and endogenous processes, however, new acids will constantly form in the paper in time. An alkaline buffer is therefore added to neutralise those acids too.

The deacidification treatment basically comprises three stages:-

- pre-drying: reduction of the moisture content
- deacidification: chemical neutralisation with Mg-ethylate/Ti-ethylate in HMDO
- post-drying: removal of solvents from the paper.

Battelle's optimised method has an enormous technological margin against former processes and systems. No selection is necessary.

The Battelle process can be used for:-

(A) All kinds of books:

- no limitation in size
- no limitation in book paper (including coated paper)
- no limitation in book cloth or other covering material (including leather-bound books, books with metal clips and plastic book jackets)
- extremely damaged books.

(B) All kinds of archival material:

- no side effects on printing inks, stamps and colours
- bound and unbound archive material
- archival material in closed paper boxes
- brittle archive material.

(C) All kinds of maps.

FEATURES OF THE BATTELLE PROCESS

The Battelle method uses hexamethyldisiloxane (HMDO) as a solvent. This colourless organic silicon compound is harmless to the environment, non-toxic and compatible with all common materials used in books and archives. It is used in the cosmetic industry, for nail polish and after-shave.

The active substance contains alkoxides of magnesium and titanium, *i.e.*, compounds of the two metals with ethanol. Dissolved in HMDO they form thin-bodied solutions with very low surface tension, which is important for the impregnation of bound books.
With the Battelle-developed method it is possible to strengthen already damaged papers while neutralising the acid. This is accomplished by the highly reactive titanium component of the deacidifying solution, which interacts with the cellulose fibres of some papers, not of all. Depending on what kind of paper is treated, strength increases up to 50% are possible.

The strengthening effect can be further enhanced by means of isocyanates, which also can be dissolved in HMDO and which are applied to the paper in an additional process step. Isocyanates are toxic compounds and Battelle started research to find a non-toxic substitute. If work is finished, we hope the end of next year, a dream will be fulfilled for most of the librarians: then not only deacidifying books and archival materials is possible, but also a significant strengthening of the paper.

FUNCTIONAL CHARACTERISTICS OF THE FACILITY

The books and/or documents to be treated require sorting and packing by the customer into Battelle's treatment baskets. I ttelle makes available these treatment baskets in three different sizes: octavo,

quarto and folio. The baskets are to be locked and sealed by the customer. Therefore, the materials remain unopened in these baskets during the deacidification procedure and the transport.

In the Battelle facility, pre-drying, impregnation and post-drying are done in one chamber. During the pre-drying procedure, the books and documents are slowly heated carefully under vacuum to no more than 50°C. We use heat plates, flooded by warm water, and also the chamber wall is heated by warm water. The temperature of the water is limited to 50°C. The pre-drying is completed after 48 hours. Owing to the very low pressure, all the air is extracted from the pores of the paper.

When pre-drying is finished, the chamber is filled with the alkaline deacidifying solution. This vacuum impregnation guarantees that the solution enters very fast into all pores of the paper. The paper is completely filled with the liquid, even closed books and documents in boxes being entirely impregnated. As a consequence, the acid neutralisation and alkaline buffering processes take only a few minutes to be completed.

Then the solution of the treatment chamber is emptied and the post-drying starts. During this process the solvent is completely removed from the paper.

Like pre-drying, the post-drying of the impregnated books and documents takes place in vacuum, with simultaneous heating. Also at this step, the temperature is controlled to a maximum of 50°C. The exhaust vapours from the drying chamber are cooled in the solvent recovery unit, the condensation being collected and recycled.

The post-drying duration needs a maximum of 24 hours. After that time the treated material is solvent free. The re-establishing of the normal moisture content is completed after approximately three weeks. During this time, ethanol is continuously emitted. This depends on the reaction of the distributed Mg-Ethylate/Ti-Ethylate and the moisture.

The pH-value after treatment depends on different factors, for example the type of paper, the age and the original acid content. Normally the neutralisation raises the pH value to the alkaline range around 8,5 and 9,5. The alkaline buffer consists in 1,0 to 2,0% of magnesium carbonate.

The whole treatment is completed after 72 hours. Including the follow-up processing, the books and archival materials can be sent back to the libraries after approximately four weeks.

RESULTS

By the neutralisation treatment, at least the following listed characteristics are achieved:-

pH value

- Increase of the pH value in the neutral or alkaline range, with a pH above 7,0 at 98% of the treated material.
- Increase of the pH value in the neutral or alkaline range, with a pH above 7,5 at 95% of the treated material.

Alkaline range/buffer capacity

- Increase of the alkaline buffer of 2,0% of magnesium carbonate at 95% of the treated material.

In rare cases, the following changes can appear in the treated materials:-

- slight yellowing of the paper
- strippings by plastic laminated book covers

- slight odour of evaporating alcohol
- minor deformation of book covers
- darkening of heat-sensitive papers (FAX, etc.)
- sticking of photographic materials
- slight browning of leather.

Patents are pending for both the treatment method and the chemical substances.

BATTELLE'S CAPABILITIES

Battelle is an international technology organisation that serves industry and public institutions in developing, managing and commercialisation technology. With a wide range of scientific and technical capabilities, it helps to put technology to work for clients in 30 countries.

The close co-operation of Die Deutsche Bibliothek and Battelle has resulted in a mass deacidification method which is well proven and truly meets librarians' and archivists' requirements.

FACILITIES AND ASSISTANCE

The Battelle Ingenieurtechnik GmbH has the necessary technical know-how and the equipment to build further mass deacidification facilities.

Why not benefit from Battelle's considerable experience and know-how on paper conservation? In particular, Battelle seeks to establish a demonstration relationship with selected libraries and other entities. Such a relationship would consist of an agreement by book owners to provide a prescribed number of books, shipping such books to Frankfurt, treatment by Battelle and return shipment. Battelle would treat such books at a below-cost basis in recognition of the additional costs of shipping and the need to demonstrate the effectiveness of the process. You are invited to contact Ulrich Behrens for more information.

Use Battelle's Papersave service and belong to the first who stop the decay of their book and archival collections.

THE APPLICATION OF THE BATTELLE MASS DEACIDIFICATION TREATMENT IN THE GERMAN LIBRARY, LEIPZIG

Joachim LIERS

Deutsche Bücherei (Germany)

INTRODUCTION

It has long been widely acknowledged that paper produced industrially since the middle of the 19th century is endangered by decomposition.

What causes this decomposition process? Since 1826 the traditional gelatine sizing of paper began to be replaced by rosin sizing invented by Illig. Using this method, acid aluminium sulphate, which releases sulphuric acid, enters the paper. The acid decomposes the cellulose fibres by catalysing a hydrolysis reaction.[1]

Additionally, in the second half of the 19th century, wood became the main raw material for paper-making. Wood contains 15 to 30% lignin. The decomposition of lignin produces organic acids which speed up the ageing process.[2]

Unsuitable storage conditions, such as excessive heat and humidity and inadequate air-conditioning, accelerate the decomposition process as well. It may take only 50 to 80 years until a book or document can no longer be handled.

In the forties of our century, the first deacidification methods were developed by Schierholtz[3] and Barrow[4] and improved in the following years. The general idea of these methods is to neutralise the acids contained in the paper by an aqueous solution of earth alkali salts (*e.g.*, barium or calcium bicarbonate) or earth alkali hydroxides. Such deacidification methods are based on the individual treatment of each document. Methods of this type are used frequently by restorers but they require much time and labour. Therefore the treatment of books on a large scale, such as for an entire library, requires a new kind of process.

In the early seventies, the first mass deacidification processes, the DEZ process[5] and the Wei T'o process[6,7], were developed. Whereas the DEZ process works with the gaseous diethyl zinc, the Wei T'o process uses a solution of methoxy magnesium methyl carbonate as the deacidification compound. In the following years, these processes were improved and some new ones developed.[8] In 1987, the German Library began looking for a method to deacidify its books. A test comparing several mass deacidification treatments showed that none of the existing methods was able to effectively treat all library materials without adverse affects.[9]

Therefore the Battelle Institute in Frankfurt was engaged to develop a new mass deacidification process. The basis of their research was the Wei T'o process. The first German paper deacidification facility, which worked with a substantially improved version of this method, was put into operation at Battelle in 1990. After a further improvement of the Battelle deacidification method, a facility for the German Library was built in 1993. After a three-month test at Battelle, the equipment was moved to Leipzig and rebuilt in the basement of the German Library. On June 22, 1994, the Battelle mass deacidification equipment was put into operation.

THE BATTELLE MASS DEACIDIFICATION PROCESS

THE EQUIPMENT

The main components of the equipment are the treatment chamber, two vacuum pumps - for pre-drying and post-drying, a solvent recovery unit, and the storage tanks (*Figure 1*). Because of the flammability of the solvent used, the whole deacidification equipment had to be built explosion-proof. The mass deacidification facility in the German Library has a modular design and allows the installation of a planned additional treatment chamber.

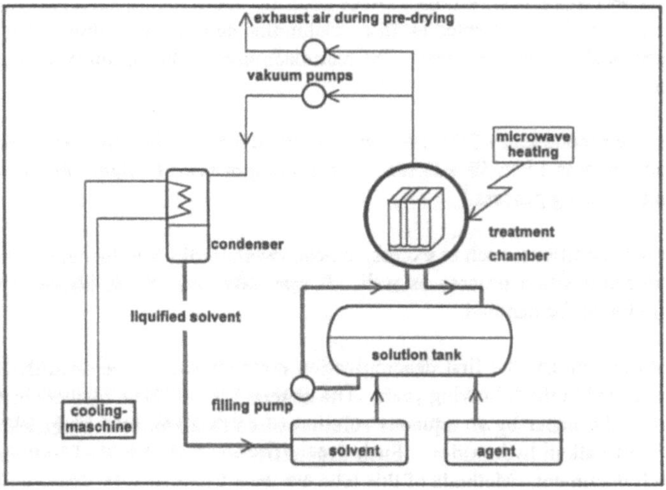

Figure 1 Scheme of the Battelle mass deacidification equipment.

The treatment chamber has a cylindrical shape with a diameter of 60 cm and a length of 4.5 m. It is equipped for microwave heating. The chamber is directly connected to the vacuum pumps. They realise a vacuum down to 1 mbar. The vacuum system for post-drying is directly coupled with a condenser to recover the solvent.

The storage tanks are located outside the German Library and lie underground. They consist of 4 tanks with a total volume of 50 m^3. The number of tanks permits a re-circulation of the used chemicals and a variation of the concentration of the deacidification compound. The tanks are sealed with nitrogen to prevent vapour leakage and also to keep air from flowing in when the volume in the tanks changes.

Because of the solvent recovery and the re-circulation of the used chemicals, this equipment allows a closed circulation of the chemical compounds.

The process control of the equipment takes place via a SPS (stored-programme controller) produced by Siemens. This programme control is suitable for complex industrial controlling problems. The whole process is displayed on, and operated through, a visual display system on a monitor. The SPS allows automatic, semi-automatic, and manual control of the equipment.

THE TREATMENT

For the deacidification treatment, the books must be selected and cleaned. Covers which contain metal are unsuitable for the deacidification treatment. Treatment of such materials is the topic of research at the moment.

The books and documents to be treated are placed in plastic baskets on a slide and moved into the treatment chamber. After closing the chamber, the deacidification treatment can be started.

To prepare the paper for deacidification, its normal moisture content of 7-8 wt.-% must be reduced to about 1 wt.-% in a pre-drying step.

Customarily, books are dried in a warm air dryer and in a vacuum dryer with conventional heating (*e.g.*, MMC-drying procedure). This drying procedure is not very efficient, requiring about 36 hours, because of the poor heat transfer in the vacuum. Therefore Battelle developed a new technology of book- and paper-drying - a vacuum dryer combined with microwave heating. In this way, it is possible to warm the books rapidly and evenly in a vacuum.

Infrared-sensors monitor the temperature of the books in the different baskets and control the microwave heating. In this way, even books containing different kinds of paper are dried evenly. The infrared-sensors ensure that the temperature of the book surface does not rise above 50°C. Former experiments have shown that, by keeping this surface temperature, the temperature inside the books does not rise over 60°C. It takes about one to two hours to pre-dry the books.

After pre-drying, the impregnation of the books starts. The chamber is completely evacuated before the impregnation begins. Through this process all the air is extracted from the pores of the paper.

When the chamber is filled with the alkaline solution, the papers absorb the liquid very quickly like a "sponge", even though the books and documents are enclosed in the baskets. The pre-drying step and vacuum impregnation guarantee that the solution quickly enters all pores of the paper. Therefore the impregnation process takes only a few minutes to be completed.

After the treatment chamber is drained, the deacidification solvent is pumped back into the storage tanks and can be re-used.

The impregnated books contain solvent in the range of their dry weight. Therefore the saturated books must be dried. The post-drying process takes place in a vacuum with simultaneous microwave heating as in the pre-drying step. Because of the evaporation enthalpy of the solvent, a temperature drop of the treated material in the vacuum takes place. However, effective warming by microwave heating prevents the books from freezing and allows fast post-drying. This process requires about half-an-hour.

The exhaust vapour from the drying chamber is cooled in the solvent recovery unit and the obtained condensate is collected and recycled.

After post-drying, the chambers are ventilated and the books are removed from the chamber.

At the moment, the whole deacidification process takes about two to three hours. It is possible to deacidify about 150 - 300 books per run.

THE CHEMICAL PROCESS

The chemicals used in the solvent phase of the Battelle deacidification process are ethylates of magnesium and titanium and isopropylates of titanium. These alkoxides are dissolved in hexamethyldisiloxane **(I)**. Whereas the ethylate of magnesium acts as the deacidification compound, the alkoxides of titanium are only solutizing agents.

By using the environmentally safe hexamethyldisiloxane as the solvent, it was possible to substitute conventionally used chlorofluorocarbons (*e.g.*, by the Wei T'o process).

Our solvent is compatible with all materials commonly used in books and archival materials. This colourless organic silicon compound has no effect on adhesives, plastics, printing inks or dyes. It leaves no odour and produces no marks or changes in the treated books.

From the deacidifying process the alkoxides of magnesium and titanium remain finely distributed in the paper. They react with the water and with the carbon dioxide of the air by producing magnesium carbonate, titanium dioxide and ethanol **(II-IV)**. The acids are neutralised by the compounds of magnesium **(V)**. Because of the formation of ethanol, the treated books have to stay in a separate room for about 14 days before they can be moved to the stacks.

$(CH_3)_3 - Si - O - Si - (CH_3)_3$ **(I)**
hexamethyldisiloxane

$Mg(C_2H_5O)_2 + 2\,H_2O \rightarrow Mg(OH)_2 + 2\,C_2H_5OH$ **(II)**
magnesium ethylate → magnesium hydroxide, ethanol

$Mg(OH)_2 + CO_2 \rightarrow MgCO_3 + H_2O$ **(III)**

$Ti(C_2H_5O)_4 + 2\,H_2O \rightarrow TiO_2 + 4\,C_2H_5OH$ **(IV)**
titanium ethylate → titanium dioxide

$Mg(OH)_2 + H_2SO_4 \rightarrow MgSO_4 + 2\,H_2O$ **(V)**
sulphuric acid → magnesium sulphate

RESULTS OF THE DEACIDIFICATION

The deacidification process not only results in the effective neutralisation of the acids in the paper, but also raises the pH value to around 8 to 9. This process also gives an alkaline buffer to the paper which consists of 1 to 2% magnesium carbonate. Thus the treated paper is additionally protected against a further formation of acids.

The effectiveness of the deacidification was investigated by treating test-paper. The test-paper was a 20-year-old, acid-sized, wood-containing paper. Some sheets of the treated and the untreated test-paper were artificially aged up to a maximum of 60 days in a climate chamber with a temperature of 80°C and 65% relative humidity.

Paper samples were investigated in the very beginning of the ageing test and after a definite ageing time. The pH-value, the content of acids or alkalis, and the strength of paper, were determined from these samples.

Figure 2 shows the behaviour of the pH-value, and the content of acids or alkalis of treated and untreated paper, throughout the ageing process. To illustrate the content of acids or alkalis in the paper, these values were converted into a deficit or a surplus of $MgCO_3$.

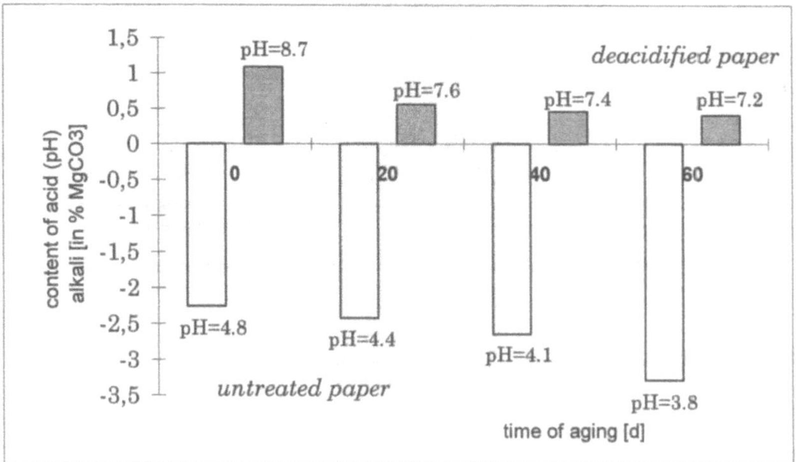

Figure 2 Content of acids or alkalis and the pH-value of the paper related to the time of ageing

Whereas untreated, unaged paper has a pH-value of about 4.9, the pH-value of the deacidified sample is about 8.8. The untreated paper has a deficit of about 2.2% $MgCO_3$. After treatment the paper contains an alkaline buffer of about 1.2% $MgCO_3$.

During the ageing time, the pH-value and the content of the alkaline buffer decrease in the treated paper, whereas the deficit of alkalis increases in the untreated paper. But, after an ageing time of about 60 days, the pH-value of the deacidified paper did not fall below 7.

The next diagram (*Figure 3*) shows the behaviour of the tensile strength of the treated and untreated paper in the ageing process. The strength was measured, as well, after folding the paper using the method of Bansa.[9]

The strengths of the treated paper are higher than those of the untreated paper. Whereas the strengths of the deacidified paper are nearly unaffected by the ageing process, the strengths decrease for the untreated paper.

These results show that the deacidification is able to decelerate the ageing rate of paper.

Tests to investigate the influence of deacidification on the rate of ageing are continuing.

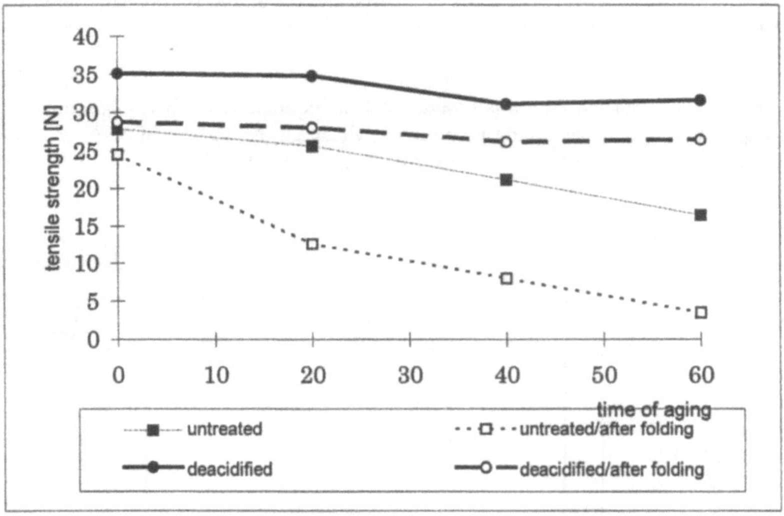

Figure 3 Paper strength related to the time of ageing.

CONCLUSIONS

With the Battelle mass deacidification equipment the German Library has an excellent tool for saving its stock of books from acid deterioration. This new process allows the effective deacidification of a large number of books and archival materials. It has no adverse effects on the treated materials and is environmentally safe. Therefore, this new technology is a milestone in preservation in libraries and archives.

ACKNOWLEDGEMENTS

The whole project of developing and building the first German mass deacidification equipment was founded by the *Bundesministerium für Forschung und Technologie.*

REFERENCES

1. Brandt, Astrid-Christiane. *La Désacidification de Masse du Papier.* Paris: Bibliothèque Nationale, 1992.

2. Bund-Länder-Arbeitsgruppe Papierzerfall. *Bericht ... vom 15. Juni 1992.* Berlin: Deutsches Bibliotheksinstitut, 1992.

3. Schierholtz, O.J. U.S. Patent no. 2.033.452 (1936).

4. Barrow, W.J. and Reavis C. Sproull. "Permanence in Book Papers", *Science*, 129:3356 (Apr. 24, 1959), pp. 1075-1084.

5. Williams, J.C. and G.B. Kelly. U.S. Patent no. 3.969.549 (1976).

6. Smith, R.D. "Design of a Liquified Gas Mass Deacidification System for Paper and Books", in: *Preservation of Paper and Textiles of Historic and Artistic Value.* (Advances in Chemistry Series, 164) Washington, D.C.: American Chemical Society, 1977, pp. 149-158.

7. Scott, M. "Mass Deacidification at the National Library of Canada", *Restaurator*, 8 (2/3), 1987, pp. 94-99.

8. Schwerdt, P. *Massenkonservierung für Archive und Bibliotheken.* (Zeitschrift für Bibliothekswesen und Bibliographie, Sonderheft 49) Frankfurt am Main: Vittorio Klostermann, 1989.

9. Bansa, H. and H.H. Hofer. *Das Papier*, 34 (8), 1980, pp. 348-355.

MASS DEACIDIFICATION OF ARCHIVAL MATERIALS: THE BATTELLE AND DEZ PROCESS COMPARED

John B.G.A. HAVERMANS

Ronald J. P. VAN DEVENTER

TNO Paper and Board Research (The Netherlands)

INTRODUCTION

One of the main causes of the deterioration of our paper-based cultural heritage is 'acidification'. The stored papers are becoming more and more acid, causing discoloration and deterioration of the paper. In some cases, the deterioration is so severe that the stored documents can no longer be consulted: the paper breaks when touched. There are various causes of this acid degradation. One of the reasons is the paper-making process: an acid (sulphuric acid) or an acidic salt (alum) was added to the pulp in order to make the sizing agent (resin) effective. Another reason is the uptake of acid-producing contaminants present in the ambient air in which the materials are stored.

Because paper is still one of the main carriers of information, it is extremely important that our paper-based cultural heritage can be used and consulted for much longer than our own lifetime. For example, the cultural heritage of the past is now the seeds of our scientific and cultural activities. Therefore papers have to be preserved for the future. Considering the amount of paper stored in the major archives and libraries (approximately 25,000 km of records equivalent to 1 billion books), manual methods can no longer in a short time protect these materials. Therefore mass treatment is necessary. This was also one of the main conclusions of a study performed as a commission of the Dutch National Preservation Office, C.N.C. (Hol and Voogt 1991). The need for mass deacidification of its 19th and 20th century archives induced the Dutch State Archives to take a closer look at available mass-deacidification systems. A preliminary desk-research was performed by the Dutch National Preservation Office (Neevel 1991), which arrived at the conclusion that deacidification of archival materials with a gas-phase process is to be preferred over a liquid-phase process.

During the last 15 years, many mass-conservation methods were developed aiming at stopping the deterioration of paper. Two of these methods are:

1. the treatment of paper with DiEthylZinc (DEZ) gas (U.S.Congress 1988). This three-step diffusion process, drying-permeation-rehydration, not only neutralises the acids in the paper, but also forms an alkaline buffer in the paper for preventive purposes (Miller 1993),
2. the treatment of paper with a solvent of alkoxides (METE) in hexamethyldisiloxane (HMDO). From this multi-stage process, the alkoxides of magnesium and titanium remain distributed in the paper. They not only neutralise the acids in the paper, but also form an alkaline buffer in the paper for preventive purposes (Wittekind 1994).

In 1993, a detailed experimental study concerning the application of the DEZ-deacidification for archival and newsletter materials by TNO (Havermans and van Deventer 1993; van Deventer and Havermans 1993) was finished. It was concluded that the alkali reserve after the treatment was homogeneous and that the general performance of the materials used was good after the treatment. Scanning Electron Microscopy (SEM) showed a homogeneous distribution of the zinc oxide, ZnO, particles around the fibres. MacInnes and Barron (1992) drew the same conclusions concerning the uniformity of the deposition of the ZnO using the same techniques (Barron 1993). Even after exposure of the deacidified papers to a thermal ageing process, the deacidified papers deteriorated more slowly than the non-deacidified papers. However, the authors also concluded that the packaging of the materials to be deacidified has to be improved. The use of closed archive boxes was the main reason why papers stored in the boxes located in the middle of the deacidification room showed a higher emission of volatile carbon compounds like butanol and other alcohols. Another important study was on the different types of crystals that could be formed after a DEZ-treatment and after the uptake of, for example, sulphur dioxide (Schoute 1993). From this case study it was concluded that the type of crystals formed after the DEZ-treatment and the type of crystals which could form after reacting with sulphur dioxide will not contribute to the deterioration of the paper. During the European STEP-project, the DEZ process was studied on its protection of paper against air pollutants (Havermans, Deventer *et al.* 1994). The researchers found positive and negative points. The distribution of the alkaline compounds in the paper was not homogeneous, however this was finally improved due to process parameter changes. The formed ZnO protected all types of papers against the acid attack caused by air pollutants.

Concerning the Battelle process, a little literature is known describing the effects of this process related to the increase of life-span of papers. One of the latest and most interesting research published was by Wittekind from Battelle GmbH. New and old papers were deacidified using METE. Scanning Electron Microscopy of the papers deacidified was carried out and some chemical and mechanical changes of the materials were measured and discussed. Because Ti-compounds can stimulate the photo-induced deterioration of paper, extra attention was given to the crystalline structure of these compounds. The author found that, even after 100 days artificial ageing at 85°C and 65% relative humidity, the strength of the deacidified papers was nearly unchanged, while the untreated papers showed a continuous loss. The pH of all papers used increased after the treatment. For example after the treatment with a solution containing 6.0 g Mg per litre solvent, the pH varied from 7.0 - 9.4. After intensive exposure of the treated paper to ultraviolet light, no significant changes in the strength of the paper used were found.

After these studies, the Dutch National Preservation Office decided to carry out an intensive study on effects of the Battelle process on the durability of paper.

This paper describes the results and conclusions concerning the deacidified reference test-materials and the stability of these deacidified materials against acid contamination. The study was carried out as a commission of the Dutch State Archives and the Dutch National Preservation Office by TNO Paper and Board Research.

DEACIDIFICATION WITH DEZ AND BATTELLE, PRINCIPLES AND PRACTICE

The DEZ Process

The diethylzinc process is based on gas diffusion. DEZ molecules penetrate the leaves in an archives case or the pages of closed books. The process treatment is the result of a 20-year development history and its origin was put into practice for the first time by chemists of the Library of Congress Preservation Research and Testing Office in Washington DC, USA. Nowadays, papers which were treated at that time are presently in a very good shape (Harris 1993).

The process was licensed by AKZO Chemicals Inc. and performed at the plant located at Deer Park, Houston, Texas (Miller 1993)

The principle of the deacidification and other reactions of DEZ can be summarised as follows:

DEZ reacts very rapidly with the organic as well as the inorganic compounds present in paper, *e.g.*, hydroxyl groups and carboxylic groups of cellulose, the residual moisture present in the paper, and the sulphuric acid formed due to hydrolyses of the alum sulphate present in the paper.

The main reactions which will take place during the deacidification are:

- Reaction with the hydroxyl groups of cellulose

$$2R_{cell}\,COH + (C_2H_5)_2Zn\,(g) \rightarrow (R_{cell}CO)_2Zn\,(s) + 2\,C_2H_6\,(g \qquad (1)$$

- Reaction with the carboxylic groups of cellulose

$$2R_{cell}COOH + (C_2H_5)_2Zn\,(g) \rightarrow (R_{cell}COO)_2Zn\,(s) + 2\,C_2H_6\,(g) \qquad (2)$$

- Mixed reaction with the hydroxyl groups and carboxylic groups of cellulose

$$R_{cell}COOH + R_{cell}\,COH + (C_2H_5)_2Zn\,(g) \rightarrow (R_{cell}CO)(R_{cell}COO)Zn\,(s) + 2\,C_2H_6\,(g) \qquad (3)$$

- Reaction with sulphuric acid

$$H_2SO_4 + (C_2H_5)_2Zn\,(g) \rightarrow ZnSO_4\,(s) + 2\,C_2H_6\,(g) \qquad (4)$$

The zinc sulphate formed remains in the paper, while the ethane gas is removed.

- Reactions with water

$$H_2O + (C_2H_5)_2Zn\,(g) \rightarrow ZnO\,(s) + 2\,C_2H_6(g) \qquad (5)$$

$$ZnO\,(s) + H_2O \rightarrow Zn(OH)_2 \qquad (6)$$

Because the paper to be deacidified is pre-dried, *i.e.* the moisture content of the paper is lower than 0.5%, it is to be expected that most of the access of DEZ will form ZnO, which will remain in the paper as an alkaline buffer. The solubility of ZnO in water is 1.6 mg/l (25°C), and the pH of the water extracts of the treated paper will therefore be approximately 7.5. ZnO is amphoteric, dissolving in acids to form salts and in alkalis to form zincates, such as $[Zn(OH)_3]^-$ and $[Zn(OH)_4]_2^-$. ZnO can also react with alkaline compounds. Therefore the pH of the extract of the treated paper can never exceed the value of 9.5 according to the following reaction:

$$ZnO + 2\,OH^- + H_2O \rightarrow [Zn(OH)_4]^{2-} \quad (7)$$

The remaining ZnO protects the paper from the alkali-catalysed oxidative and hydrolyses reactions of the cellulose.

The mechanism of ZnO dissolution (hydroxylation) has been discussed by several authors and varied from a dissociative one to a redox one (Sengupta, Ahluwalia *et al.* 1975; Sengupta, Ahluwalia *et al.* 1979) as shown by water adsorption studies onto ZnO (Logtenberg 1983).

$$(ZnO)_n + H_2O \rightarrow \text{-}ZnOH\text{-}O\text{-}ZnOH\text{-} \quad (8)$$

- <u>Reaction with oxygen</u>

One of the disadvantages of the use of DEZ it the violent exothermic reaction with oxygen according to

$$7\,O_2 + (C_2H_5)_2Zn\,(g) \rightarrow ZnO\,(s) + 4\,CO_2 + 5\,H_2O \quad (9)$$

And the treatment is therefore carried out in an inert atmosphere.

The whole DEZ-treatment, a three-stage process, is summarised below:

Drying phase

The first stage of the process is drying. Warm dry nitrogen is flushed through the deacidification chamber, and this dries the paper and consequently leads to an increase in the amount of water in the vapour phase. Using vacuum and a so-called "cold finger", the water in the vapour phase is removed. The final water content of the paper after the drying stage is lower than 0.5% by weight. The drying is actually a multi-stage process on its own. In general, four heating and cooling stages were performed from 35°C to a maximum of 54°C. During heating, the pressure is changed from 1000 to 0.65 torr. After the drying phase, liquid nitrogen is flushed through the system in order to make the environment inert.

Permeation

During the permeation step, solvent-less DEZ is introduced into the deacidification chamber to deacidify the papers. The pressure was approximately 15 torr while the temperature increased from approximately 21°C to 54°C. After the permeation step is completed, excess DEZ is removed by purging with nitrogen while the temperature is decreased to approximately 15°C.

Rehydration

Rehydration is the final stage in the whole process. Moisture is injected into the deacidification chamber at approximately 54°C to increase the moisture content of the deacidified materials before the deacidification chamber is opened. After this stage, a 3-day humidification is carried out.

The Battelle process

In 1987 the Battelle Ingenieurtechnik GmbH in Frankfurt was engaged to develop a new mass deacidification process by Die Deutsche Bibliothek. The aim was to find the most useful method, in order to improve this method for starting a new and better deacidification method. After using the liquid phase method with Magnesium-Methoxi-Carbonate (MMC), a new active compound was found. Besides, a new more environmentally friendly solvent was used.
Reactive organo-metal compounds in a flammable silicon oil are used. This silicon oil, hexamethyl disiloxane (HMDO) with its formula $(CH_3)_3SiOSi(CH_3)_3)$, is suitable as a solvent for the effective compounds used, magnesium and titanium alkoxide. Although the silicon oil used is highly flammable, it also shows a very inert behaviour towards most organic substances. A full chemical description of the chemicals used is given by Wirttekind (1994). A summary of the compounds is given below, including the possible reactions which may occur during the deacidification.

- Reactions of the alkoxides

The principle of alkoxides, the raw materials involved in the Battelle process, is their fast hydrolyses reaction, which occurs even if traces of water are present. In general, a polymer compound will be formed whereas the monomeric compounds are bonded by -OH- of -O- bridges.

The initial hydrolysis of the compounds is the addition of the H_2O to the metal ion according to

$$H_2O + M(Oet)_x \rightarrow M(OH)(OR)_{x-1} + R - OH \qquad (10)$$

The next step, in presence of the remaining water in the paper, both alkoxide compounds ($Mg-(O-C_2H_5)_2$ and $Ti-(O- C_2H_5)_4$) will hydrolyse under formation of a metal hydroxide.

$$M - (O - C_2H_5)_n + nH_2O \longrightarrow M(OH)_n + nH - O - C_2H_5 \qquad (11)$$

Here M is the metal-ion Mg of Ti, and n will have the value of 2 respectively 4.

Under the influence of CO_2 and O_2, which are present in the air, a third reaction will occur and $MgCO_3$ respectively TiO_2 will be formed. The remaining excess of $MgCO_3$ can be seen as the alkali reserve, protecting the paper against further acid-deterioration.

During the reactions, ethyl-alcohol is formed, giving the paper a sweet alcoholic odour. According to Wittekind (1994), the TiO_2, a well-known precursor for photodeterioration reactions, will not harm the paper. The main reason given is the crystalline form of the polymorph TiO_2. After the deacidification treatment the allotrope anatase will be formed and not the reactive form rutile. However, it is possible that phase transitions may occur. Thus anatase TiO_2 can form rutile TiO_2. Factors influencing this phase transition are, for example, the surface area, the temperature relative to equilibrium transition temperature and activation energy bond strength (West 1984).

The deacidification power of $MgCO_3$ respectively TiO_2 can be found in previous papers by several authors.

The Battelle-treatment, also a multi-stage process, is summarised below:

Drying stage

The drying stage used during the research described in this paper, was based on conventional drying. The moisture content of the paper was therefore reduced to approximately 1%. After placing the papers to be deacidified in plastic crates, the materials were dried using high vacuum at 60°C for about 2 days.

Impregnation

The impregnation of the active compounds takes place under vacuum. The materials, present in the deacidification chamber, are impregnated for a few minutes using the liquid active deacidification compounds.

Pre-drying

After the impregnation stage, the liquid is removed, while the temperature will be increased somewhat. Using again vacuum, the excess of liquids will be removed from the papers.

Pre-conditioning

After the pre-drying stage, a pre-conditioning stage is started. The papers are therefore removed from the deacidification chamber, and placed in a well-conditioned and ventilated room. Because during the deacidification treatment the formation of alcohol takes place, the pre-conditioning period is set to approx. 3 weeks. By using a high ventilation rate in the pre-conditioning chamber, the excess of alcohol is removed.

MATERIALS, METHODS AND LOGISTICS

During the deacidification treatments, original and test papers were included.

For the DEZ, 5 treatments were used, whereas for the Battelle deacidification, only one treatment was carried out.

Table 1 The deacidification treatments

Treatment code	Deacidification	Date of treatment
Run-0 (Pre-run)	DEZ	October 1992
Run - 1	DEZ	June 1993
Run - 2	DEZ	September 1993
Run - 3	DEZ	October 1993
Run - 4	DEZ	February 1994
Run - 5	Battelle	June 1994

The test materials used were a bleached sulphite softwood paper (code paper-1) and an acid mechanical pulp paper (code paper-3). The first paper (initial pH = 6.7) contained no additives, fillers or sizing agents. The second paper was made of groundwood-containing pulp and was alum-rosin sized (initial pH = 5.9). Both papers had a grammage of 80 g/m^2.

The materials were wrapped in archival boxes and stored in different locations in the whole batch of original archives, which was prepared by the Dutch State Archives for the deacidification.

For the DEZ-treatment, a container was filled with the materials to be deacidified, and this container was sent to Houston, Texas for the deacidification treatment. At Houston, the containers were kept unopened until the start of the treatment. The archival boxes containing the archival materials and the test materials were placed on a specially developed rack in the deacidification chamber without any repackaging of the materials. The lid of each archival box was previously removed by the Dutch State Archives. During transport, the temperature and relative humidity in the container were recorded continuously by remote control sensors.

For the Battelle-treatment, a corrugated box was filled with the materials to be deacidified, and this box was sent to Frankfurt, Germany, for the deacidification treatment. At Hamburg, the papers were partially repackaged into specially made crates, and placed into the deacidification chamber for the treatment.

Directly the materials had been returned to The Netherlands, the boxes with the test materials were transported to the research lab of TNO, and stored in the dark at 23°C and 50% relative humidity. *Table 1* shows the dates of the different deacidification treatments.

The deacidified materials were investigated with respect to visual changes in the materials including microscopic research for possible deformations and salt-deposition on the paper. The homogeneity of the distribution of the alkaline compounds was examined by measuring the zinc content for the DEZ-treated papers, and the magnesium and titanium content for the Battelle-treated papers. Also the alkali-reserve according to ASTM D 4988 of the papersheets was measured.

Deacidified specimens and their references were subjected to accelerated ageing by storing the papers for 12 days at 90°C and 50% RH. Also deacidified paper and their references were exposed for 4 days against air pollution using concentrations of NO_x = 20 ppm and SO_2 = 10 ppm at a climate of 23°C and 50% RH. These artificial pollution conditions were similar to the conditions as used in the European Research Project (Havermans, Deventer *et al.* 1994). In these experiments, 98 sheets of one type of paper (size A4) were placed vertically in a Plexiglas exposure cabinet. The air flow containing the air pollutants was introduced into this chamber through a perforated wall. The concentrations of air pollutants were continuously measured by SO_2 and NO_x analysers (Havermans 1992; Havermans 1992).

Finally deacidified papers were subjected to a light source, in order to determine the relative rates of photo-oxidation. The paper samples were exposed to a light source (150 W high pressure mercury lamp). The source was provided with an immersion tube and water cooling, both of Duran 50 glass, transmitting wavelengths above 300 nm. The sample is placed in the outer wall of the cooling tube in front of the light source. The gas, an oxygen-air mixture, is kept at 40°C. The vessel is in open connection with a gas burette. By using this system, the oxygen consumption during the exposure towards light can be measured. The whole system is based on the assumption that essential all pressure changes are due to consumption of oxygen. Therefore all major volatile photo-oxidation products, mainly CO_2 and H_2O, are absorbed into molecular sieves, which are added to the closed gas system.

Before and after the accelerated ageing and artificial pollution, analyses were performed. The pH of the cold water extract of the paper shows not only the alkalinity of the deacidified papers, but also indicates that absorption pollution and the formation of acid compounds occurred during the artificial pollution experiments (NEN 1981). The pH was determined using a 0,1 M NaCl solution to examine the alkaline compounds inside the fibres (Scallan 1990). Deterioration products that can be formed after an artificial deterioration experiment were examined using the alkali-extractable fraction according to ASTM D 4988 (ASTM 1992). The equilibrium moisture content shows the morphological changes in the paper before and after each treatment (TAPPI 1990). The mechanical performance of the paper was examined by measuring the tear resistance and folding endurance (Kohler Mohlin) of the papers (ISO 1978). On additional samples, Scanning Electron Microscopy (SEM/EDXA) with X-ray analyses was carried out to look at the homogeneity of the distribution of the alkaline zinc compound on the fibres. Before and after the artificial pollution, two extra chemical tests were carried out. Firstly the copper number (Cu-No.) or the contents of reducing groups present in the cellulose of the paper were measured (TAPPI T 430), and secondly the degree of polymerisation (DPv) of the cellulose present in the paper according to TAPPI T 254 (TAPPI 1985; TAPPI 1988). Here the measured viscosity is related to the chain length or molecular weight of the cellulose.

In this paper, a summary of the results obtained with the DEZ treated-materials will be given. A full description of the DEZ treated-materials will be published separately.
The sampling and testing schedule is given below (*Figure 1*).

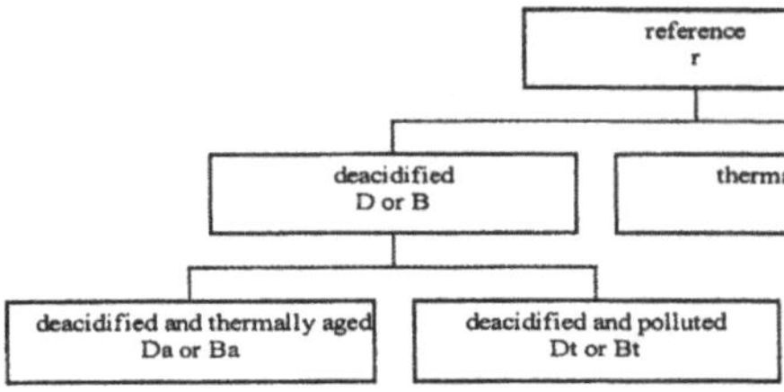

Figure 1 Sampling and testing schedule, here D stands for DEZ-treated paper and B for Battelle-treated paper

RESULTS AND DISCUSSION

Visual judgement was carried out on the original materials only. It was found that both treatments gave a slight odour, other than that of old paper.

It was also found that the texture of the *Battelle-treated* papers differed from the untreated papers. They feel more glassy. There was no change in texture found in the *DEZ-treated* papers.

Old manuscripts and books, which were also sent to both deacidification treatments, showed that coated paper may give problems, especially for the Battelle treatment. The deacidification compounds did not transfer into the paper, but remained on the surface. On occasional papers, Newton-rings were found on both the *DEZ-* and *Battelle-treated* papers.

Finally, it was found that some red inks were fully deteriorated after the Battelle-treatment.

The homogeneity of the deacidified papers

The distribution of Zn, Mg and Ti in the paper was examined using atomic absorption spectroscopy.

The investigations showed that the distribution of the Zn, Mg and Ti was homogeneous. This is shown in *Figure 2*. The graph also shows the difference between the middle and the margin of a sheet. The margin of a papersheet is here defined as a cut strip of 5 cm around a papersheet while the middle is defined as the remaining part of the papersheet, after removing the strip of paper from the margin.

It was also shown in *Figure 2* that the acid mechanical paper (paper-3) contained more Zn than the softwood sulphite cellulose paper (paper-1). This can be attributed to the fact that the acid mechanical paper is more acid (average initial pH = 5.9) than the softwood sulphite cellulose paper (average initial pH = 6.7). SEM/EDXA analyses showed that the ZnO particles were distributed homogeneously around the fibres, indicating that the fibres are protected from external contaminants.

Figure 3 shows the average amount of Mg and Ti, measured in the margins and the centres of the sheets of the *Battelle-treated* papers. It can be seen that by weight the amount of Ti is approx. 2 times higher than Mg. It was also found, that the distribution of the compounds was relatively homogeneous. SEM/EDXA analyses, however, showed that the alkaline particles were not homogeneously distributed around the fibres. Most of the particles are situated clustered in the empty spaces around the fibres.

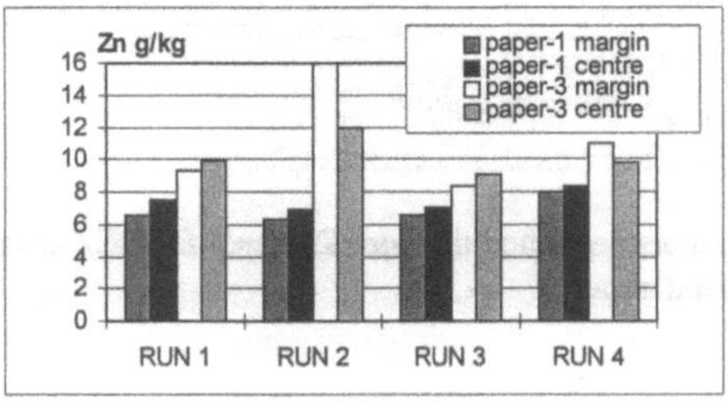

Figure 2 The Zn content of the deacidified sheets in g Zn per kg oven dry paper

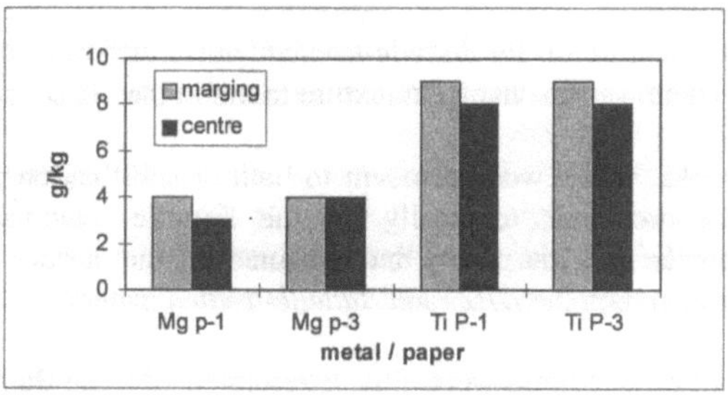

Figure 3 The Mg and Ti content of the deacidified sheets in g per kg oven dry paper 1 (p-1) and paper 3 (p-3)

Acidity and alkali reserve

It was found that the measured pH value of the cold water extract from the deacidified sheets was independent of the location of the sheet in the archive box. The average pH (from the margins and middles of these sheets) is shown in *Figure 4*. In general, the DEZ treatment gave a neutral deacidification (pH around 7), while Battelle gave a high alkaline deacidification (pH around 10). According to Whitmore, pH levels higher than 9 must be avoided, as it may stimulate the alkaline deterioration of paper under light.

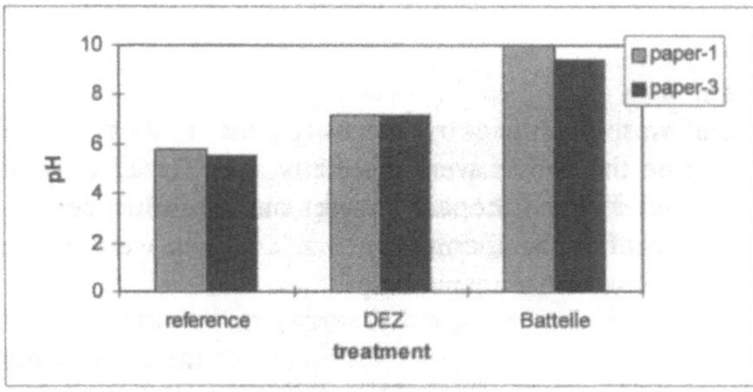

Figure 4 The pH of the cold water extract of the sheets from both the softwood cellulose and acid mechanical paper, before and after the deacidification

The pH of the extract using a 0.1 M NaCl solution to measure the pH inside the fibre wall of the papersheets showed an even more homogeneous distribution. No significant differences were found among the different DEZ-runs.

The average is shown in *Figure 5*. Again it can be seen that the reference papers are slightly acid (the pH of the acid mechanical paper is 5 while the pH of the sulphite softwood cellulose paper is 5.7). After deacidification, the pH of both paper extracts was 7.2, which was slightly decreased after the accelerated ageing.

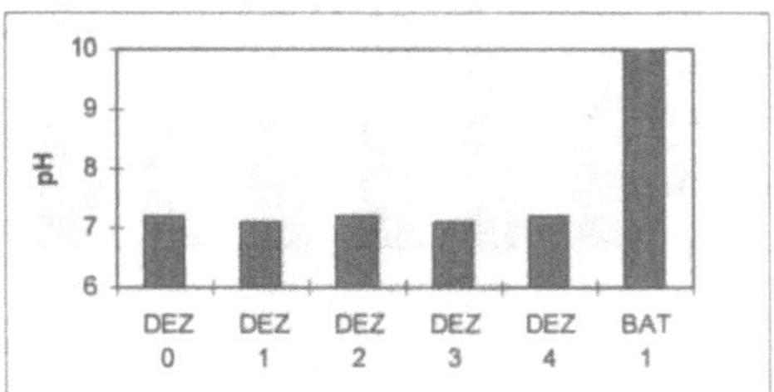

Figure 5 The pH of the cold water extract using 0.1 M NaCl solution of the 5 DEZ-treatments and the Battelle(BAT)-treatment of paper-1

The data for the alkali reserve show that all the *DEZ-treated* papers were given an alkali reserve of about 0.3 - 0.4 mol/kg. The *Battelle-treatment* gave results higher than 0.4 mol/kg.
The homogeneity of the alkali reserve of all the deacidified papers can be seen as good and effective.

The moisture content (mc) of the deacidified papers was affected only by the *DEZ-treatment*. The average mc of the *DEZ-treated* papers decreased about 2%, while the mc of the *Battelle-treated* papers was unchanged. The main reason of the decrease in mc is the combination of the drying stage and relative short reconditioning stage of the *DEZ-treatment*.

Summarised, both treatments gave an acceptable result on deacidification, although questions may arise on the high pH value of the cold water extract of the papers, deacidified by Battelle. *DEZ-treated* papers need a longer reconditioning time, before releasing them from the treatment.

Durability behaviour

The durability behaviour was examined by means of the stability of the papers against an accelerated ageing. Therefore the papers were thermally aged for 12 days at 90°C and 50% RH. Similar conditions were used in the European project on the influences of air pollutants on the ageing of paper. Before and after the thermal ageing, analyses were performed to indicate any deterioration of the papers after thermal ageing only.

The alkali-extractable fraction AEF (see *Figure 6*) represents the amount of extractable poly- and oligosaccharides that is soluble in a 1% alkali solution and is therefore an indication of the amount of deterioration products formed, the higher the AEF the higher the amount of degradation. Since no significant difference was found between the AEF of the reference and that of the deacidified papers, it can be concluded that the deacidification treatment does not affect the materials.

The results obtained show that the AEF increased after the deacidified papers had been accelerated-aged (see *Figure 6*). So a slight deterioration effect occurred. The *DEZ-treated* groundwood containing paper showed a somewhat higher AEF compared to the *Battelle-treated* paper.

The differences in the total amount of extractable compounds between the acid mechanical and sulphite softwood cellulose papers are due to the use of different raw materials. Groundwood-containing papers always contain more extractables than the woodfree papers.

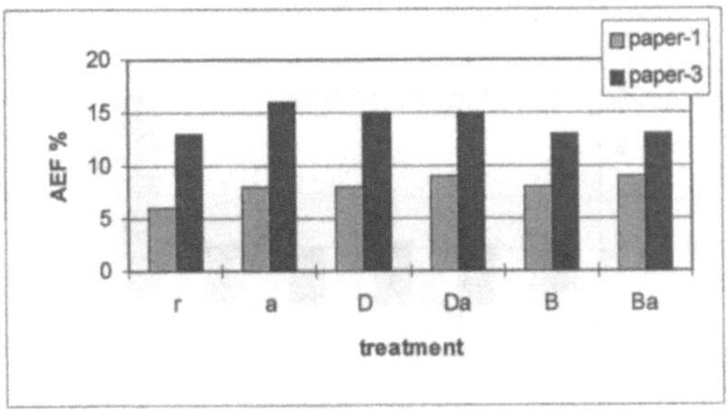

Figure 6 The alkali-extractable fraction as a percentage of the oven dry paper before and after deacidification and after thermal ageing. The codes used are: r=reference, a= thermally aged, D= *DEZ-treated*, B= *Battelle-treated*, Da= *DEZ-treated* followed by thermal ageing and Ba= *Battelle-treated* followed by thermal ageing

Since chemical properties only cannot represent the behaviour of the paper during normal use, two types of mechanical analyses were performed, the tensile strength and the folding endurance.

The mechanical properties of the papers before and after the ageing experiments were determined in the two principal directions: the machine direction (MD) and the cross machine direction (CD). From these values, the geometric mean of the properties X was calculated according $X = \sqrt{X_{MD} \times X_{CD}}$. The geometric mean value X_{gm} corresponds to the value for an isotropic sheet, and its use facilitates the comparison of sheets with different mechanical anisotropies.

From the results obtained, the retention values, *i.e.*, the value of the actual value divided by its reference value, were calculated. In *Figures 7* and *8* these values are presented for the tensile strength in the machine direction of the acid mechanical paper and the softwood sulphite cellulose paper respectively.

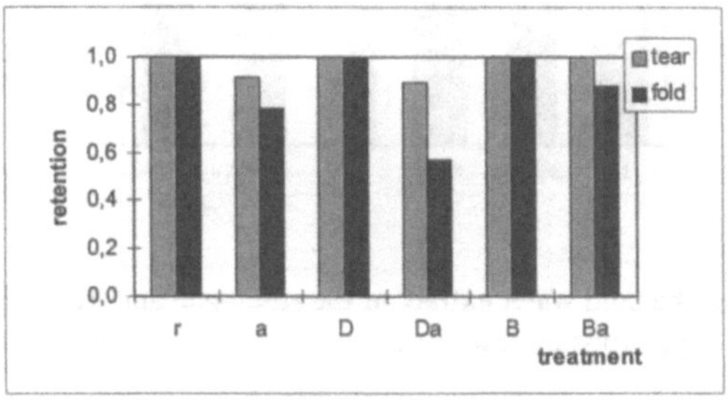

Figure 7 the retention in tear and fold number of paper-1, represented by the ratio of the measured values before and after deacidification and after thermal ageing

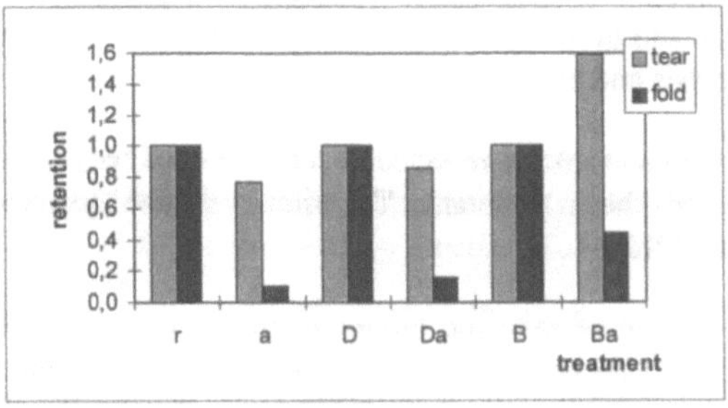

Figure 8 The retention in tear and fold number of paper-3, represented by the ratio of the measured values before and after deacidification and after thermal ageing

From the *Figures 7* and *8* it can be seen that both papers loose their mechanical strength properties after the thermal ageing. Similar results were found for the papers after DEZ-deacidification.

Battelle-deacidification showed an increase in the tear strength properties, while the fold (or flexibility) properties were reduced after the thermal ageing.

Stability towards air pollutants

After 4 h of artificial exposure towards 20 ppm NO_2 and 10 ppm SO_2 at 23°C and 50% RH, the pH of the cold water extract of both the exposed sulphite softwood paper-1 and acid mechanical paper-3 decreased, as can be seen in *Figure 9.* The pH after the exposures is about 6.5, thus again slightly acidic. It should be noted that the pH of the deacidified papers was higher than their reference values. This indicates the protective work of the alkaline compounds.

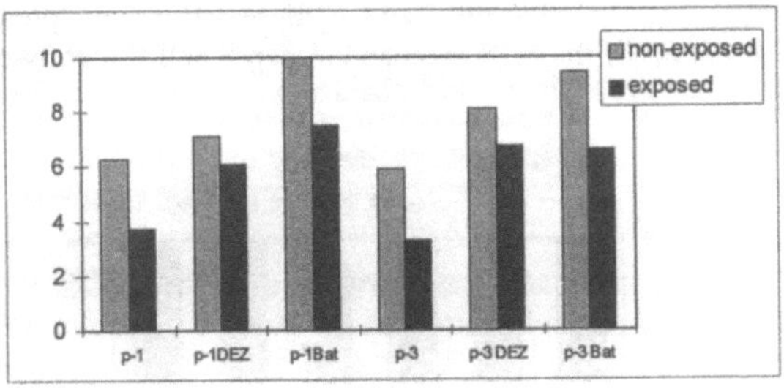

Figure 9 The pH of the cold water extract of the reference and deacidified papers before and after a 4 days exposure towards 20 ppm NO_2 and 10 ppm SO_2 at 23°C and 50% RH

To gain more insight into the observed degradation due to air pollutants, the alkali-extractable fraction, the degree of polymerisation and the copper number were determined. The reducing properties of the paper were examined by the **copper number,** *Cu-No.* The copper number indicates the presence of reducing aldehydes and reactive keto groups and therefore the copper number indicates the amount of degradation. The papers exposed to air pollutants showed an increase in both the AEF and in the *Cu-No.* indicating a substantial deterioration took place caused by acid-catalysed hydrolysis and by oxidation.

From the *Cu-No.* it was evident that more reducing aldehydes and reactive keto groups were formed due to the exposure towards the air pollutants. The primary alcohol groups of the cellulose at the C6 position are possibly involved.

It was found that the amount of reducing groups of the exposed *DEZ-treated* sulphite softwood cellulose paper was comparable to that of its untreated reference, whereas in the case of the acid mechanical paper, the increase in reducing groups was less in the *DEZ-treated* paper than in the untreated paper (see also *Figures 10a* and *10b*). In case of the *Battelle-treated* papers, the *Cu-No.* was in all cases lower than that of the reference papers, possible indicating that the reactive groups are shielded by the treatment.

After exposing the papers to the air pollutants it was found that the *Cu-No.* increased enormously for the untreated papers only. Paper-1, the pure cellulose paper, showed in all cases an increase of the *Cu-No.*, indicating that deterioration took place. In case of paper-3, the groundwood-containing one, it was found that for the *DEZ-treated* paper, the *Cu-No.* remained similar to that of the reference paper, while the Battelle treatment lowered the *Cu-No.* comparable to the non-exposed papers.

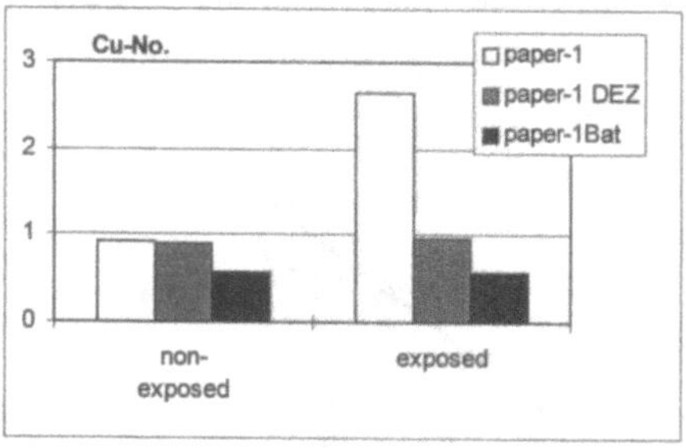

Figure 10a The Cu-No. of paper-1 reference and deacidified papers before and after the exposure to air pollutants (4 days at 20 ppm NO_2 and 10 ppm SO_2 and at 23°C and 50% relative humidity)

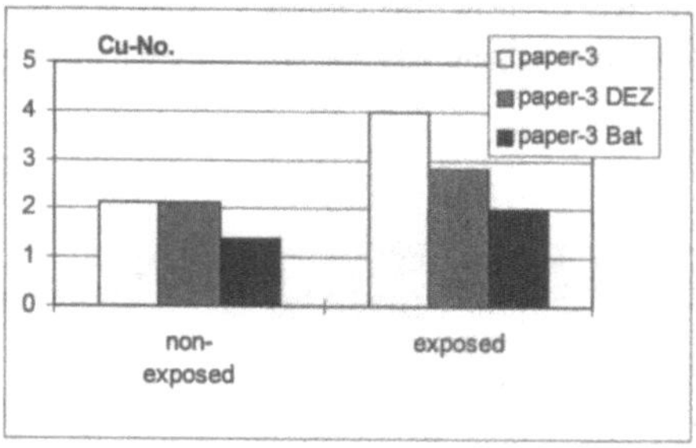

Figure 10b The Cu-No. of paper-3 reference and deacidified papers before and after the exposure to air pollutants (4 days at 20 ppm NO_2 and 10 ppm SO_2 and at 23°C and 50% relative humidity)

Using the AEF, the effect of lowering the deterioration can be shown. Here the approach was made that the deterioration followed first order reaction kinetics. To calculate the relative deterioration rates *(k·t)*, the formula $\ln\left(\frac{[P_t]}{[P_o]} = k \cdot t\right)$ was used. Here $[P_o]$ is the AEF at t=0 or the AEF or the reference $[P_r]$, and $[P_t]$ is the AEF after each deterioration experiment. The calculated relative deterioration rates *(k·t)* for paper-1 are projected on the y-axis in *Figure 11* and for paper-3 on the y-axis in *Figure 12*. On the x-axis the *(k·t)* values of the bleached sulphite softwood cellulose, paper-1, (internal standard) only are projected. An increase in the relative deterioration rate results in an increase in the angle with the x-axis. The solid line in both graphs represents a 1:1 ratio.

Figure 11 shows that the deterioration rate for the pure softwood cellulose paper, paper-1, was reduced for both the DEZ- and Battelle-treated papers.

Figure 12 shows that the deterioration rate of the groundwood paper, paper-3, was higher than that of the pure softwood cellulose paper, paper-1. However, after the deacidification the deterioration rates decreased enormously especially for the Battelle-deacidified papers.

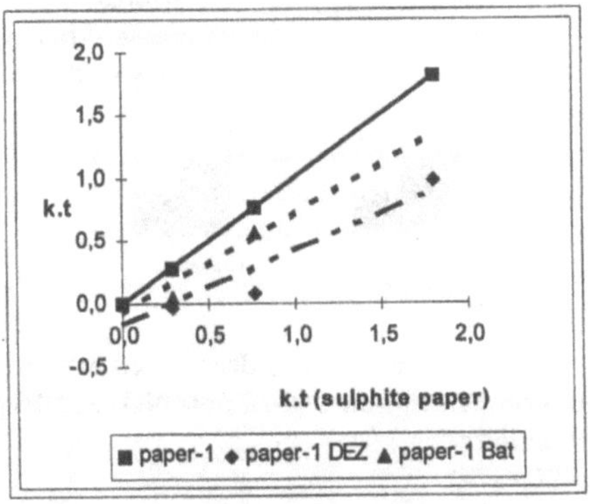

Figure 11 The calculated relative deterioration rates *(k·t)* of the softwood paper, paper-1, and that of the DEZ-deacidified and Battelle-deacidified papers (paper-1 DEZ and paper-1 Bat).

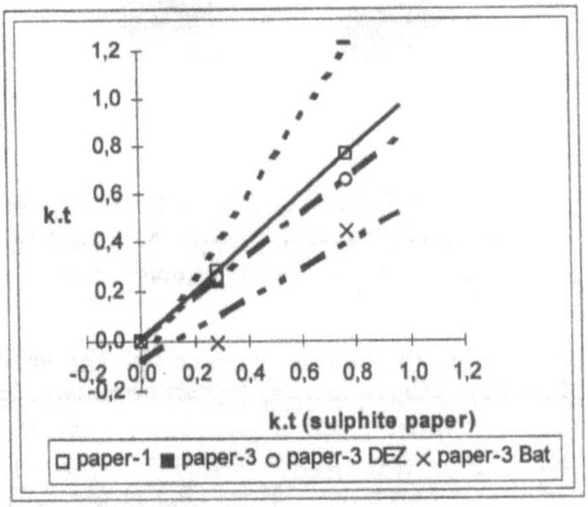

Figure 12 The calculated relative deterioration rates *(k·t)* of the groundwood paper, paper-3, and that of the DEZ-deacidified and Battelle-deacidified papers (paper-3 DEZ and paper-3 Bat).

Stability towards light

It is a fact that groundwood-containing papers do discolour more than bleached papers, therefore the results of paper-3 will be discussed here only.

Paper-3 was subjected to a light source at 50°C, in order to determine the relative rates of photo-oxidation. The results are shown in *Figure 13*. On the x-axis the exposure time is given, while on the y-axis the so-called sorption-ratio is given. The value of 1 represents the maximum ratio of the burette used. The experiment is then stopped.

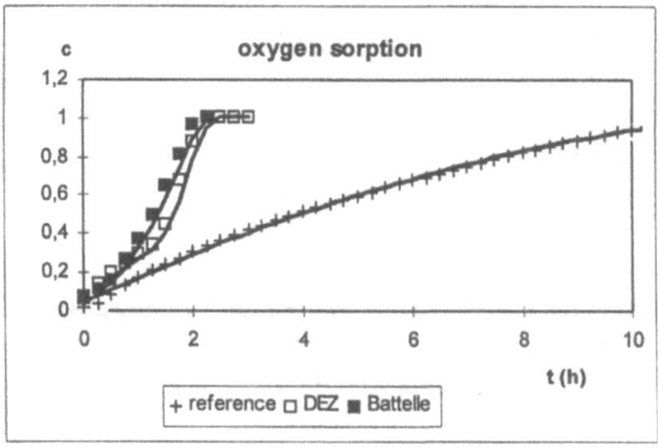

Figure 13 The deterioration caused by light, as measured by the oxygen sorption of the groundwood-containing paper-3. The papers were subjected to a light source for a maximum of 10 hours and/or the sorption ratio of 1 was reached.

From *Figure 13* it can be seen that, after the deacidification the papers became more sensitive to light deterioration. From this study it was calculated that, after the deacidification, the papers deteriorated approximately 5 times faster than the untreated papers, while there is no significant difference between the deterioration of the *DEZ-treated* paper and the *Battelle-treated* paper. Only the pathway differs somewhat: the *Battelle-treated* paper showed an almost continuously oxidative deterioration, while the *DEZ-treated* paper showed a lower initial deterioration followed by a faster second stage.
This effect will be studied more extensively in our future research programme.

FINAL DISCUSSION, DEZ AND BATTELLE COMPARED

From the results obtained in this study it must be clear, that paper deacidified by DEZ and Battelle will be protected for acid deterioration, however there is an enormous increase in sensitivity towards deterioration by light. This can be due to the ZnO and TiO_2 particles, which can stimulate the light-induced oxidative deterioration. Although it looks that after the *Battelle-treatment* an increase of the paper-strength properties was found, there was a decrease of the flexibility properties. DEZ lowered in all cases the mechanical properties somewhat.
Remarkable was the change in texture of the *Battelle-treated* papers, while for the *DEZ-treated* papers no change in texture was found.

Figure 14 shows a compilation of all the chemical results obtained. The x-axis represents the Battelle-values while the y-axis represents the DEZ-values. Linear regression shows that DEZ = 0.7 Battelle, thus both treatments will give comparable chemical protection against acidification; however more research has to be carried out in order to establish the results obtained.

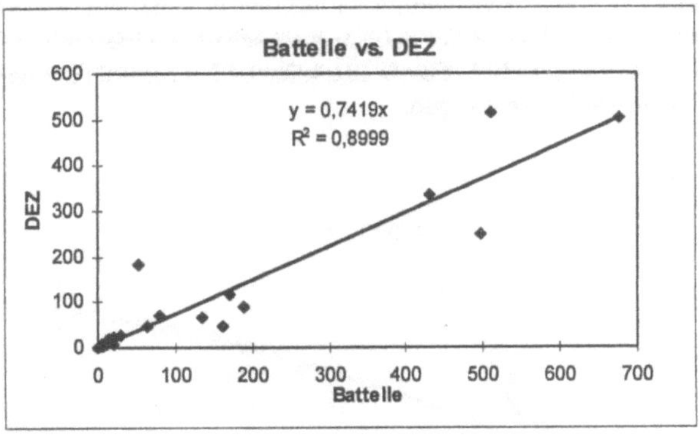

Figure 14 The chemical results of the *DEZ-* and *Battelle-treated* paper-1 and paper-3 compared. The results are obtained before and after thermal ageing, artificial exposures and thermal ageing after the artificial exposures

CONCLUSIONS

It can be concluded not only that a homogeneous deacidification occurred with the DEZ process but also that the treatment is indeed very effective if archive papers are subsequently exposed to air pollutants. No pre-selection has to be made, when only paper is inside the archival boxes. The package of each archival box is apparently to be considered as not too tight.

It was also shown that the reproducibility of the DEZ-treatment is very good and that, in all cases, an effective amount of alkaline compounds was introduced into the paper. The amount of zinc introduced was not representative of the homogeneity because, during the treatment, DEZ reacts with the acid compounds present and turns them into alkaline compounds. It was proven that the measured pH value of the cold water only does not stand for an effective treatment, but that the alkali reserve does, and this can be seen as the most important factor for the protection of the paper against acid attack. The performance of the paper can be slightly affected when the papers are treated with DEZ due to the change in the equilibrium moisture content, but after an effective time the moisture content of the deacidified paper will be recovered.

Deacidification with Battelle also gave a homogeneous deacidification; however the active particles were not homogeneously distributed around the fibres. The pH of the paper deacidified was high, approx. 10. An effective amount of alkaline compounds was introduced into the paper. The treatment is very effective if the papers are subsequently exposed to air pollutants, this protection was even better than for the *DEZ-treated* papers. It is preferable to use the crates as developed by Battelle, instead of the papers in their original package. The performance of the paper increased somewhat after leaving the *Battelle-treatment*, which can possibly be ascribed to the remaining silicon compounds. This effect has to be investigated further.

RECOMMENDATIONS

It is recommended to carry out further research on the effects of the Battelle-deacidification, before it will be generally used for deacidification of irreplaceable materials. Research has to be carried out on the reproducibility of the process in order to guarantee the quality of the process. Also the change in texture of the paper has to be further investigated, while special attention has to be given to the light-induced oxidative deterioration of the paper.
As AKZO closed the DEZ-plant at Houston, opening again and using it has to be reconsidered. it has to be reconsidered, after optimisation of the whole process, as one of the possible deacidification procedures.

ACKNOWLEDGEMENT

The financial assistance of the Dutch State Archives and from the Dutch Preservation Office CNC, Den Haag, The Netherlands, is greatly appreciated. The hospitality of Battelle GMBH, Germany, and AKZO, Houston, USA, is gratefully acknowledged.

REFERENCES

ASTM (1992). ASTM D 4988; Determination of alkalinity of paper as calcium carbonate (alkaline reserve of paper).

Barron, A. (1993). Personal Communication about DEZ. Harvard University, Cambridge, Mass.

Harris, K. (1993). Personal Communication about research on DEZ. Washington D.C.

Havermans, J. B. G. A. (1992). *The experimental set up - Part 1.* The Air-Pollutants. The influence of air pollutants on the accelerated ageing of cellulose containing materials. STEP project CT 90-0100. Second Workshop, Paris, France, Centre TNO for Paper and Board Research.

Havermans, J. B. G. A. (1992). *The experimental set up - Part 2.* The Equipment and Conditions. The influence of air pollutants on the accelerated ageing of cellulose containing materials. STEP project CT 90-0100. Second Workshop, Paris, France, Centre TNO for Paper and Board Research.

Havermans, J. B. G. A., J. P. van Deventer, R. van Dongen, F. Flieder, F. Daniel, P. Kolseth, T. Iversen, H. Lennholm, O. Lindqvist, and A. S. Johansson (1994). *The Effects of Air Pollutants on the Accelerated Ageing of Cellulose Containing Materials - Paper.* EC/DGXII/STEP Project CT 90-0100. BU3.94/1068/JH, TNO, Delft.

Havermans, J. B. G. A., and J. P. van Deventer (1993). Voorstudie DEZ. Het ontzuren van twee referentiepapieren. PK 93.2001, TNO, Delft.

Hol, R. C., and L. Voogt (1991). *Endangered Books and Documents.* Den Haag, CNC.

ISO (1978). ISO 5626; Paper - Determination of folding endurance.

Logtenberg, E.H.P. (1983). *The Relation Between the Solid State Properties and the Colloid Chemical Behaviour of Zinc Oxide.* Thesis Technical University Eindhoven.

Miller, R. (1993). The deterioration of modern records and books, and the DEZ vapor phase process. AKZO, Deer Park.

Neevel, J. G. (1991). Methoden voor Massaconservering. Analyse en evaluatie. Den Haag, CNC.

NEN (1981). NEN 2151; Bepaling van de pH van een waterige suspensie.

Scallan, A. M., Ed. (1990). *The pH inside the Fibre Wall.* Cellulose and Exploitation: industrial Utilization, Biotechnology and Physico-Chemical Properties. London, Ellis Howard.

Schoute, M. F. E. (1993). *Kristallen in ontzuurd papier.* Chemiewinkel, Laboratorium voor kristallografie, Universiteit van Amsterdam.

Sengupta, G., H. S. Ahluwalia, and S. P. Sen. (1975). "Zinc oxide - water vapor system. Mechanism of adsorption from electrical conductivity studies." *Journal of Catalysis* **36**(1) Jan 1975: 111-113.

Sengupta, G., H. S. Ahluwalia, S. Banerjac and S. P. Sen. (1979). "Chemisorption of water vapor on zinc oxide." *Journal of Colloid & Interface Science* **69(2)** April 1979: 217-222.

TAPPI (1985). TAPPI T 254; Cupriethylenediamine disperse viscosity of pulp (falling ball method).

TAPPI (1988). TAPPI T 430; Copper number of pulp, paper, and paperboard.

TAPPI (1990). TAPPI T 412; Moisture in paper and paperboard.

U.S.Congress (1988). Book Preservation Technologies. Office of Technology Assesment, Washington D.C.

van Deventer, J. P. and J. B. G. A. Havermans (1993). Effectiviteit DEZ-proces. Evaluatie met ingebonden Nederlandse kranten. PK 93.2001, TNO, Delft.

West, A. R. (1984). Solid State Chemistry and its Applications. Chinchester, John Wiley & Sons.

Wittekind, J. (1994). "The Battelle Mass Deacidification Process: a New Method for Deacidifying Books and Archival Materials." *Restaurator* **15**: 189-207

THE BOOKKEEPER PROCESS
A REAL SOLUTION

Richard SPATZ

Preservation Technologies Inc. (USA)

BACKGROUND

The self-destruction of paper products is well known in both the library and scientific communities. The causes have been pinpointed, beginning around the 1850's when chemical pulp manufacture was begun to satisfy the increasing demand for printing papers. In addition, paper fibers had to be treated with chemicals to accept inks and dyes and to increase paper opacity. As time passed, environmental conditions contributed to the problem. In papers and books, these acidic processes were described as "auto catalytic", and the effect over time has been a catastrophic loss of paper strength to a state of brittleness. Simple solutions were offered and are still used for neutralization of acids in individual documents or papers.

But mass deacidification of books and papers has been an elusive problem. For decades, scientists have tested and tried several chemical solutions - all of which had some shortcoming or disability that made them unacceptable. Residual odor and negative impact on inks or adhesives were all problems that seemed to defeat the proposed solutions.
Uncontrolled chemical reactions in most of the proposed processes produced unwanted side effects in the books. In the United States, several processes were tried. The Library of Congress began a program to develop its own process, using gaseous diethyl zinc as the reactant which produces the neutralizing agent, zinc oxide. After the expenditure of substantial funds and a complete test cycle of all of the methods available, the Library reached the conclusion that some other solution must be sought.

In 1993, the Library of Congress announced an invitation to all those owning mass deacidification technology to submit the processes for testing by the Library and a team of independent experts. The only company offering to submit to this procedure was Preservation Technologies, Inc., which had developed and patented the Bookkeeper process.

The Library test run was conducted in 1993. In December of 1994, the Library issued its final report concluding that the process did have the potential to meet the mass deacidification requirements established by the Library.

LIBRARY OF CONGRESSS EVALUATION

The Technical Evaluation Team did a thorough examination of the Bookkeeper deacidification process as it related to the Library of Congress specifications. These specifications address both technical and ethical considerations and the findings indicate that the process has many advantages. It should also be understood that the tests were completed in August, 1993, and there have been substantial changes since that have improved the process, including the design and construction of a higher capacity machine.

The efficacy of the treatment is perhaps the most important technical consideration. The findings of the Team indicated that treated papers showed less degradation of mechanical properties than did untreated paper during accelerated aging. Treated papers from the LC test books generally retained their desirable performance properties for 3-5 times longer in oven aging, comparable to the 3 fold improvement required in the LC specifications. Overall performance in the oven tests showed the benefits of the treatment. The treatment did not affect the physical appearance of the papers in the Library test books.

The findings of the Team also indicate that all of the three paper types were completely deacidified and that pH values of all the sheets were raised from a moderately acidic pH of 5.7 to 6.5 to alkaline levels of 9-10. Subsequent oven-aging of the treated sheets caused the pH to fall only slightly to 8.0-9.5. The alkaline reserve in this evaluation was also reported to be somewhat lower (but acceptable) than the LC specification although this may have been due to the test used rather than a low alkaline reserve.

The alkaline reserve was also found to be permanent as the initial values did not fall during the 30 days of oven aging. All books treated for LC and others since the tests have easily met the original standards.

With the efficacy of the treatment adequately demonstrated, the next consideration is uniform coverage of the pages. Test results indicate that the Library test book papers contain an overall uniform distribution of magnesium oxide across the entire sheet with the exception of the gutter areas.

Since the LC tests were completed in 1993, a new machine was designed and built, Bookkeeper III. Most recent tests done with the Library have shown an average of 99% of all pages are deacidified. New design changes will provide steady improvement.

Another important point that was considered was damage. The LC specification states that there can be no damage to processed materials and media, and the findings of the Team in this area were very positive.

1. The treated books had no odor. Even those demonstrating a pretest musty odor lost that odor during the treatment process. The ability of the process to remove dirt and debris from the books suggests the process has a "dry cleaning" effect. Because of this effect, filters had to be installed in the process.
2. There was no observable adhesive loss or damage on book spines or to shelf labels, security strips, book pockets, or plates.
3. There was no damage to book cloth or other covering material. A typical plastic book jacket acquired a light dusting of magnesium oxide. There was no softening of plastic or change of color. There was no damage to pamphlet binders. There was no damage to the leather on the two leather bound books.
4. There was no change in dye color, book cloth or in printing ink, internally or externally. There was no damage to gold tooling or gilded edges. Marker ink used for underlining text did not change color or bleed, with the exception of a pH sensitive marking pen.
5. There was no cockling of paper or distortion of boards, pamphlet binders or text blocks. The Team also found that the Bookkeeper process had the potential to treat books on a mass scale. A distinct advantage was the modest start- up costs for a new treatment facility. Since the treatment

is not hazardous, a plant could be located in a library or related facility. It is also portable and could be installed in a mobile unit and moved to different sites to treat books.

In June, 1995, Preservation Technologies and the Library of Congress signed a two year contract for the deacidification of books and papers. PTI. will treat 72,000 books at its plant over a two year period while working closely with the Library in refining the process. Provisions are included to expand the number of books to be treated. Now, in early 1996, the process refinements are complete and the Library of Congress is shipping books from its general collections. We expect to be treating four to five thousand books per month this summer.

BACKGROUND OF THE PROCESS

The Bookkeeper process was developed and patented by the Koppers Company in the mid - 1980's. Koppers was a diversified American chemical company with headquarters in Pittsburgh, Pennsylvania. One of its businesses was the chemical preservation of wood products. It used chemicals such as creosote, pentachlorophenol, and salts to preserve and extend the life of wood products such as piling, railroad ties, utility poles and lumber. The slow growth of these products caused the company to begin a search for new products. After some three years it developed and patented a process for deacidifying books and paper products, which has become known as the Bookkeeper process.

Koppers was subsequently the target of an unfriendly buy-out. At the time, Richard Spatz was President of the Koppers Forest Products Group. When neither Koppers or the new company had shown any interest in the process, he offered to buy it and this sale was culminated in 1990. Further product development was conducted and resulted in the formation, in 1991, of a new company, Preservation Technologies, to which the original process was licensed.
The process involves the deposit of sub-micron sized particles of magnesium oxide into the structure of the paper product. These particles are carried into the cellulose fibers in a dispersion using an inert chemical known as perfluroalkane, which is a non-reactive fluorocarbon that is non-toxic and has no ozone depletion potential. The magnesium oxide particles adhere to the structure of the paper by electromagnetic forces. The magnesium oxide particles combine with water from the books and the atmosphere to form magnesium hydroxide - the alkaline agent which neutralizes the migrating acids in the paper.

The latest chapter in the development of the process has been the engineering design and construction of a machine to "mass" treat books in a multiple form. The patented machine treats and dries the books in vertical cylinders. The current machine, which treats for universities and the Library of Congress at a plant located just outside of Pittsburgh, Pennsylvania, has a capacity to treat over 100,000 books per year. The machine is capable of expansion at a minimal cost. The current machine occupies a space of approximately 20 square meters. It has no effluent or discharges that are environmental problems and requires only 100 amp electrical service to be operational. PTI continues to improve the recovery of the chemical carrier, which improves the economic viability of the process.

The process has been successfully tested by the Library of Congress and the National Library of Belgium. It is currently being used by several libraries in the United States. Spray products, using the same patented chemistry, are sold in both the United States and Europe.

HOW DOES THE BOOKKEEPER PROCESS WORK?

There are actually two deacidification machines in the Pittsburgh plant.
One is limited to structurally sound books which do not exceed a size of 12" x 9" x 2 1/2" (Bookkeeper III). The majority of books in most collections will meet this requirement. The other machine can handle larger books, books with loose bindings and loose archival papers. (Bookkeeper II).

In Bookkeeper III, a work tank is filled with the dispersion which contains 3 ingredients - sub micron sized magnesium oxide particles, a liquid perflouroalkane carrier and a dispersant. The treatment section of the machine is four vertical cylinders. The book covers are fastened to a book holder outside the cylinder. Each holder retains 4 books with the spines held together and the pages loose. Each cylinder holds 8 books. The book holders are then inserted into the cylinder over a center shaft. The cylinders are sealed and the dispersion is pumped from the work tank into the treatment cylinders. The book-holders are then moved within the dispersion. The nature of the dispersion causes the pages of the books to float open like a fan
and the magnesium oxide is carried across each page and into the gutter of the book. The treatment phase takes 30 minutes. The dispersion is then pumped from the cylinder. A vacuum is then drawn on the cylinder and the carrier is recovered in one and a half (1 ½) hours.

ADVANTAGES OF THE BOOKKEEPER PROCESS

The advantages of the Bookkeeper process are several:-

1) The pH of treated acidic papers is raised above the minimum of 6.8, typically between 7.5 and 9.5.
2) The magnesium particles are distributed throughout the paper in an amount sufficient to leave a reserve in the paper to counteract future acidic attacks, both from the storage environment and from within the book itself.
3) In numerous tests, the process has demonstrated that, on the average the treated books will have a life extension of at least 3 times the life of untreated books.
4) No pre-drying of books is necessary, and no heat is used in the recovery step, thus saving the energy costs and avoiding unnecessary heat that might damage or weaken the paper.
5) The Environmental Protection Agency of the United States has examined the process and found it to be without substantial risk. It is non-toxic. non carcinogenic, non-flammable and does not contribute to ozone depletion.
6) The process, after treatment of thousands of books, has demonstrated no harmful effects on inks, covers, colors, adhesives, bar codes or any of the many other materials found in bound volumes.
7) The process leaves no odor in the books or paper and actually cleans the books of debris and musty odors.
8) The mass deacidification machine occupies only a small area and can be used in the confines of a library without the danger of a chemical or environmental hazard. There are no waste streams associated with the product.
9) The process is economical. PTI now mass deacidifies books in the United States for approximately $8 per pound or about $12 per volume We anticipate that ongoing improvements in the recovery phase of the process and in the automation of equipment may allow even lower operating costs.

10) The process is simple. There are no complicated chemical reactions taking place - except for the deacidification of the book itself. No by-products are created that must be controlled. It is certainly capable of being operated by library staff after minimum training.

BOOKKEEPER SPRAY PRODUCTS

Preservation Technologies also manufactures and sells spray products used for deacidifying individual books or papers. The ingredients in these products are essentially the same as those used in the mass process. They are packaged in 454 gram aerosol spray cans or in 1,078 gram pump spray bottles. The dispersion can also be purchased in larger containers. The principal distributor of these products in Europe is La Route du Papier located in Brussels, Belgium.

ARCHIVAL MATERIALS

The plant in Pittsburgh also has facilities for the mass treatment of loose papers and oversized books. The so-called Bookkeeper II machine is constructed to treat books or containers of papers. The machine is designed to treat books using the same methods described for Bookkeeper III, except that the movement of the books is horizontal. The drying of the books or papers is done in a separate vacuum dryer. PTI has also designed a special crate or box with open sides that will allow the treatment of loose papers on a volume or mass basis.

FUTURE OF THE BOOKKEEPER PROCESS

PTI plans to expand and operate its plant in Pittsburgh, Pennsylvania. The present combined capacity exceeds 150,000 books per year and will undoubtedly increase. Other plants will be built as the market dictates - serving other regional or geographic areas.

Plants will be licensed to libraries or binderies on an individual basis and the designs of the machine will be tailored to the specific needs.
In Europe and Asia, PTI plans to make the same opportunities available, licensing plants to libraries or entrepreneurs. It is also possible that the company may construct a plant(s) in Europe where the library community prefers a service contract.

NEW DEVELOPMENTS IN CONTROLLED ATMOSPHERE TECHNOLOGY

Colin P. SMITH

Rentokil Ltd. (United Kingdom)

INTRODUCTION

Insect and mold infestations in books, manuscripts and other documents of cellulose based organic material can be difficult to control, particularly when collections are held in large libraries or stores. Such materials can provide a rich source of nutrition and once an infestation occurs it can spread rapidly causing serious damage.

Other items potentially at risk include paintings, tapestries, icons and clothing. Some traditional methods of eradication such as fumigation with methyl bromide or phosphine are fast and effective. However, apart from concerns for safety and environmental damage, there is the potential for materials to be changed over time due to chemical interaction or poor application technique.

Infestations often found in collections are:

- Carpet beetles,
- clothes moths,
- furniture beetle,
- termites,
- silver fish, and
- book lice.

Other traditional methods such as direct application with para dichlorobenzene, benzene hexachloride (also known as BHC or 1,2,3,4,5,6-hexachlorocyclohexane) and ethylene oxide, can be effective. However their use is no longer permitted in most countries due to health and safety and environmental concerns. Therefore, there has been the need in recent years to initiate research programs to develop more environmentally acceptable techniques.

This paper describes methods for controlling infestations in collections which have resulted from recent research.
In this paper we consider the two scenarios which normally confront pest controllers involved in this work:

1. Deep seated infestations already established throughout a collection.

2. Collections currently pest free but with the potential of becoming infested.

DEEP SEATED INFESTATIONS ALREADY ESTABLISHED THROUGHOUT A COLLECTION

Established infestations of insects in, for example a library or archive, present the pest controller with a difficult task, particularly if the infestations have been active over a long period. In these situations infestations could be found throughout the collection and in the structure of the building. Certain insects such as *Anobium punctatum* and termites will show preference to wooden shelving, paneling and other cellulose material whilst others such as *Dermestes maculatus* will prefer leather book bindings or linen covers.

Prior to undertaking any pest control treatment, it is crucial to conduct a detailed survey to establish the level of infestation and identify the insects involved. A suitable treatment for such situations is to place the entire collection in fumigation-bubbles with a view to eradicating all life stages of infestation using inert atmospheres.

Bubbles are purpose built, portable gas tight structures which can be fabricated in any size from a heavy duty gas tight polyethylene or they may be fabricated as an *in situ* bubble, from a disposable aluminum laminate oxygen barrier film.

The choice of bubble and gas depends on the situation. Normally if the collection is relatively small, carbon dioxide is used in a silver coated heat retaining polyethylene bubble fitted with a unique gas tight zip.

Normal carbon dioxide treatments last for up to 30 days at 20°C with a CO_2 concentration of 60%. This is particularly important if *Anobium* or *Anthrenus* are the target pests.

To shorten the exposure time the bubble can be connected to an environmental control system which will warm the entrapped atmosphere to a chosen temperature. Research has shown that raising the temperature will decrease the exposure time for both CO_2 and nitrogen treatments. (see *Tables 1* and *2*).

Alternatively if there are many items to be treated, time is not a problem and there is the perceived risk of a reaction with carbon dioxide, (for example treatments involving paintings where vegetable based pigments have been used) then nitrogen would be the preferred gas.

Modes of action

Carbon dioxide

Carbon dioxide when used at a concentration of 60% kills insects because of the toxicity of the gas at that concentration. The chosen concentration of 60% allows an oxygen concentration of approximately 7% to remain which allows the insects to continue to respire until they succumb to anoxia. This concentration is also sufficient to kill insect eggs provided sufficient exposure time is allowed. Some eggs and larvae (particularly those which tunnel in wood) can be difficult to control. It is therefore sensible to extend treatments for as long as practical.

Nitrogen

Nitrogen is used as an asphyxiate with the intention of preventing insects from respiring. Nitrogen is not toxic to insects and will not be effective if more than a trace of oxygen is present. If oxygen concentrations are not maintained at less than 0.2% for the treatment period, there is a chance that insects will survive.

The nitrogen method

Items to be treated can be loaded onto support shelving which is carefully placed on a large sheet of aluminum laminate. More aluminum laminate sheet is then draped over the structure and the leading edge is heat welded to the bottom edge to make a gas tight seal. The sides are then welded to form a gas tight structure. To date, bubbles with a capacity of up to 90 ^{3} have been constructed using this technique.

Once the bubble is sealed a powerful vacuum pump is connected to a port and the entrapped air is withdrawn until the sides of the deflating bubble begin to make contact with the item(s) being treated.

It is important when treating delicate items that the vacuum is carefully controlled as the external pressure could cause damage to items such as paintings if they had to support atmospheric pressure over a large cross sectional area. Such items should be protected in a frame or case.

Pure nitrogen is slowly introduced into the bubble through a humidification regulator, which ensures that the humidity inside the structure is the same as the ambient. Once the bubble has fully inflated the gas is removed and the process is repeated.

With large structures it has been found that it is necessary to perform at least 6 'flushings' before the oxygen readings fall into the range of approximately 0.2%.

An accurate trace oxygen monitor is required to monitor the oxygen concentration. Samples are take through gas tight septum fitted to various locations on the bubble. The oxygen meter should be a non invasive device capable of accurately measuring to 0.01% oxygen. It is important to ensure that the gas tightness of the film is not compromised by the gas sampling, all readings should be taken through gas tight septum.

Once the oxygen concentration is within the target parameters, oxygen scavengers normally comprising a mixture of iron oxide and activated carbon are quickly placed inside the bubble, prior to the final nitrogen fill.

A further oxygen reading is taken during the final nitrogen fill. If it is confirmed that the oxygen level is at or below 0.2% no further readings need to be taken for 24 hours. After this period, regular readings must be taken as the oxygen readings can change. The oxygen concentration must stay below 0.2% throughout the treatment period. (Table 3).

There are four major reasons why the oxygen concentration can change:

1) The adsorption of interstitial oxygen from the item being treated. (This is particularly noticeable with treatments involving large wooden items or a pile of books).

2) Pockets of unmixed oxygen yet to equilibrate.
3) Diffusion of oxygen from the atmosphere into the bubble.
4) Accidental damage to the film.

Reasons 1 & 2 are normally detected and resolved in the short term. Reason 3 happens slowly throughout the treatment due to the large surface area of the films, confirming the need for regular monitoring. Reason 4 should not be a major problem if the treatment is conducted in a suitable location and sufficient warning notices are on display.

The exposure period can vary depending on the insects involved. Generally a 30 day exposure is required to ensure that all life stages have been controlled and to make provision for the idiosyncratic behavior of some insects under controlled atmosphere conditions. Preferably items should stay in the bubble for as long possible or until they are required.

Data loggers which record temperature and humidity continuously throughout the fumigation period are placed in the bubble at the same time as the oxygen scavengers to confirm the treatment parameters have been maintained.
At the end of the treatment the data logger is 'down-loaded' through a PC.

Once the collection is safely protected inside the bubbles, insect infestations can now be removed from the building. This will involve the deep cleaning of the walls, crevices, shelving, ceiling and floors. A full building fumigation using one of the traditional fumigants may also be required particularly if the building is constructed of wood and the infestation has been established for some time. Low toxicity residual insecticides, which would not be applied directly to the collection, may be sprayed onto all uncoated wooden surfaces to prevent re-infestation.

Note:

Fumigation gives no residual action, this is also the case with controlled atmosphere treatments. Therefore at the end of the bubble treatment it is essential to ensure that the collection is not returned to an infested building as reinfestation will occur.

Once a suitable residual insecticide has been applied to the shelving and structure it will be quickly absorbed and when dry it will be safe for the collection to be returned.

If the building is not air conditioned and the windows and doors have to be open, insect screens should be fitted to prevent infestation due to casual insect intruders.

Pheromone traps and electronic fly catchers should be placed strategically throughout the building to enable continuous monitoring.

COLLECTIONS CURRENTLY PEST FREE BUT WITH THE POTENTIAL OF BECOMING INFESTED

Where collections appear to be currently pest free there is also a need for regular monitoring and surveillance throughout the building. This will include the use of pheromone traps and fly screens.

Once a treatment has been conducted as in scenario 1 the result will be that the level of infestation should be the same as scenario 2. However, there is the need in both cases to maintain the status quo. There is always a risk of re-infestation if new additions are added to the collection. Therefore a strict quarantine procedure should be instigated.

Another version of the bubble technology is available for this function. In this case we recommend a free standing system which is basically a bubble fabricated in heavy duty polyethylene supported on a purpose built frame.

Bubbles of this type can be installed in a store room away from the collection. As new additions are acquired and exhibition items are returned, they can be placed in the bubble irrespective as to whether an infestation is apparent. (Infestations of many insects are difficult to see, particularly if only eggs are present). It is therefore sensible to work on the basis that all new additions are infested. At any time the bubble can be filled with a chosen gas and the infestations eradicated. Only then should the item be added to the collection.

Mold control

Due to the lack of suitable chemicals for the control of molds, de-humidification is becoming an important technique.

Free standing bubbles fitted with a zip closable door with a de-humidifier installed inside are now used for the storage of books and other items at risk of mold damage due to damp storage conditions. Most molds cannot reproduce in environments where the relative humidity is below 40%. Such storage conditions will prevent molds spreading. However, if the conditions change and the RH increases the spores will germinate. Therefore, it is important that bubbles in this mode are well maintained and monitored.

De-humidification

Bubbles can be made to any size. The largest one made to date has a capacity of 500 m^3 and has been installed in a damp warehouse which could not be economically kept dry. The relative humidity in the bubble is maintained at a constant 40%.

The techniques used today for conservation are slower and require more knowledge than the traditional methods to apply. However, they are safer, environmentally more acceptable, and will not damage collections in the short or long term. Further research is required to generate data on the susceptibility of more insect species to controlled atmospheres, and for the development of more techniques for the control of molds.

Table 1 Taken from Rust and Kennedy (1993).
25.5°C, 55% RH, <0.1% oxygen (achieved by flushing 4 l. chambers, containing *Ageless*, with pure nitrogen).
Phase III Woodborers in vials inside 8 x 8 x 14 cm softwood blocks (separated from free space by minimum 12.7 mm thick solid wood). Other insects in containers under 10-13 cm packed flour.

Species	Stages tested	Days to 100% mortality
Thermobia domestica	e n a	<2
Periplaneta americana	o	5
Tineola bisselliella	e l p a	4+
Anthrenus flavipes	e l p a	<3
Dermestes lardarius	e l p a	<4
Tribolium confusum	e l p a	<4
Trogoderma inclusum	e l p a	5
Lasioderma serricorne	e l p a	<8
Incisitermes minor	n	4*
Lyctus spp.	a l p	<5
Trogoxylon prostomoides	a	<6

Notes
e = egg, n = nymph, a = adult, o = ootheca, l = larva, p = pupa
+ = larva in cocoon may be most tolerant stage
** = delayed 100% mortality occurred after 2 day exposure*
< = indicates shortest exposure used gave 100% mortality

EFFICACY OF LOW OXYGEN/HIGH NITROGEN ATMOSPHERES V. ARTHROPODS

Taken from: Annis (1986) "Towards rational controlled atmosphere dosage schedules: a review of current knowledge" *Proc 4th Int Work Conf Stored-Prod Protn*

Arthropods of stored grain - times to >95% mortality at 20-29°C
Most species - <10 days at both <0.1% and 1% oxygen
Exceptions: *Trogoderma granarium* larvae - 12 days at <0.1%
Sitophilus oryzae pupae - 20 days at <0.1%
> 14 days at 1%
Sitophilus oryzae adults - 16 days at 1% oxygen

Table 2 *Minimum number of days* exposure to atmospheres containing normal 60% carbon dioxide which gave 100% mortality of mixed stage cultures of insects and mites at various temperatures*

Temperature Exposure Periods (days)	15 °C 14, 28	23 °C 1, 2, 4, 8, 14+	35 °C 1, 2, 4, 7, 14
Species			
T. Putrescentiae		1	14
A. siro	14	1	1
P americana	14	2	4
T. granarium (larvae)		-	14
S. oryzae	28	14+	4
A. verbasci (larvae)	14	14+	2
O. mercator	14	4	1
T. castaneum	14	4	4
L. serricorne	14	4	1
D. maculatus	14	4	-
P. tectus	14	1	4
E. cautella	14	4	2
L. patruelis	-	14++	-
L. bostrychophilus	-	8	-
A. punctatum (larvae)**	14	1	14

Notes

*For a given temperature, no insects or mites survived exposures longer than the minima tabulated above.
** 5 year old larvae used at 15 and 23°C, 10 to 12 month old larvae used at 35°C.
\+ at 25°C.
++ minimum exposure period tested.

REFERENCES

BANKS, H.J., A review of recent studies of the effects of controlled atmospheres on stored product pests. *Controlled Atmosphere Storage of Grains,* Elsevier, Amsterdam (1980) 101-118.

BANKS, H.J., Modified atmosphere and hermetic storage - effects on insect pests and the commodity. *Proceedings of the Australian Development Assistance Course on the Preservation of Stored Cereals.* Ed. B. R. CHAMP and E HIGHLEY, CSIRO Division of Entomology, Canberra (1984) 521-532.

BATEMAN, P.L.G., and SMITH, C.P. Unique 'Zip-up' Fumigation System. *Journal of the Society of Archivists.* (1994) 15 (2) 215-218.

BROKERHOF, A.W. Control of fungi and insects in objects and collections of cultural value. *Central Research Laboratory for Objects of Art and Science,* Amsterdam, Netherlands (1989) 77pp.

GILBERG, M., Inert atmosphere disinfestation using Ageless® oxygen scavenger. *ICOM Committee for Conservation, 9th Triennial Meeting,* Dresden (1990) 812-816.

GILBERG, M, Inert atmosphere disinfestation of museum objects using AGELESS oxygen scavenger. *Bulletin of the Australian Institute for the Conservation of Cultural Materials* 16 (1990) 27-34.

GILBERG, M., Inert atmosphere fumigation of museum objects. *Studies in Conservation* 34 (1989) 128-148.

GILBERG, M. The effects of low oxygen atmospheres on museum pests. *Studies in Conservation* 36 (1991) 93-98.

GILBERG, M., and ROACH, A. The use of a commercial pheromone trap for monitoring *Lasioderma serricorne* (F.) Infestations in museum collections. *Studies in Conservation* 36 (1991) 243-247.

MAEKAWA, S. Personal communication. *The Getty Conservation Institute.*

NEWTON, J. Carbon dioxide fumigation in a heated portable enclosure. *Proc. 5th Int. Working Conference on Stored-Product Protection,* Bordeaux, France. Ed. F FLEURAT-LESSARD and P DUCOM, September (1990) Vol II 877-885

NEWTON, J. Carbon dioxide as a fumigant to replace methyl bromide in the control of insects and mites damaging stored products and artefacts. *International Conference on Insect Pests in the Urban Environment.* Cambridge, UK 30 June-3 July 1993.

PATON, R. 7 CREFFIELD, J.W. The tolerance of some timber insect pests to atmospheres of carbon dioxide and carbon dioxide in air. *International Pest Control* 29 (1980) 10-12.

PAYTON, R., and STARLING, K. The use of carbon dioxide for fumigation at the Museum of London. *Conservation News.* March (1994) 53, 16-17.

REICHMUTH, C. New techniques in fumigation research today. *Proc. 5th Int. Working Conf. On Stored Product Protection.* Bordeaux, France. Ed. F FLEURAT-LESSARD and P DUCOM) September (1990) Vol II, 709-725.

RUST, M.K. & KENNEDY, J.M. The feasibility of using modified atmospheres to control insect pests in museums. Final Report July 1, 1989 - December 12 *University of California, Department of Entomology.*

SMITH, C.P. Fumigation - a new concept. *Proc. 8th Brit. Pest Control Conf.* Stratford-upon-Avon, UK June (1988), 2nd session, Paper 3, 15pp.

SMITH, C.P. & NEWTON, J. Carbon dioxide : the fumigation of the future. *Seminar on Research in Conservation, Columbia University,* New York, 26th May (1991).
VALENTIN, N., ALGUERO, M & de HIJAS, C. Evaluation of disinfecting techniques for the conservation of polychrome sculpture in Iberian museums. Madrid, September 1992.

VALENTIN, N. & PREUSSER, F. Insect control by inert gases in museums, archives and libraries. *Restaurator* 11 (1990) 22-23.

VALENTIN, N. Insect eradication in museums and archives by oxygen replacement: a pilot project *ICOM Committee for Conservation, 9th Triennial Meeting,* Dresden (1990) 821-823.

IN THE TREATMENT OF BRITTLE PAPER, DOES THE FUTURE BELONG TO MECHANICAL OR CHEMICAL REINFORCEMENT?

Astrid-Christiane BRANDT

Bibliothèque Nationale de France

INTRODUCTION

Wood pulp and rosin sized papers have a very poor durability. They are acidic and some are already in a very brittle state. Millions of library and archival documents on this type of paper cannot be handed over to the readers any more.

Numerous collection surveys have contributed to raise awareness of this problem. At first, collection keepers encouraged research to develop mass deacidification and strengthening processes which are able to deal with the huge quantity of documents. Now mass treatment has become reality, and it is necessary to develop an economical approach and to evaluate the impact of mass treatments on the management of the collections.

To answer the question whether the future of the treatment of brittle paper does belong to mechanical or chemical reinforcement, I will focus my analysis on economical factors. The results of the collection survey the Bibliothèque Nationale de France realized in 1990 will serve as a basis for my argumentation.

COLLECTION SURVEY AND ANALYSIS OF THE NEEDS

Before setting up a long-term strategy for the treatment of a collection, it is necessary to assess the extent and the kind of degradation for the different types of documents.

The collection survey of the Bibliothèque Nationale de France was conducted with a sample of 21.185 documents corresponding to 0.21% of the printed collection of the library of nearly 10 million books and periodicals.

The state of preservation of paper was evaluated as follows:

good condition	paper resists manipulation
poor condition	paper is yellow and embrittled on the edge of the page
bad condition	paper is yellow and so brittle that it cannot be manipulated without the loss of fragments

The documents in a poor condition can be handed over to the readers with some precautions, but those which are in bad condition cannot.

Three classes of acidity were documented:

paper with a	$pH > 7$	alkaline
paper with	$5.5 < pH > 7$	slightly acid
paper with	$3 < pH > 5.5$	acid

If we only take into account the period running from 1870 to 1960 and corresponding to the augmentation of paper in a bad condition, the results of the survey are the following:

Table 1 State of preservation and acidity of paper from the period of 1870-1960 (43% of the total collection: 4,3 million documents)

State of preservation of paper	%	Number of documents (millions)
good	38.4	1.6
embrittled	26.6	1.1
brittle	35.0	1.5
Acidity of paper		
alkaline		
slightly acidic		
acidic	80.0	3.4

If the priority is given to documents published in France belonging to the period running from 1870 to1960 representing 62% of the 4.3 million documents, 2.6 million documents have to be treated including l million periodicals.

Treatment needs can be divided as follows:

1) ***documents which need deacidification***

urgent need (acidic paper)	80% (2.1 million documents)
medium treatment needs (slightly acidic paper)	20% (0.5 million documents)

2) ***documents which need strengthening***

urgent need (brittle paper)	35% (0.9 million documents)
medium treatment needs (embrittled paper)	26.6% (0.7 million documents)

DETERMINATION OF APPROPRIATE TREATMENTS AND COSTS

To plan a mass treatment process, it is necessary to have evaluated the needs of the collection and the output of treatment (equipment, staff).

The analysis of the needs makes it possible to determine several treatments according to the state of preservation and the use of the document.

To simplify, microfilming is not taken into account in my argumentation. Nevertheless, in a real situation a choice has to be made between transfer of information and physical treatment of the original document.

Table 2 The choice of a treatment according to the state of preservation of the document

State of preservation of the paper	Type of treatment	Millions of documents Concerned
acid but not brittle or embrittled paper	deacidification and chemical reinforcement (optional)	1.0
acidic and embrittled paper	deacidification and chemical reinforcement	0.7
acidic and brittle paper	deacidification and mechanical reinforcement	0.9

Mass deacidification already works. The national libraries of Canada, France and Germany have an in-house facility. Acids included in the paper are neutralized and an alkaline reserve is let in the paper. Laboratory studies have shown the benefits of this treatment, but deacidification cannot restore the loss of mechanical strength of the paper.

This is the reason why several national libraries like the British Library, the Bibliothèque Nationale de France, and Die Deutsche Bibliothek have commissioned industrial firms to develop mass strengthening treatments. The methods under development are based on the impregnation of the documents by polymers or monomers which will be polymerized. These treatments are especially designed for embrittled papers, but not for brittle ones.

In this respect, the Bibliothèque Nationale de France has signed an agreement with SEPAREX, a French company, to develop a new process of book treatment aiming at extracting the products responsible for paper deterioration, then impregnating them with neutralizing and strengthening products dissolved in supercritical carbon dioxide (CO_2).

Brittle paper needs a sheet by sheet treatment. At present two methods are used in conservation workshops: lamination and splitting. In the case of lamination, the paper is laminated on both sides by a synthetic fiber web containing an adhesive. The following data show the output of the lamination treatment in three workshops of the Bibliothèque Nationale de France.

Table 3 Annual production for lamination in the 3 workshops of the Bibliothèque Nationale de France

Workshop	Number of sheets/year	Number of volumes/year	Number of persons
Sablé : treatment of books	97,000	1.350	4.5
Provins : treatment of newspapers	72,000	1.000	6
Richelieu : treatment of newspapers	24,000	333	2

Basis: *1 book in 8°, 288 pages (72 sheets); 220 working days/year.*

It is obvious that this method cannot treat in a reasonable time all the documents which need reinforcement.

In the case of the paper-splitting method, the paper is split into two parts, then a resistant fiber web is included and the two parts of the document are sized together. The manual process is rather time-consuming and requires special skill. Recently the German firm BECKER Preservotec has developed a paper-splitting machine with a capacity of 2000 to 5000 sheets per day, equivalent to 6,000 to 15,000 books per year (on a basis of 220 working days). The objective is to treat 10,000 sheets per day.

The mechanical reinforcement is the only way to treat acid and brittle paper, because the bindings are most often in a very bad condition and need to be replaced. This method fits also very well with the needs of unbound newspaper collections.

The precise analysis of the needs, the knowledge of the best adapted treatment, as well as the capacity of treatment, will allow a financial approach to the treatment and an evaluation of the time needed.

As far as chemical reinforcement treatments are concerned, costs are based on estimations, because these processes are still under development.

The data for the paper-splitting machine were calculated by BECKER Preservotec, the firm which has developed this machine for the workshop of the Deutsche Bibliothek in Leipzig. The number of sheets treated is supposed to be about 10,000 sheets per day, equivalent to 36,500 books per year.

Table 4 Capacity and costs for chemical and mechanical reinforcement

Treatment	Number books/ year	Cost per book ($)	Number of persons	Total number of books	Number Of Years	Total Costs (Million $)
deacidification + strengthening (R&D, BNF)	150,000 (BNF) + 150,000 (other libraries)	14 (estimated)	2			
acidic paper (BNF)				2.6 M	17	37
embrittled paper (BNF)				0.7 M	5	13
mechanical splitting (BECKER/Deutsche Bibliothek)	36,500	76(1)* 50(2)*	3**			
brittle paper (BNF)				0.9 M	25	46-70

Remarks:

(1) including equipment costs

(2) running costs

***Basis:** 1 book in 8°, 288 pages (72 sheets); 220 working days/year.*

* *Further costs have to be added : preparation of the documents, deacidification, binding. Three persons are involved in these operations.*

** *1 person for maintenance of the equipment.*

CONCLUSION

According to the present state of development, the mechanical reinforcement method is the only way to treat brittle and embrittled paper, but the capacity of the treatment remains quite low, even for the paper-splitting machine. Nevertheless, as the costs for the treatment itself and for complementary treatments (removing of the binding, deacidification, re-binding, etc.) remain high, the development of a mass process which combines deacidification and reinforcement is necessary.

Chemical reinforcement processes will probably be only useful for acidic and embrittled paper to prevent further degradation. It is illusory to believe in one treatment which will be adapted for all kinds of documents. Libraries and archives need several treatments completing each other.

In the future, more attention must be paid to the selection of the documents. Methods which enable a quick diagnosis to determine the kind of treatment according to the state of preservation and the use of the document have to be developed.
The collection management has to be evaluated beforehand, in order to supply enough documents for mass treatments. The staff necessary for all these operations has also to be considered correspondingly.
Moreover, the capacities of complementary treatments have to be adjusted, because they are still a limiting factor. These treatments imply a lot of time and a certain amount of staff.

In this context, the development of mechanical binding methods is particularly important, to meet the requirements of libraries and archives for an extensive treatment at low costs.

THE IFLA SECTION ON CONSERVATION: LIBRARY PRESERVATION AND CONSERVATION IN THE 90s

Ralph W. MANNING

National Library of Canada

In the past 2 days we have listened to almost 20 presentations dealing with many aspects of preservation and conservation. Some of the topics we have heard about are permanent paper, registers of reproductions, digitization and access, conservation techniques and the inherent contradiction of preservation in a institution where access to information is fundamental.

The IFLA Section on Conservation acts as a forum for discussion on all of these issues and provides a potential conduit to the many other Sections of IFLA which deal with issues related to preservation and conservation. Some of the Sections to which I refer are the Section on National Libraries which has a keen interest in the preservation of the national heritage of each country; the Section on Library Buildings and Equipment which is interested in the structures used to store and preserve library materials; and, for obvious reasons, the Section for Rare Books and Manuscripts.

In the next presentation, Marie-Thérèse Varlamoff will speak to you about the IFLA Preservation and Conservation Core Programme. This core programme with its five regional centers throughout the world is the keystone to IFLA's efforts to preserving the world's library and archival heritage. The IFLA Section on Conservation has a very keen interest in the work of the Core Programme and we have been developing a strong link to this programme so that we may work together in fulfilling our mutual goals.

The Section on Conservation represents the worldwide concern for the protection and preservation of the recorded knowledge which forms an important part of our universal cultural heritage. Recording of knowledge and information has been integral to the development and sustenance of literate cultures, but records are generally impermanent. Awareness of the need for active preservation has been growing throughout the world in recent years. The Section therefore brings together librarians, documentalists and conservation managers from all countries interested in the preservation problem and in the need to provide a better understanding of the professional issues which it poses. These words are taken from the IFLA Medium-Term Programme as it relates to the Section on Conservation.

IFLA member bodies choose to join any number of IFLA Sections as part of their membership to IFLA. At the present time, 114 institutions and associations have chosen to join the Section on Conservation making it one of the more popular Sections in IFLA. This clearly attests to the importance of Preservation to the international library and archival communities and I think demonstrates the pervading influence of preservation on all aspects of library science.

May I remind you of the first objective of IFLA which is to promote international understanding, cooperation, discussion, research and development in all fields of library and information service activity.

In my opinion, the preservation and conservation of library and archival materials is of vital concern to us. We must work to play our individual roles in the worldwide effort to preserve the world's intellectual heritage.

The IFLA Section on Conservation draws its membership from 45 different countries representing every continent (except *Antarctica*!). This provides a rich and varied pool of expertise that can be used to promote the activities of IFLA in the field of preservation and conservation. It is also an important vehicle for disseminating information about preservation and conservation to libraries and archives around the world.

I would like to summarize the objectives of the Section on Conservation:

- Promote an awareness of preservation problems and factors;
- Promote the assessment of the extent of conservation problems;
- Promote the effective use of conservation and preservation options;
- Encourage national and international programs;
- Promote the production and use of permanent paper;
- Encourage further research.

The Section on Conservation is guided in its work by a Standing Committee. There are currently 15 members of the Standing Committee for the Section on Conservation and an additional 4 observing or corresponding members. This represents a national representation from 13 different countries. Once again, we can take some pride in our ability to draw from a vast expertise from around the world.

We have a ways to go, however. As much as we can take pride in a respectable share of the IFLA membership, we need additional members of both the Section and its Standing Committee to be able to respond effectively to our goals and objectives.

The need to share information and assistance is great and I believe there is a particular need for input from the developing countries of the world. We need to better understand how IFLA can help developing countries and how the Section on Conservation can work with the Core Programme on Preservation and Conservation to provide necessary assistance. Last year the IFLA Conference was held in Havana, Cuba, and we were able to see at first hand the great need for financial assistance in Cuba while at the same time the level of technical understanding was already improving. The IFLA Section on Conservation is in a good position to facilitate communication throughout the world.

At the present time, the Section has been working hard to renew itself and establish a firm base upon which further work can be accomplished.

We have just completed the publication of a brochure on Disaster Planning which we hope to make available to libraries throughout the world with a view to helping these libraries find the information and resources that they need to prevent disasters and to cope with disasters when they occur.

We are also working on a brochure on permanent paper which we hope to disseminate to publishers throughout the world. It is important that the world learn from its mistakes and the monumental mistake of the past 100-150 years has been the explosive growth of publishing on paper which self-destructs. This has cost libraries and archives around the world tremendous amounts of money in efforts to contain the loss of information that occurs when the paper on which it is recorded simply turns to dust. The Section on Conservation feels that a significant contribution can be made by promoting the use of permanent paper.

In addition to our close working relationship with the IFLA Preservation and Conservation Core Programme, we have established close ties with the International Organization for Standardization subcommittee which is responsible for the physical materials on which information is stored.

Last year, the Section initiated a Newsletter which has now appeared in two issues. The third issue should appear in the early autumn of this year. The Newsletter appears to have been well-accepted and is only one of many methods of communication available to libraries and archives in the field of preservation.

Much work remains to be done and we look forward to an increased participation of interested libraries in the Section and of active and interested individuals on the Standing Committee of the Section on Conservation.

The IFLA Section on Conservation has the flexibility to provide assistance and knowledgeable input from countries throughout the world. It is, however, only with the active participation of individuals and libraries that we can make a truly effective contribution to the preservation of the world's heritage.

I therefore invite all of you to investigate the possibility of joining the Section on Conservation and standing for election to the Standing Committee when elections are next held.

THE PAC CORE PROGRAMME

Marie -Thérèse VARLAMOFF

Bibliothèque Nationale de France

Most of you have heard of PAC. Nevertheless, it will not do any harm to recall why it was created and how it works before we list its main activities and present its medium-term programme.

HISTORICAL BACKGROUND AND PAC STRUCTURE

Officially created during the IFLA meeting in Nairobi in 1984, the IFLA Core Programme "Preservation and Conservation" (PAC) was effectively launched in Vienna by the Conference on the Preservation of Library Materials sponsored by the Conference of the Directors of National Libraries, with IFLA and UNESCO.

It took about three years to finally give PAC its present structure. Contrary to other IFLA Core Programmes, PAC has been originally conceived on a decentralized pattern. An international focal point manages the programme, co-ordinates activities, and is responsible for the general strategy and the promotion of the programme among professionals, institutions or associations already dealing with preservation or susceptible of being interested. Five regional centres, hosted by a national library, represent PAC in different regions of the world and are responsible for their own choices and policies.

The first international focal point was hosted by the Library of Congress in Washington and two regional centres were created: one in France, at the Bibliothèque Nationale in Sablé, which was responsible for Western Europe, Africa and the Middle East, and another one hosted by the Deutsche Bücherei in Leipzig (Democratic Republic of Germany), responsible for Eastern Europe. Though it was a good start, it was not enough, since a large part of the world was not represented. This is the reason why, in 1988, the Biblioteca Nacional de Venezuela, in Caracas, proposed to host the regional centre for Latin America and the Caribbean and, in 1989, the National Diet Library in Tokyo, and the National Library of Australia, in Canberra, became respectively regional centres for Asia (Central and East) and for Oceania and South East Asia. PAC could start working on solid and efficient bases.

In 1992, the international focal point was transferred from the Library of Congress to the Bibliothèque Nationale in Paris. The Library of Congress became the regional centre for the United States and Canada, while Paris went on taking care of the above-mentioned area.

Last September, I was appointed the new director of PAC to replace Jean-Marie Arnoult, who had left the Bibliothèque Nationale de France a few months earlier. The present directors of the regional centres are:

- Wolfgang Wächter, in Leipzig
- Jan Lyall, in Canberra
- Diane Kresh, in Washington
- Ramón Sánchez, in Caracas
- Takao Shimamura, in Tokyo.

The PAC directors met in Budapest on Monday. We are thinking about a new geographical division between centres in order to stick to economic, cultural and linguistic priorities as well as to the state of the art concerning preservation activities in each region. The creation of new centres (especially in Eastern Europe and Africa) will be proposed for discussion and approval to the IFLA Executive Board.

PROGRAMME OBJECTIVES

The IFLA PAC Core Programme has one major goal: to ensure that library materials, published and unpublished, in all formats, will be preserved in accessible form for as long as possible.

Three major principles support this goal:-

- the preservation of library materials is essential to the survival and development of culture and scholarship;
- national and international interdependency exists in the preservation of library materials; and
- national strategy should be guided by the principle that each country must accept responsibility for the preservation of its own imprints and for the preservation of other library materials of its own civilization and culture.

In order to reach its objectives, PAC must:-

- raise the consciousness level of government officials, of the general public, and of library administrators and staff, about the issues of preservation in libraries;
- educate library administrators and staff about the theories and practices of library preservation;
- inform users of library materials of the need for preservation and conservation, and of the role they can play in extending the usable life of library holdings;
- encourage and facilitate the training of library administrators and staff in the proper care and handling of all library materials, and of technicians and professional conservators in the preservation and conservation of library materials;
- encourage scientific research on the causes of deterioration in library materials and on the application of science and technology to the prevention and treatment of deterioration;
- promote the development of national and international standards and laws that pertain to and support the production, preservation, and treatment of library materials; and
- promote, through co-operation and collaboration, the development of national and international preservation activities that support the goals and objectives of the IFLA Section on Conservation and the other IFLA Core Programmes.

ACTIVITIES, PAST AND PRESENT

Much has already been done by my predecessors, and it would take too long to give a detailed enumeration.

Let us mention the following:-

The Seminar on Preservation and Conservation held in Loughborough and London in September 1990, and the Pan-African Conference on the Preservation and Conservation of Library and Archival Materials held in Nairobi in 1993, in co-operation with the ALP (Advancement of Librarianship in the Third World) Core Programme and the RSCA (Regional Standing Committee for Africa). IFLA has just published the *Proceedings of the Pan-African Conference*, available in French or in English from the Headquarters in The Hague.

The publication, twice a year, of a newsletter, *International Preservation News*, widely distributed, and which presents, among other things, the most recent developments in research (mass deacidification or splitting activities).

The publication of the brochure about PAC. (This is available in English so far, but is awaiting translators. A French version is already in print.)

The regional centres of Washington and Caracas have initiated the publication of preservation packets, such as: *Care, Handling and Storage of Photographs,* by Mark Roosa, Vosper Fellow, or *Disaster Preparedness*, by Sally Buchanan.
The Canberra centre asked Wendy Smith, Vosper Fellow, to produce a distance-learning training manual on conservation for Asian librarians. Recently, Jan Lyall, the director of the centre, wrote the *Guidelines for the UNESCO Memory of the World Programme.* I would like to thank her again for the excellent work she has been doing.

The survey for the "Memory of the World" Programme, launched through a questionnaire elaborated by Jan, has required the co-operation of all the PAC centres (translations and mailing). The answers are being computerized and will allow us to locate the holdings of national significance by inputting and updating these in a database on preservation and conservation activities, existing or being set up, in order to hand these holdings over to future generations in the best possible state of conservation,

either in their original carrier or in other formats. May I thank here all the libraries which answered the questionnaire.

Moreover, each centre, or should I say each library hosting a regional centre, responds, according to its possibilities, to the various demands from the region: translations and dissemination of professional literature, such as *Conservaplan* published by Caracas, organization of symposia or conferences, like Tokyo, which organizes each year a forum on preservation.

Of course we must not forget to emphasize the role of the PAC centres in the formulation and organization of numerous training classes and internship programmes.

SHORT- OR MEDIUM-TERM PROJECTS

I shall concentrate here on the major ones.

- The safeguarding of photographic collections preserved in libraries or archives, in collaboration with the International Council on Archives. This project has been proposed to UNESCO for the "Memory of the World" Programme. It is a very ambitious project which aims at locating, cataloguing and safeguarding the photographic holdings prior to 1900 kept in libraries and archives and significant for the history of a nation, region or culture. The centre of Caracas has been asked to develop this project in Latin America. According to the success encountered, the project will be extended to other regions.
- I have been asked to prepare a draft resolution on permanent paper to be presented at the UNESCO General Assembly in December.
- In 1993, the regional centres of Tokyo and Canberra have been conducting surveys in their regions to assess the expectations from the PAC centres. The results indicate that they meet the objectives of the programme, namely:
  - to be informed regularly on preservation news, research and development, through publications, seminars and workshops;
  - to be trained in the techniques in use, with education materials, manuals, guidelines, standards....

This is why it is important to stick to the revision of out-dated but still useful documents such as the *Principles for the Preservation and Conservation of Library Materials*, and to continue formulating such documents and organizing workshops and other training sessions, until the trainees can become trainers and train other people, and so on.

- The revision of the *Principles for the Preservation and Conservation of Library Materials* by J.-M. Dureau and D.W.G. Clements, in collaboration with the Section on Conservation. May I insist here on the necessity for your co-operation. The more comments we receive, the better the final version will be and probably the more satisfied you will be.
- The translation of those *Principles*, not only into IFLA's official languages, but into rarer languages too, in order to make them accessible to most, especially those do who not master foreign languages. You are most welcome to bring your personal support to this project.

The ECPA (the European Commission on Preservation and Access) and PAC will co-operate to make it possible.

The following are the projects foreseen for the next five years, provided that we manage to fund them:-

- The organization in Paris of an international conference - it could take place during the Spring of 1998 - on The Economics of Preservation Policies. This will be for many participants the occasion to visit the new premises of the Bibliothèque Nationale de France, especially the Technical Centre for Conservation in Marne-la-Vallée.
- The regional centre in Caracas suggested, when I visited it last April, the publication of a sort of Who's Who listing all those involved in either preservation or conservation. This seems to be an excellent idea to be discussed before we start implementing the project. Should it concern all the regions? Should all the people dealing with preservation or conservation be listed? Or should the repertory include only specialists or managers?

Should the repertory list people according to their location or to their specialty or both? Should this repertory be computerized in order to be easily updated? Who would then be in charge of the updating? etc., etc. ..... There are so many questions about such a repertory that I propose to give us one more year to think about it and to discuss the matter next year in Beijing.

- The publication of a sort of *vade-mecum* for those who must undertake surveys on the conditions of preservation in a library. Such a document would save time in the final writing of the report and unify the presentation. Moreover, for those who are not acquainted with this kind of report, it would remind them of the points that have to be taken into consideration. This project has appealed to the ECPA. which could assist us technically, but we still need to find a strong financial support.
- Of course, we intend to issue more brochures, leaflets and videos susceptible of raising awareness among the greatest number of people, at each level and for the largest public, on the importance of preservation.

COOPERATION AND COMMUNICATION ARE THE KEYS TO OUR SUCCESS

As you may have noticed, PAC has been and intends to be fairly active, but, to be honest, most of the activities that were programmed in the past and those which are planned for the future have received or will need the support and the co-operation of other structures, associations, or NGOs. Beatrix Kastály and I have decided to strengthen the links between PAC and the Section on Conservation. This is the reason why the annual meeting of the PAC directors took place, here in Budapest, just before the IFLA Satellite Meeting on Library Preservation and Conservation in the 90s. In addition to the convenience of the location which enabled PAC directors to attend the Satellite Meeting and save travel costs, it was a symbol of a new start on a more co-operative basis. Our task next year will be to identify the activities headed by PAC from those undertaken by the Section.

As we are talking about co-operation, I would not like to end without saying a few words on communication.

It seems obvious that what people mostly ask for is information about the development of preservation activities conducted outside their own library. There is a gap between the level of communication according to the language in use. English-speaking librarians have no problems whatsoever getting information out of newsletters, brochures, leaflets, manuals, reports or other professional publications. I truly believe that, when the necessary information is published, one of the major goals for PAC should be to make this information available to what we call in French "the silent majority", that is, to all those who do not practice English and who, for the same reason, cannot get the information they need to extend their field activities. So, I urgently beg you to bring your contribution to PAC in helping us translate into rare languages the information everyone should be able to get.

MEMORY OF THE WORLD: PRESERVING THE DOCUMENTARY HERITAGE

Abdelaziz ABID

UNESCO (France)

INTRODUCTION

The collective memory of the peoples of the world is of vital importance in preserving cultural identities, in bridging the past and the present, and in shaping the future. The documentary heritage residing in libraries and archives constitutes a major part of that memory and reflects the diversity of peoples, languages and cultures. But that memory is fragile.

A considerable proportion of the world documentary heritage disappears through "natural" causes: acidified paper that crumbles to dust, leather, parchment, film and magnetic tape attacked by light, heat, humidity or dust. The cinema, for instance, is in danger of losing most of the works that have made it the art of the century, just when it is celebrating its centenary. Thousands of kilometres of film could just fade away unless they are restored and preserved as soon as possible. Nitrate fires in France and Mexico, for example, have caused important losses.

As well as natural causes, accidents regularly afflict libraries and archives. Floods, fires, hurricanes, storms, earthquakes ... the list goes on of disasters which are difficult to guard against except by taking preventive measures. The recent catastrophe in Japan immediately comes to mind.

It would take a very long time to compile a list of all the libraries and archives destroyed or seriously damaged by acts of war, bombardment and fire, whether deliberate or accidental. The Library of Alexandria is probably the most famous historical example, but how many other known and unknown treasures have vanished in Constantinople, Warsaw, Florence, or more recently, in Bucharest, St. Petersburg and Sarajevo? There are so many more, and sadly the list cannot be closed - not to mention holdings dispersed following the accidental or deliberate displacement of archives and libraries.

The sheer scale of the effort needed to preserve what is part of this irreplaceable "Memory of the World" requires the implementation of a consistent protection programme which will pool endeavours and make use of state-of-the-art technology.

PRESERVATION AND ACCESS

One of UNESCO's basic missions is to help maintain, increase and diffuse knowledge by assuring the protection of the world's documentary heritage and making it accessible to as many people as possible. Impelled by its responsibility to develop culture and protect the world cultural heritage, UNESCO recognised that urgent action was required to ensure that the world's documentary memory was not further deteriorated, and launched in 1992 the "Memory of the World" Programme to protect and promote the world documentary heritage.

UNESCO's reinforced long-standing commitment to the safeguarding of the world's documentary heritage came originally from a growing awareness of the perilous state of preservation of, and bad conditions of access to, documentary heritage in various parts of the world. War and social upheaval, as well as severe lack of resources to carry out preservation and dissemination activities, have aggravated the problems that have existed for centuries.

The "Memory of the World" Programme is designed as a new approach to safeguard the world documentary heritage, democratise access to it, and raise awareness of its significance and the need to preserve it.

The Programme has the following four objectives which are complementary and of equal importance:

a) to facilitate preservation by the most appropriate techniques of the world's documentary heritage;

b) to assist in enabling access to it, without discrimination against any users;

c) to increase the awareness world-wide of its existence and significance;

d) to promote the Programme and its products to the widest possible public.

The main objective of the Programme is to ensure the preservation, by the most appropriate means, of documentary heritage which has world significance and to encourage the preservation of documentary heritage which has national and regional significance.

A twin objective is making this heritage accessible to as many people as possible, using the most appropriate technology, both inside and outside the countries in which it is physically located.

Preservation of documentary heritage and increased access to it complement one another. Access facilitates protection and preservation ensures access. For example, digitised materials can be accessed by many people and demand for access can stimulate preservation work.

Another element of the Programme is to raise awareness of UNESCO Member States of their documentary heritage, in particular aspects of that heritage which are significant in terms of a common world memory.

Finally, the Programme seeks to develop products based on this documentary heritage and make them available for wide distribution, while ensuring that the originals are maintained in the best possible conditions of conservation and security. High quality text, sound and image banks could be compiled and made available on local and global networks, and reproductions could be derived in all sorts of forms such as compact discs, albums, books, postcards, microfilms, *etc.* Any proceeds from the sale of related products will then be ploughed back into the Programme.

PROGRAMME SCOPE AND STRUCTURE

The scope of the Programme is, therefore, quite vast and will involve a variety of partners, ranging from students, scholars and the general public, to owners, providers and producers of information, and manufacturers of end products. An International Advisory Committee for the "Memory of the World" Programme was appointed by the Director-General of UNESCO to guide the planning and implementation of the Programme as a whole and make recommendations concerning fund-raising, the allocation of funds, and the granting of the "Memory of the World" label to the projects selected, including those not receiving financial support from the Programme. The International Advisory Committee held two meetings (Pultusk, Poland, September 1993 and Paris, France, May 1995). The Committee recommended, at its first meeting, that the concept of documentary heritage be extended to include, besides manuscripts and other rare and valuable documents in libraries and archives, documents in any medium: in particular, audio-visual documents, computerised recordings and oral traditions, the importance of which varies from region to region. In all these fields there is a need for protection, sometimes as a matter of urgency, if we are to prevent collective amnesia and set up world cultural exchange.

The Programme should make governments aware that they must protect their documentary heritage, release potential for action, support the activities of professional, national, regional and international organisations, and stimulate initiatives.

At the national level, it is recommended that a committee be appointed, firstly to select projects according to the criteria agreed upon and submit them to the International Advisory Committee and, thereafter, to follow them up. The committee membership should include experts able to make an active contribution to the projects and representatives of the users. Persons submitting projects must ensure that the rights of the owners of the holdings or collections are protected. In addition, each project will set up its own scientific committee of specialists to determine the general thrust of the project and to supervise its organisation. A "Memory of the World" National Committee is now set up in ten countries (Belarus, Cape Verde, China, Colombia, Croatia, Cuba, Finland, Hungary, Malawi and Mauritania) and five countries (Canada, Denmark, Germany, Spain and Zaire) are considering the creation of such a Committee. Jordan and Syria indicated that national institutions are already performing the role of National Committee.

Lastly, whenever the need arises, a regional committee will be required to select projects of a regional nature, taking local characteristics into consideration, with a view to submitting them to the International Committee.
An example of efficient regional follow-up to the establishment of the Programme is the Experts Meeting held in December 1994 in Kuala Lumpur for the definition of an Asian component of the "*Memory of the World*" Programme. Participants from 20 countries discussed problems facing custodians of national documentary heritage materials which are generally endangered because of neglect, adverse physical and climatic conditions, political instability ... The situation is very bleak for least developed countries, because precious and rare documents are endangered now, and, if no action is taken in a few years, they will be lost for ever, while others that are still in a more or less stable condition now will be endangered in a few years if no programme for their preservation and conservation is carried out. The meeting agreed to take steps in ensuring that Member States will establish a mechanism at the national and regional levels to identify projects receivable under the "Memory of the World" Programme, as well as establish individual country inventory of documentary heritage materials, prepare a programme for preservation and conservation of such

materials, and promotion and marketing strategies to generate resources to finance the programme.

Similar conclusions were reached by a sub-regional meeting on the "Memory of the World", held in Budapest from 9 to 10 March 1995. The meeting was attended by participants from Austria, Croatia, the Czech Republic, Hungary, Romania and Slovakia. While digitisation is a powerful tool to facilitate access and thereby helping to preserve the originals, participants stressed that it has limits and could not substitute for conventional preservation work. During the meeting, a co-operative sub-regional project was designed. Mobile digitisation equipment will be shared by the participating countries, a digital version of a selection of historical documents of interest to several countries will then be made available. It is expected that the project will enable the participating institutions to test digitisation techniques and equipment and assess the related financial, legal and dissemination aspects.

"MEMORY OF THE WORLD" REGISTER

The participants in the Second Meeting of the International Advisory Committee, held in Paris in May 1995, agreed that a "Memory of the World" Register be developed. This Register will list all documentary heritage which has been identified by the International Advisory Committee as meeting the selection criteria for world significance, similar to UNESCO's World Heritage List.

The "Memory of the World" Register will be a significant document in itself, as well as an inspiration to nations and regions to identify, list and preserve their documentary heritage. Listing will serve as a significant tool in raising awareness of governments, non-governmental organisations, foundations and the public at large, to the importance of their heritage and will serve as an incentive to obtain funds for its preservation.

Individual countries are encouraged to set up their own documentary heritage registers in parallel to the "Memory of the World" Register. National registers identify the documentary inheritance of the nation. The national registers will increase awareness of the importance of the national documentary heritage, and the need for a co-ordinated and integrated policy to ensure that endangered documentary heritage is preserved.

Groups of nations may compile regional registers to list documentary heritage which is integral to their collective memory.

SELECTION CRITERIA

Each register - World, Regional and National - must be based on clearly-defined criteria for assessing the cultural value of documentary heritage. These criteria relate to influence, time, place, people, subject, form and style, and social value. Documentary heritage may need to meet only one criterion for inclusion in the World Register, but it is more likely to be assessed by reference to several criteria.

The criteria are:

> **Criterion 1 - Influence**: Documentary heritage is of world significance if it had a major influence on the history of the world, transcending the boundaries of a national culture.

Criterion 2 - Time: Documentary heritage is of world significance if it reflects in an outstanding way a period of momentous change in world affairs or makes an outstanding contribution to our understanding of the world at a particularly important time in its history.

Criterion 3 - Place: Documentary heritage is of world significance if it contains important information about a locality or region which made a crucial contribution to major developments in world history or culture.

Criterion 4 - People: Documentary heritage is of world significance if it has a special association with the life or works of a person or people who have made an outstanding contribution to world history or culture.

Criterion 5 - Subject/Theme: Documentary heritage is of world significance if it documents in an outstanding way an important subject or major theme of world history or culture.

Criterion 6 - Form and Style: Documentary heritage is of world significance if it is an important example of an outstanding form or style.

Criterion 7 - Social and Cultural Value: Documentary heritage is of world significance if it has outstanding cultural and social or spiritual value which transcends a national culture.

Secondary Criteria: In addition to these seven major criteria, two further criteria should be taken into account. These may enhance the world significance of documentary heritage, though they are not sufficient in themselves to establish its significance.

a) *Secondary Criterion 1 - Integrity*: The significance of documentary heritage may be enhanced if it has a high degree of integrity or completeness.
b) *Secondary Criterion 2 - Rarity*: The significance of documentary heritage may be enhanced if it is unique or rare.

The criteria will be tested by the International Advisory Committee and weighting factors will be developed to reflect the relative importance of the criteria.
The criteria for documentary heritage to be entered on National or Regional Registers are to be decided by the relevant National or Regional Committees. It is recommended, however, that the World Register criteria be used as a model.

Proposals for documentary heritage to receive resources through the "Memory of the World" Programme may be made by National and Regional Committees, by Governments, by NGOs, by the International Advisory Committee, or by other professional bodies in the country or region. Documentary heritage proposed for support will be of World Register status. Support will require the documentary heritage to meet criteria to be set by the International Advisory Committee.

Restrictions on access to documentary heritage will not systematically prevent entry on a Register but may reduce the possibility of receiving support through the "Memory of the World" Programme.

Furthermore, the Pultusk meeting recommended that some degree of priority be given to operations affecting several countries, national projects with a regional or international dimension, and projects carried out in co-operation or in partnership, while not overlooking minorities and their cultures. Particular attention will be paid to reconstructing the memory of peoples in the case of collections or holdings that have been displaced or scattered.

SOME CURRENT PROJECTS

1) Prague

A digitisation programme was launched by the National Library in Prague, in co-operation with a private firm, Albertina Ltd. A demonstration CD-ROM was first published in 1993, featuring some of the most precious manuscripts and other documents in the historic collections of the National Library, with annotations in Czech, English and French. In addition, a CD-ROM series has been starting with the release of the first two discs in early May 1995.

Digitising the most beautiful manuscripts and old prints of the National Library will facilitate access to these treasures without exposing the originals to heavy use, thus contributing to their preservation. In addition, while colours and ink react with paper, parchment, silk and other traditional media, digital information does not fade with the passing of time and could be easily transferred from CD-ROM to more durable media to come in the future.

2) The Radzivill Chronicle

Written in old Russian, this monumental work reveals the history of Russia and its neighbours from the 5th to the early13th century in pictorial form, representing events described in the manuscript with more than six hundred colour illustrations. Known to the scholarly community according to its ownership in the 17th and 18th centuries, the Radzivill, or Kenigsberg Chronicle, is the most ancient surviving example of the art of Russian illuminated chronicle. It is a 15th-century copy of a 13th-century archetype held by the Library of the Russian Academy of Sciences in St. Petersburg (BAN). The Radzivill Chronicle's combination of text and illustration places this manuscript in the company of such acknowledged masterpieces as the Madrid copy of the Greek Illuminated Chronicle of Ioann Scilipa, the Vatican copy of the Bulgarian Translated Chronicle of Konstantin Manassia, the Budapest copy of the Hungarian Illuminated Chronicle, and the copies of the Big French Chronicles. Among these, the Radzivill is distinguished for the richness and quantity of its illustrations.

The text of the manuscript has been published many times. However, the illustrations have been published only once, at the turn of the century, as part of a black and white reproduction of the entire Chronicle. In the centuries since its creation, the manuscript has sustained significant damage. Its binding has been replaced several times, the edges of leaves have been cut, and the painted miniatures have been worn by age and use. The Radzivill Chronicle was restored on two occasions in this century.

The increasing fragility of the original manuscript, together with its pre-eminence in the Russian literature, has left BAN to share a dilemma faced by libraries around the world charged with the care and wise use of cultural treasures. Handling of the Radzivill Chronicle, itself, must be restricted to preserve its material well-being. At the same time, the scholarly and scientific enterprise to which the Library is dedicated argues for access to this important document for serious research.

This is why the Library has turned to a digital medium - to display the manuscript in full colour while preserving the original. A prototype Photo CD is produced with the support of UNESCO and the Library of Congress, as a pilot project and a demonstration of the use of digital media in the service of preservation.

3) *Saint Sophia*

Devised by a group of Bulgarian and French writers, the "Saint Sophia" project is an attempt at a multimedia edition of Bulgarian manuscripts on an interactive compact disc. The disc evokes the symbolic figure of Saint Sophia, patron saint of Sofia, capital city of Bulgaria, in Bulgarian history, literature and civilisation from the 11th to the 17th centuries.

The documents selected include primarily the facsimile reproduction, in the form of digital images, of Bulgarian manuscripts, including the oldest one known: the 11th-century *Book of Apostolic Epistles of Enina*. They are supplemented by reproductions of illuminations, frontispieces and decorative motifs, and by photographs of various historic and archaeological sites. There are also printed transcriptions in Old Bulgarian of some manuscripts and their translations into modern Bulgarian, English where such translations exist, and French.

4) *The Sana'a Manuscripts*

In 1972, after heavy rain, a section of the wall of the Great Mosque of Sana'a collapsed. Work on the roof brought to light manuscripts which had been concealed in the ceiling in ancient times. They are parchment and paper fragments representing approximately one thousand different volumes, the oldest of which date back to the first century of the Hegira. Most are extracts from the Koran and are of considerable interest for the linguistic, religious and palaeographic study of the literature of the early centuries of the Hegira and of the Arabic language. The fortuitous and extraordinary discovery of these documents and their unique character make this find a remarkable event which will mobilise efforts and expertise on an international scale. Thanks to the active participation of Germany, a plan of work on the fragments was begun, which led to the construction of a House of Manuscripts, the restoration of some 12,000 fragments of parchment (out of 15,000), their storage, identification and classification, and the training of Yemeni restorers and photographers.
Research work on illuminated fragments and on bindings was carried out with a grant from the Getty Institute. This work, together with papers read at congresses and articles in academic journals, shows just how remarkable the collection is. The Yemeni authorities concur in the view that the collection is the equivalent of an historic building of exceptional heritage quality. A UNESCO mission visited Sana'a at their request to consider including a pilot project on the Yemeni collections in the "Memory of the World" Programme.

The collections of manuscripts that it has been possible to examine have been outstandingly rich, justifying their status as a "Memory of the World" project. Their historical, archaeological, scientific and documentary quality is such that they have all the features of collections worthy of heritage status.

A National Committee for the project has been set up to identify the most suitable documents. A demonstration disc based on a selection of manuscripts including some of the Koranic fragments should be published soon, in co-operation with the Regional Information

Technology and Software Engineering Centre (RITSEC), Cairo, Egypt.

5) *Memoria de Iberoamérica*

In November 1992, the "Asociación de Bibliotecas Nacionales de Iberoamérica" (ABINIA) submitted a project called "Memoria de Iberoamérica" to UNESCO for the "Memory of the World" Programme.

A pilot stage of the project is concerned with protecting the 19th-century press published in Latin America and improving access to it for historians and interested members of the public.

ABINIA had previously organised a series of activities on the occasion of the Five Hundredth Anniversary of the Encounter between Two Worlds, in response to the desire to encourage appreciation of the documentary heritage of the Iberian world.

Among these activities was the compilation of a database indexing 90,000 books from the 16th to the 18th centuries, a travelling exhibition, and the reissue of the most important historical works in the context of the Five Hundredth Anniversary. The national libraries of seven countries (Brazil, Colombia, Costa Rica, Cuba, Nicaragua, Puerto Rico and Venezuela) are taking part in the project on the 19th-century press. It has led to the drawing-up of a computerised inventory of some 2,000 newspaper titles and other press organs.

The second phase of the project will be to arrange for the conservation of the listed collections and their transfer to microfilm with a view to exchanges between national libraries, the organisation of exhibitions, and special publications.

6) *Manuscripts of Kandilli Observatory*

The aim of this project is the preservation of a collection of about 950 works on astronomy in three languages (Turkish, Persian and Arabic) held in the Library of Kandilli Observatory and Earthquake Research Institute at Bogaziçi University in Istanbul.

UNESCO's contribution covers the preparation and publication of the catalogue of these manuscripts, maintenance of the catalogue in a computer-readable form, using CDS/ISIS software package, microfilming of the manuscripts, and production of a CD-ROM consisting of the catalogue and sample pages from each manuscript.

7) *Memory of Russia*

This project deals with preserving and improving access to the collection of XVth and XVIth Century Slavic manuscripts held by the Russian State Library in Moscow. It also includes the archives of many of the major Russian authors such as Dostoevsky and Pushkin.

Several other projects are under consideration.

METHODOLOGICAL FRAMEWORK

From the examples mentioned above, it emerges clearly that the two basic principles which guide the "Memory of the World" Programme are the preservation of documents, holdings and collections, and the democratisation of access to them. The two principles are intrinsically linked, since access is conducive to protection and preservation ensures access.

The essential steps for carrying out any project in the "Memory of the World" programme are: selecting and preparing the documents, ensuring that they are placed in a suitable physical environment, photographing them where necessary, digitising them, describing and annotating them, providing the staff to perform these tasks with appropriate *ad hoc* training where necessary, translating bibliographical descriptions where necessary or even the texts themselves, and ensuring that the resultant product is distributed as widely as possible.

Provision has been made for the establishment of two sub-committees, the first to make regular assessments of the technology that might be used by the Programme, and the second to study methods for marketing and selling the Programme's products throughout the world. The first Committee held two meetings devoted to digitisation of documents. It reviewed recent developments in digitisation and prepared draft technical guidelines with a table showing, for each type of carrier (texts and still images on the one hand and sound and moving images on the other hand), the recommended digitisation standards for access and preservation. It was suggested that a programme of digitisation of documents is the best compromise between the conflicting demands for wider access to collections and for greater protection of the documents. As to the Sub-Committee on Marketing, it will hold its first meeting in 1996, when all the mentioned pilot projects have achieved concrete results.

Lastly, so that UNESCO can play its role to the full as co-ordinator and catalyst, three inventories in the form of regularly updated databases are being created in co-operation with IFLA, ICA and other competent professional bodies such as FID, FIAF, FIAT and IASA. They will be as follows:

1) an inventory of library collections and archive holdings which have suffered irreparable destruction since 1900;
2) an inventory of ongoing operations to protect documentary heritage; and
3) a world list of endangered library collections and archive holdings.

These three lists will take the form of databases periodically updated and will constitute the indispensable basis for the "Memory of the World" Programme. To date, institutions from more than 100 countries have replied to the first inventory, and some 50 countries have proposed collections and holdings to be included in the list of endangered documentary heritage.

Finally, in recognition of the impact of cinema on the world, it was decided, as part of the centenary celebration, to compile and publish, in the context of the "Memory of the World" Programme, a list of approximately 15 films each country considers to be representative of its most significant national cinematographic heritage.

Furthermore, UNESCO will shortly publish guidelines on the Programme's technical, legal and financial framework and its working structures. This text will be widely distributed in all UNESCO official languages.

LEGAL AND FINANCIAL CONTEXT

Working in partnership in an international context means that a legal framework is an absolute necessity if "Memory of the World" is to be managed in a properly accountable manner. The framework must nevertheless remain sufficiently flexible to guarantee the originality of each project and take account of the diversity of national legislation.

It is essential that the rights of the owners of the collections and holdings in a project are respected, and that the relationship between the owners and the technical and commercial users is clearly defined, particularly with regard to the division of rights among the various parties, the allocation of rights of ownership to the images produced, and the sharing of the profits from the sales of products made from images. It also seems clear, however, that excessive protection which might limit access to the documents would run counter to one of the Programme's fundamental principles. The International Advisory Committee recommended, at its second meeting, that UNESCO pay careful attention to legal questions affecting the intellectual heritage in the new context of increasing use of electronic storage media in libraries and archives, in particular to provide for freedom of access within the limits set by national and international legislation. A working group of legal experts and of representatives of NGOs, will be set up, in co-operation with other interested parties, including the European Commission and the G7 Working Party on "The Electronic Library" pilot project.

Finally, with regard to financial support, an international fund is being set up within UNESCO to finance some of the Programme's projects. These will include, as a priority, projects with a regional or international dimension. Other projects which meet the agreed criteria could use the "Memory of the World" label without necessarily receiving aid from UNESCO or the fund. A UNESCO special account has been opened for the "Memory of the World" (Ref. 406 INT 61).

A set of promotional material highlighting the aims of the Programme is being widely distributed. This material will also be used to attract funds for the Programme. A two-tier approach is envisaged: a programme-oriented campaign and a project-oriented campaign.

Each "Memory of the World" project will be an entity in itself, especially as far as finance is concerned. While profit can never be a prerequisite for carrying out a project, each project must strike a financial balance between, on the one hand, the investment needed for digitising, reproducing, and distributing products, and for preparing the reproduced collections and holdings for conservation and, on the other, initial contributions from local or outside funds and royalties from possible sale of products. This balance will not be achieved without the participation of sponsors and technical and financial partners. The search for partners is an important, not to say decisive, phase of all "Memory of the World" projects.

CONCLUSION

As soon as it was launched, the "Memory of the World" Programme began to arouse great interest. Requests for assistance, sometimes even appeals for help, regularly reach UNESCO. It is a daunting task and only the mobilisation of all the parties concerned can translate declarations of intent into a vast world workshop to rescue, reproduce and disseminate endangered documentary treasures.

From that point of view, the economics of the operation and the considerable investment it will require cannot be stressed enough. The twofold aim - securing the survival of the heritage and facilitating access to this collective memory so that it is within the grasp of as many people as possible - necessitates new approaches to funding, particularly through co-operation with the private sector.

SOURCES

"Memory of the World" Programme - First Meeting of the International Advisory Committee, Pultusk, Poland, 12-14 September 1993. Final Report. (PGI-93/WS/17) Paris: UNESCO, 1993.

"Memory of the World" Programme - Second Meeting of the International Advisory Committee, Paris, France, 3-5 May 1995. Final Report. (CII-95/CONF.602/3) Paris: UNESCO, 1995.

"Memory of the World" Programme - Draft General Guidelines to Safeguard Documentary Heritage. (CII-95/CONF.602/1) Paris: UNESCO, 1995.

"Memory of the World" - Experts' Meeting - Asia Pacific Region, Kuala Lumpur, Malaysia. 12-14 December 1994. Final Report. Kuala Lumpur: National Archives of Malaysia and Malaysian National Commission for UNESCO, 1994.

BUILDING BRIDGES: THE ROLE OF THE EUROPEAN COMMISSION ON PRESERVATION AND ACCESS

Yola DE LUSENET

European Commission on Preservation and Access (The Netherlands)

Those professionally concerned with the issue of preservation of our cultural heritage are daily confronted with the issue of how the past bears upon the present and the future in a concrete way. They are faced with the task of keeping collections that are a record of times past, reflecting the actions, achievements, knowledge, thoughts and dreams of previous generations, accessible to the future. This requires not only an understanding of the historical material itself, of the way it was produced and of its contents, but also an assessment of its future use and value. In this way, those working in the preservation field are standing at the cross-roads of the times, building the libraries and archives of the future from what is left of our past.

Librarians and archivists cannot fail to see the wide-ranging implications of this task. Unfortunately, outside this circle there are still many people who underestimate the scope and urgency of preservation work, and in particular the fact that material is deteriorating through the use of acidic paper over the last 150 years is little known. For most people it is self-evident that old and rare books, precious manuscripts and unique documents, require expert care from preservation specialists, and this is what they will think of when they come across terms like preservation and conservation. Even scholars and scientists who depend on 19th- and 20th-century material for their research often are not sufficiently aware that a considerable part of the comparatively recent written record is being threatened with irreversible decay, and hardly anyone has any conception of the scale of the problem. Moreover, those who do know about it sometimes display a disconcerting light-heartedness about the ways it could be solved. In this digital age, all too often the misconception arises that a high-tech solution must be within easy reach: why not just scan everything, digitize it, put it on a computer disc? Surely for big institutions like university libraries and archives this must be a simple thing to do?

For users, digitisation not only seems relatively easy but also so much more attractive that they find it hard to understand why one would still resort to what they regard as the clumsy and old-fashioned medium of microform. Strange but true, the magic of the digital age is such that, even though computer users themselves may frequently experience problems in exchanging data because of the incompatibility of various systems, they are often too enthralled with the seemingly infinite possibilities of the new media to see how short the life-span of every digital solution is at the moment. The same person who has a shelf full of long-playing records at home that can no longer be used on a modern CD-player may regard scanning and digitisation as the ultimate solution for preserving published material - failing to realise that the format that it would be stored in might easily get outdated even more quickly than those long-playing records were.

Paradoxical though it may seem to many people, digitisation is in fact the least permanent of possible methods for preservation, instead of the simple way to store documents safely, quickly, once and for all, that they take it to be.[1] Whereas digital material is revolutionary in its potential to bridge long distances, with networks providing easy access to material on the other side of the globe, it is far inferior to a mediaeval manuscript in its resistance to the test of time: the latter we can still read when centuries have gone by, but we may not be able to read the text on a specific kind of computer disc 10 years from now.[1] It is ironic that this gain of accessibility in one direction, this triumph over the limitations of space, should be accompanied by restrictions in accessibility in another direction. The risk of losing access to information over time will have to be counteracted, at great cost, by periodical refreshing and conversion of digital material - so that, more than ever, time becomes a determining factor in collection management. For preservation specialists, these issues are of central concern, and ways and means to come to standards and protocols for digital archiving are discussed continually, but most users focus on the short-term advantages without thinking about long-term dangers.

In short, outside the world of libraries and archives, there is little awareness of the complexities involved in preserving large collections of older material. Yet the situation is so serious that the institutions charged with the responsibility for our cultural heritage cannot be expected to shoulder the burden on their own. What is at stake is not only preservation of rare books and documents of obvious cultural-historical value, but also of a vast amount of knowledge and information accumulated over centuries. This daunting task will require an immense investment of expertise, time and money, for which a widespread recognition of the problem and strong support from the general public and governmental bodies are prerequisites.

In the United States, the Commission on Preservation and Access (CPA), established in 1986, has been very successful in the 10 years of its existence in bringing preservation issues to the attention of the general public and getting them on the political agenda, both inside and outside the U.S. To encourage independent initiatives in Europe and stimulate interest in the issue here as well, they organised in 1993 a meeting of 23 scholars, librarians, archivists and information scientists from 10 Western European countries and the United States, to explore opportunities for international collaboration in saving the contents of libraries from loss through embrittlement. At this meeting in Bellagio in Italy, it was concluded that a European counterpart to the CPA to address this problem would be desirable, and, as a result, in March 1994, the European Commission on Preservation and Access (ECPA) was officially established. The 14 members of the Commission are representatives from libraries, archives, universities and academies. Since May 1995 the ECPA Secretariat has been housed at the Royal Netherlands Academy of Arts and Sciences in Amsterdam.

The important contribution of the U.S. CPA to preservation work is well known. The Commission has not only fulfilled a central role in raising public awareness of preservation issues, it has also initiated many projects, for research, microfilming and bibliographic control, published reports, and helped to organise training. It has always functioned as co-ordinator and catalyst: the Commission itself does not carry out research or preservation projects, but encourages or contracts others to do so and concentrates on communicating activities and results to the field.

The ECPA, as the European counterpart of the CPA, is working along the same lines. The members of the Commission act as liaison points in their respective countries, whereas the Secretariat functions as an administrative centre. The activities can be summarised under five headings:-

1. Information for specialists
2. Information for a wider public

3. Consultation and co-ordination
4. Discussion, exchange of views and training, and
5. Research and development.

The majority of these activities will be developed within and with the collaboration of the professional world of archives and libraries, to support and expand preservation work already going on.

Over the past years, many initiatives have been taken by individual institutions, by government agencies, and by organisations such as UNESCO, the Council of Europe, the European Commission, IFLA, the ICA, LIBER, and the EFLC. The ECPA can play a role in advancing the preservation agenda by helping to create a European platform for the exchange of expertise, for discussion, and for co-operative efforts between libraries and archives in a European context. The Commission sees it as its first task to disseminate information about the situation in Europe: on research done by specialists, on projects going on at various institutions, on policies developed at an institutional, regional or national level. Talking about building bridges here means bridges between institutions to come to co-operative projects, and between, on the one hand, the specialists working in the field and, on the other hand, those responsible for general management and government policies. In stimulating the flow of information and the discussion between specialists and decision makers, the ECPA will focus on general problems and draw attention to organisational, financial and managerial aspects, as a way to further the development of overall policies. Whenever possible, the ECPA will actively seek co-operation with other organisations.

Several concrete projects are now under way. In its capacity as clearing-house for information about the preservation situation in Europe, the ECPA is presently setting up a World Wide Web site where documentation can be found. This WWW-site, EPIC (for: European Preservation Information Centre), will become operational in the Spring of 1996 and will be expanded over the next years to include news on projects, meetings and activities in European countries, bibliographic information, a database of research in progress and a discussion list. Through this electronic platform professionals all over Europe will have easy access to information on what is going on elsewhere and can share experience with their colleagues in other institutions and other countries.

A strong publications programme will be a central activity. Information collected through the WWW-site will be disseminated in printed newsletters and reports. The first report now being prepared by staff of the Royal Library in The Hague will provide an overview of mass deacidification methods and will be published jointly with the CPA in the course of 1996. A project is being set up for the translation of practical guidelines for librarians and archivists that are now only available in one or two languages, in co-operation with the ICA and the IFLA. Such introductory publications, aimed at a wide circle of librarians and archivists who encounter preservation problems in their work but who have not been trained as conservators or preservation specialists, will be linked to a programme of courses, seminars or workshops developed by institutions in various countries. In this project the ECPA, in co-operation with professional organisations of librarians and archivists, aims to build bridges between institutions with strong preservation programmes willing to share their expertise and those in need of support in setting up training courses.

A major event will be the conference *Choosing to Preserve: Towards a Co-operative Strategy for Long-Term Access to the Intellectual Heritage*, organised by the ECPA and Die Deutsche Bibliothek, which will take place in Leipzig in March 1996, during the Leipzig Book Fair. This meeting will focus on developing policies on institutional, national and international levels, and should provide another opportunity for the exchange of experience between specialists from West and East, and from the U.S. and Europe. Publishers present will again be alerted to the need for using permanent paper, and the publicity surrounding the Book Fair will help to communicate the findings of this expert meeting and the recommendations resulting from their discussions to a much wider circle.

Apart from activities primarily directed at the world of professionals from libraries and archives, it is the involvement of this wider circle that the ECPA is seeking to encourage. For building bridges within the professional community is one way to strengthen preservation work, but in the end this cannot be done effectively without broad support from the world outside. The relative lack of involvement of the general public, policy makers and the scholarly community, as sketched in the first part of this paper, is a cause of major concern for the ECPA. It is particularly puzzling that scholars, who depend on libraries for their work, are not more open to the problem. Perhaps they close their minds to the situation as long as they are not directly confronted with it. Perhaps, among some groups of researchers, the idea exists that older publications are of little value anyway because what is worth knowing has been incorporated into more recent research - a way of preserving knowledge that does not require preservation of the sources themselves. Another explanation is that the attitude of scholars is like that of consumers, in that they are mostly not interested in how libraries are run, but simply expect them to supply what they need and to solve themselves any problems they may have in meeting these needs. Whatever the explanation: if scholars are not taking active responsibility, if they do not seem to care about the imminent loss of an extensive body of knowledge, how can we expect the general public or governments to take the matter seriously?[3]

Scholars, as the most important group of library users, are an essential link in the chain: they can convincingly put the case for preservation efforts to administrators and politicians. They are in a key position to spur decision makers into action, and without their support it will be impossible to realise the extensive projects that are necessary to save this part of our cultural and intellectual heritage. Their support is also necessary because, given the scale of the problem, it seems inevitable that choices, sometimes painful choices, will have to be made that will have serious consequences for this same heritage. At the moment, most countries are still at the stage of making inventories of the damage becoming manifest in their collections. But, from the figures now available, it already transpires that there is very little chance that all endangered material can actually be restored, deacidified, microfilmed or digitised. It seems highly unlikely that the immense sums required for such a task will indeed be forthcoming. This means that somehow somewhere someone will have to start making choices.
Librarians and archivists as specialists in collection development have means at their disposal to set priorities. On the basis of technical inventories of damage, they can decide what needs to be done most urgently. By evaluating their own collections against those of others, at home and abroad, institutions can single out specific areas for preservation and try to come to co-operation with others to share the work. This, by the way, is why bibliographic control is such an important factor in preservation, and why the CPA has sponsored several big cataloguing projects and the establishment of the *European Register of Microform Masters* (EROMM)[2], in which partners from 9 European countries were participating at the end of 1995.

Such co-operation can achieve a great deal, but even extensive co-operation between institutions will not be able to prevent that, because funds are scarce, there will come a point that selecting a certain part of a collection for preservation inevitably means postponing or even abandoning work on another part - which may as a consequence slowly turn to dust. These are momentous decisions to make, and it would be unfair to leave them entirely to libraries and archives that will later be held responsible without giving them proper guidelines, while the people whose cultural heritage we are talking about, the users of the material, meanwhile continue in blissful ignorance. If we are now building collections for future research, should not the present generation of scholars have a say in the matter? None of us can look into the future, but perhaps they are in the best possible position for a bit of educated guesswork.

In libraries, preferences and interest fields of the academic community have always been taken into account by those responsible for collection development, and every library is in itself the result of a long series of choices, many of which reflect idiosyncratic judgements of scholars.[3] It would be logical to take scholarly views into consideration in preservation work as well. In its 1993-1994 *Annual Report*, the CPA reports on the work of the Art History Committee, which conducted a study to evaluate the importance of periodical literature in the field. They sent out a list of 2,000 periodicals to scholars in ten selected specialist fields and asked them to indicate which ones they considered most essential for scholarship, research and teaching. The list did not include information on rarity of the publications, age, condition, or other criteria that may be relevant for choosing a serial to be preserved. The aim was to get a pure measure of importance to scholarship; the question of which of these "most essential" periodicals were most urgently in need of preservation because of their condition was to be left to collection managers. The survey showed considerable agreement about the importance of the publications; the final result was a list of about 200 "most essential" periodicals.[5]
This is just one example of how scholarly involvement can provide libraries with tools for developing preservation policies. But users should be asked to think, not only about *what*, from their point of view, needs to be preserved most urgently, but also about *how* it could be preserved, and in particular about the role of the new media. For in spite of the problems still surrounding digitisation at the present time, the new technology will have to be explored for the advantages it has for keeping our cultural heritage alive. A creative, innovative approach opens up dazzling prospects of new applications in which material from older collections can be integrated and could thereby be given, as it were, a new lease on life. Such projects appeal to the imagination, not only of the general public, but also of scholars and scientists, for instance, because of easy access to research material kept in another part of the world. Increased access is obviously a strong argument for favouring one method over another. But then the question becomes what is desirable, what is possible, and what is affordable - issues that concern keepers and users alike and require a constructive dialogue between the two groups.

In view of the central role of scholars in the preservation debate, the ECPA will do its utmost to rally scholarly organisations and key-people in the academic community. The ECPA's commitment to this task appears already from the fact that the President and several members of the Commission are representatives of universities or academies. The message of preservation will have to be carried from this room into the chambers of power to ensure that the cultural heritage that links us to our past will still be accessible in the future. This will only be achieved by a concerted effort, if we all in our own way help to maintain this bridge between then and now - not only for ourselves, but also for those that come after us.

REFERENCES

1. Battin, Patricia. "From Preservation to Access". Paper presented at the 59th IFLA Council and Conference, Barcelona, 22-28 August 1993.

2. Rothenberg, Jeff. "Ensuring the Longevity of Digital Documents", *Scientific American*, 272:1 (Jan. 1995), pp. 42-47.

3. Commission on Preservation and Access. *Preserving the Intellectual Heritage. A Report of the Bellagio Conference, June 7-10, 1993.* Washington, D.C.: October 1993, pp. 22-23.

4. 4.Schwartz, Werner. *The European Register of Microform Masters - Supporting International Co-operation.* Washington, D.C.: Commission on Preservation and Access, May 1995.

5. Commission on Preservation and Access. *Preserving the Intellectual Heritage. A Report of the Bellagio Conference, June 7-10, 1993.* Washington, D.C.: October 1993, p. 23.

6. Commission on Preservation and Access. *Annual Report,* July l, 1993-June 30, 1994, p. 15.

EDUCATION FOR PRESERVATION: THE CHALLENGE OF ACCESS TO OLD AND NEW TECHNOLOGIES

Susan G. SWARTZBURG

Rutgers University Libraries (USA)

Since the beginning of recorded history, librarians and archivists have been responsible for the collection, organization, and preservation of the documents of society, to ensure their access for present and future generations. Throughout history, librarians have been concerned with the preservation of collections, often, in the past, to the extent that they were reluctant to make their collections easily available.

With the rise of modern institutions of higher education and the public library movement, which occurred in the 19th century at the time of the industrial revolution and the ability to mass produce books, librarians have devoted considerable energy and initiative to collecting materials, and to developing ways to organize and catalogue collections for ease of access. Consideration for the preservation of library materials became secondary, because books were so plentiful. By the end of the last century, however, librarians began to recognize the impermanence of the printed book, due to the use of acidic paper and poorly constructed bindings. Book care and repair was often included in training courses for librarianship. At the time, however, there was little understanding of the causes of the decay of materials, William Blades' "*The Enemies of Books*" (first edition 1880) excepted, and only spurts of interest in addressing the problem by the library associations in Great Britain and North America.

William Barrow's studies of modern bookstock, undertaken in the late 1950s at the Virginia State Library, USA, documented the extent of the deterioration of library collections, and the role played by acidic papers, used in book production since the mid-19th century. However, it was not until the catastrophic flooding of the Arno River in Florence, Italy, in the fall of 1966, that the international community became painfully aware of the value and the fragility of the world's documentary heritage. The flood water caused severe damage to the rich collections in the Laurentian Library, and to other rare collections. Book and paper conservators from Europe and America gathered in Florence to undertake a massive salvage operation and, in the process, they learned a great deal about the physical nature of library materials and how we can prolong their life and usefulness.

After a period of several decades during which library training programs de-emphasized or eliminated courses on the physical nature of books and bindings and their care and repair, increased interest in the preservation of library materials in the from the early 1970s onward led to the development of courses specifically addressing preservation concerns in North American and European library schools. Furthermore, preservation specialists are reminding information specialists that non-print materials are even more fragile and difficult to care for than printed materials.

Today there are excellent opportunities for library school students who want to specialize in preservation. Most North American, British, French, German, Scandinavian, and Hungarian library training programs include at least once course on the preservation of library and archival materials in their curriculum, and, increasingly, such courses are offered in other parts of the world. In Hungary, librarians and archivists owe a great debt to Beatrix Kastaly of the National Szechenyi Library, organizer of this conference, and to Gabriella Albrecht-Kunzeri at the National Archives, for the training opportunities now available in the country. Their accomplishments serve as models for other countries, contradicting the notion that it takes money to begin preservation programs, education and training. I know I shall learn of many other innovative training programs at this conference, where we have gathered to share information and to learn from one another.

In a paper, "Continuing Education in Preservation: Challenge for the '90s," which I presented before library school educators at the 1993 Conference in Barcelona, I traced the history of IFLA's recent concern with preservation and conservation and discussed continuing education initiatives. In this paper, I want to consider library school training as well as continuing education, for both are important if librarians are to ensure that materials are indeed preserved for future generations. Thanks to Barrow and other conservators and scientists, we have a clear idea of the causes of deterioration of paper-based materials, and options for their preservation, but we know little about the physical nature of non-print, electronic information media, so seductive yet so ephemeral. Thus a concern for preservation and access of these materials must be an integral part of basic library training. It is only through continued education, through courses, workshops, and symposia, that librarians will understand the nature of new information media and how we can preserve it. If we do not meet the challenge, our era may be considered another "dark age" for there will be slight record of our accomplishments. A disk is infinitely more impossible to decipher than the Rosetta stone.

In past years, the Conservation Section of IFLA has attempted to develop a model curriculum for library students in preservation, but with the ever-changing nature of library materials, this has proven to be an increasingly difficult challenge. Certainly we must include the basic information about the physical nature of printed and written materials: the nature of parchment and paper, inks, and leathers, materials that today make up the bulk of our repositories. In the past 25 years, as I have noted, we have learned a considerable amount about these materials, thanks in great part to those conservators who worked so hard in Florence, and observed, tested, and shared the knowledge gained with the world at large. (If any are at the conference, I shall publicly acknowledge them).

Moreover, we are learning a great deal about the environmental requirements for the housing of library and archival materials, learning how we can create "microclimates" to protect materials in even the most extreme climates. We are learning about "integrated pest management," non-chemical methods for curtailing insect pest infestation. We are learning that in conservation treatment less is more. In this regard, we have learned a great deal from techniques developed to protect collections by our wise "Third World" caretakers of collections. Our goal in preservation today is to stabilize collections, interfering as little as possible with an object's inherent structure which, in itself, tells the scholar a great deal about it and the conditions under which it was created. This is the theory of preservation, and it must be taught as a part of general library training.

Today much information is in electronic formats which are evolving as rapidly as I speak.
Increasingly in North America, we call librarians "information specialists" or "information scientists," reflecting the change in communication media from print to bites. It is essential that library students understand that electronic information is impermanent, and that they learn to be comfortable as they determine what is to be preserved.

I developed my syllabus for the teaching of preservation at the Rutgers library school in 1980. In many ways it looks the same in 1995, but I realize that information and communication theory are increasingly emphasized in my lectures. There is little point in teaching the physical nature of a disk or a computer program in detail because each will be entirely different, or non-existent, within a few years. The students need to understand that maintaining libraries in electronic format is enormously expensive and time-consuming. Hard choices have to be made. Print and microfilm will continue to be the desired formats for long-term preservation of information; electronics provide access only. Librarians must determine when immediate access to information justifies the cost, and how long that information is to remain in electronic format before it is "refreshed," that is, transferred to a newer electronic format; or it is transferred to print or microfilm; or, "deaccessioned," withdrawn - deleted or left to die. The hard choices that librarians now have to make (you can't decide to let the next librarian worry about it, because if you don't do something on your watch, the information won't exist for the next) has led many preservation educators to reemphasize the history of librarianship in our courses, and to dwell on the identity, the role, and the responsibility of the professional librarian.

I would like to note here that library schools in Eastern Europe and elsewhere, where the electronic technology has been less accessible, can benefit from the many mistakes made by librarians in the west, who, taken with new and exciting information technologies, failed to recognize the cost of properly implementing and maintaining them. This has resulted in considerable loss of information, and the waste of millions of dollars in producing information products that have not, or will not, survive.

The American Library Association has recently published the 7th edition of *its Preservation Education Directory*, listing programs and courses offered in preservation at North American library schools. The University of Pittsburgh library school now offers a formal specialization in preservation administration within its graduate library school program; at Rutgers, training in preservation is less formal and more individualized.

The University of Texas at Austin is now the home of the Conservation and Preservation programs, which originated at the Columbia University School of Library Service. The Conservation Program is two years, plus internships, designed to train book conservators. The Preservation Program is designed to train specialists; this is the post-graduate program that has prepared the majority of the librarians that have gone forth to establish themselves in careers in preservation in the past decade. It also trains book and paper conservators who receive the M.L.S. degree in addition to their certificate in conservation upon completion of two years' coursework and internships. Although this innovative program has had a difficult first decade as it struggled to find its direction and faced a move from one institution to another, I believe that there is a place for such a post-graduate training program. I believe that under the leadership of an experienced preservation educator, Karen Motylewski, formerly with the Northeast Document Conservation Center, this program will find its way, survive, and thrive. It has already trained a number of librarians and conservators from Latin America, Europe, and Japan, who have returned to implement programs to preserve the documentary heritage of their native countries.

It is through continuing education, however, that most librarians will learn to meet the challenges of new technologies and new information media. Specific courses of one to three days' duration, taught by experts in the field, will upgrade skills and understanding of new approaches to the collection, organization, preservation, and access to information. The Rutgers School of Communication, Information and Library Studies has one of the most respected academic professional development programs for practising librarians in North America. Instructors are selected carefully and course content must meet the University's academic standard. Participants in these courses are librarians in the field who need to enhance skills.

Nearly a decade ago, we recognized the need for a strong continuing education program offered by the library school to address preservation needs. Working with the State Library and our state's Historical Commission, which was concerned about the preservation of the state's documentary heritage, we identified a series of critical topics in preservation for librarians and archivists and specialists in our region who were qualified to teach continuing education courses. The Historical Commission had learned from past experience that bringing in experts from other parts of the country to conduct workshops was not successful. Librarians, archivists, and museum personnel needed a continuing series of courses with qualified instructors from our region who were willing to be of assistance to institutions beyond the classroom. The school and the instructors made a commitment to work together to strengthen the courses as the program developed and to continue to identify specific curricular needs.

We also decided, at the outset, that all people working with cultural property could attend the courses. The M.L.S. degree is not a pre-requisite for the Rutgers Professional Development Certificate Program in Preservation. Participants have included non-professional staff working directly with library materials, volunteers, museum and historical society personnel, conservators, dealers, vendors, even collectors. The participants represent a wide variety of institutions but they come together in the classroom to address a particular problem that plagues them all. We learn from one another. Several of the participants have recognized the need for further professional training and have enrolled in the M.L.S. degree program at Rutgers.

The main goal of the program is not to train preservation specialists, although Rutgers offers a certificate to people who have completed about 100 hours of coursework in the program. These people are already assuming leadership in preservation initiatives in the state. However, the need, as we see it, is to train librarians who must deal with preservation concerns amid a variety of other professional concerns, and be trained to deal intelligently with preservation problems. The majority of the librarians and archivists that attend our courses come because they meet immediate needs. On the other hand, those who have received the certificate in preservation, as well as other preservation specialists in our region, return to keep up with research and advances in preservation, conservation, and science in such areas as environmental controls, pest control, and preservation of non-print, including electronic media.

Through the Professional Development Program in Preservation, we have trained librarians in survey methodology. Participants in this course, a pre-requisite if one is to earn a Certificate in Preservation, are obliged to undertake preservation surveys of their institutions. The surveys are submitted to the instructors for review before the final seminar, where they are discussed and further actions identified and prioritized.

Training in disaster planning and recovery, which includes instruction on preparing a written disaster recovery plan, enables libraries to prepare a plan under supervision. Written disaster recovery plans are now required for grants for preservation and conservation from the State Library. An institution needs to demonstrate to agencies who will give funds for preservation and conservation that it knows how to ensure the continued care of materials.

Working in co-operation with the Northeast Document Conservation Center, the first and still the only regional conservation center in the U.S. devoted to the treatment of library and archival materials, Rutgers, with the State Library, offers a course by a member of their staff each year. The Center, working with librarian and conservator Nancy Carlson Schrock, has developed a course on basic book repair designed for the assistants who will do the repairs, not for librarians. Librarians who supervise such staff may observe. Schrock has also developed an excellent course on the repair of children's books for library assistants, which we hope to repeat at Rutgers on a regular basis. We were hesitant to offer courses with hands-on repair, for most conservators have learned that a little knowledge, gained in a workshop, can be dangerous indeed. These courses, however, concentrate on the basics, and they make clear that the repair assistant should not attempt anything beyond what has been taught, and should never work with any books that are of permanent value. The repairs are to extend the life of a book in a circulating library, not to preserve it for posterity.

The greatest compliment is to be copied. The courses that we have developed at Rutgers are today being offered at other library schools or through library agencies around the United States. Many of our instructors are teaching those courses. We hope, and believe, that other library schools will soon be offering professional development programs in preservation such as the program at the Rutgers University School of Communication, Information and Library Studies.

After assessing preservation education needs, the Commission on Preservation and Access, an independent agency charged with identifying preservation concerns and bringing them to the attention of the United States government and its citizens (we call this "lobbying", and libraries have need of such advocacy!) has sponsored a series of week-long training courses, primarily for librarians from college libraries, which are offered in the summer. Participants are selected because they will be responsible for the preservation activities at their institutions. The course provides basic training and has helped to establish a mutually supportive group of people from similar institutions with similar problems.

With a grant from the National Endowment for the Humanities, a consortium of library schools has offered week-long summer school courses with some success, but it is not clear that there is demand for an annual summer school for preservation education and training at this time. A summer program of continuing education for conservators and curators , does now exist at the Campbell Center in Illinois. This program could expand to offer more week-long courses for librarians and archivists. This is a possibility that we need to explore. It is expensive. In Europe, would people be willing to travel to the University of London for such a course; or to Munich or to Leipzig, providing that the Deutsche Bibliothek or the Bayerische Staatsbibliothek were to undertake such a program of action? Perhaps this aspect of training can be explored further at this conference. Have the Regional Centers a role to play in continuing education?

I want to describe one innovative program in the United States that will not be repeated in my country, but could well be adapted for other countries. This is the three-year initiative by the Society of American Archivists to train approximately 40 mid-level archival administrators to manage preservation programs in their institutions. The program was funded by our National Endowment for the Humanities and organized and directed by Evelyn Frangakis, who began her preservation career as a student assistant in the Preservation Office at Rutgers when she was 17 years old and has gone on to a successful career as an preservation administrator and educator. Because the focus of this training program was on the preservation of archival materials, the distinguished faculty that was assembled to help develop and teach a series of courses consisted of practising archivists and archival conservators, not librarians and book conservators.

The archivists selected for this course participated in three separate weeks of intensive coursework and training over an 18 month period. This program demanded considerable institutional commitment as the participants developed and implemented preservation programs at their institutions that were operative by the end of their training. Because of the size of the United States, separate groups of people were trained in the east, south, midwest, and the west. It was a gruelling schedule for Frangakis and her faculty, and for the participants.

Although the National Endowment for the Humanities was willing to fund another round of training for a further three-year period, it was determined that, in reality, there was no further need for such intensive, in-depth training. It is understood that the participants in this program will assume a leadership role in the education and training of other archivists, and librarians, through their own teaching of continuing education courses and workshops. We call this the "train the trainers" approach to education. The Society of American Archivists initiative is one that other countries might well follow to ensure a cadre of well-trained preservation specialists. A wealth of curricular material has been developed in the course of the Society of American Archivists program that, hopefully, will be made available in published form. I will be pleased to answer questions about this initiative during our conference. Although it was expensive, if the participants do, indeed, assume a leadership role in our country, and I believe that they will, the cost will have been worth while.

I firmly believe that post-graduate training for specialists in preservation and professional development programs that enable the continued updating of knowledge in this rapidly changing field, are essential. Because the changes in information media are so rapid and so profound, I am less concerned with the development of some agreed-upon, internationally recognized curriculum to train librarians in preservation than with the development of flexible programs that can meet the challenge of preservation in one's country in the electronic age.

I would like to talk briefly about the education and training of conservators of library and archival materials, for books and paper will continue to be the preservation medium of choice for the foreseeable future. Today the relationship between conservator and librarian is a collaborative one. In addition to the physical treatment of books, documents, and works on paper, conservators learn about collections care and management - how to prevent or retard deterioration. They are, truly, our partners in collection management.

While restorers have been with us since the beginning of time, the profession of "Conservator" of cultural property is relatively new. Formal training programs did not seriously get underway until the 1960s. The physical treatment of books and paper are specialties in conservation. There are five established graduate programs for the training of book and paper conservators in the United States and Canada, including the University of Texas, which I have briefly discussed.

The are now strong training programs in England, Germany, and France, and a developing program in Italy. Beatrix Kastaly and Gabriella Albrecht-Kunzeri have provided splendid training at the programs they have developed at the National Szechenyi Library and the National Archives. Jiri Vnoucek, who studied with Christopher Clarkson at West Dean College, England, is developing a training program at the Czech National Library. We will probably learn about other training opportunities at this conference.

The education and training of librarians in preservation and conservation is evolving as we are obliged to deal with new media. If we are to look back to the 1950s when William Barrow began his study of the causes of the deterioration of our library collections, and to what we understand about those causes today, and the marvellous developments that have occurred in the past 25 years that enable us to better preserve our collections, we should have little fear of the newer media. Through education, we will learn about their physical nature, their capabilities, and how to extend their lives. Today, we collaborate on an international basis; thus we are in Budapest today.

References

1. Blades, W., *The Enemies of Books*. London: Stock, 1880.

2. Clements, D.W.G., "Preservation and Library School Education Programmes," *Library Association Record*, 88:3 (March 1986), 136-137.

3. Cloonan. M. V., *Global Perspectives on Preservation Education*. Munich: Saur, 1994. (IFLA Publications, 69).

4. *Curriculum Development for the Training of Personnel in Moving Image and Recorded Sound Archives: A RAMP Study*. Paris: UNESCO, 1990.

5. Dureau, J.-M., "IFLA, France and the USA," *Journal of Librarianship*, 17:2 (April 1985), 75-85.

6. Fang, J. R. and A. Russell, eds. *Education and Training for Preservation and Conservation*. Munich: Saur, 1991. (IFLA Publications, 54).

7. Feather, J., and A. Lusher. *The Teaching of Conservation in LIS Schools in Great Britain*. London: British Library, 1988. (British Library Research Report, 49).

8. Swartzburg, S. G., "Continuing Education in Preservation: Challenge for the '90s," *Continuing Professional Education and IFLA: Past, Present and a Vision for the Future*. Munich: Saur, 1993, 247-252.

TRAINING FOR PRESERVATION: NEEDS AND PROVISION

John FEATHER

Department of Information and Library Studies
Loughborough University (United Kingdom)

INTRODUCTION

Preservation is concerned with both the past and the future; it is the past which has generated the documents and information which we seek to preserve, but it is for the future that we are working. To secure the future of preservation itself, we need to ensure that we are training the future managers and administrators of preservation programmes as well as the conservators, binders and other skilled workers who will undertake work at the bench. This paper considers the educational and training needs of preservation managers and others in the field, identifies some current concerns, and suggests some possible future developments.

ACTIVITIES AND DEVELOPMENTS SINCE 1986

The formal launch of the Preservation And Conservation (PAC) Core Programme at a conference held in Vienna in 1986 symbolised IFLA's commitment to preservation. It came at a time when librarians and educators in many countries, and other international bodies including UNESCO, were expressing a growing concern about the loss of preservation expertise among the rising generation of professionals, and the implications of this for the preservation of heritage documents and collections.[1] This concern was expressed in many forms. UNESCO's Records and Archives Management Project (RAMP) sponsored several studies which focused on educational issues, including a model curriculum for training conservators,[2] and guidelines for archivists and the users of archives.[3]

The proposed curriculum for conservators, by Y. P. Kathpalia, was concerned with the training of conservation practitioners, but other studies addressed the needs of library managers. An international survey was conducted for PGI and UNISIST by Clements and others to examine training needs in preservation and how far these needs were being met; the results were published in 1989.[4] At the same time, a joint Working Group of the Section on Conservation and the Section on Training and Education, under the leadership of Josephine R. Fang, was developing guidelines for a curriculum for professional education in this field. This was published by IFLA in 1990.[5]

As a result of this period of considerable activity, a broad consensus has emerged on the educational requirements for preservation. It is common ground among specialists that all professional librarians need to have a basic understanding of preservation issues, and of the significance of preservation in the context of the management of libraries. It is also agreed that in some libraries it is desirable to have full-time preservation managers at a senior level, and that the holders of such posts will need more detailed training at some time in their careers. The IFLA Guidelines of 1990 proposed a three-level approach of basic, intermediate and specialist courses. This approach developed largely out of the Working Group's knowledge of existing practice, but the Group also took realistic account of the capacity of library schools to accommodate the subject. There is some evidence that in the United Kingdom, and perhaps the United States, the basic level of preservation awareness is to be found in many, and perhaps most, library school programmes,[6] and that this is beginning to be reflected in user education programmes in some libraries.[7] There have, inevitably, been fewer developments in the field of specialist programmes, although some do exist in the USA.[8]

CHANGING PERSPECTIVES ON NEEDS AND PROVISION

The whole field of preservation has undergone significant change since the mid-1980s; education and training have, no doubt, played a part in these changes, but so have many other factors. In particular, there is a far greater awareness of the preservation issues relating to media other than those which are based on paper, and on the use of new technologies as a preservation tool in their own right. Michèle Cloonan, in the report of the work which she undertook as IFLA's Vosper Fellow, has rightly identified the fundamental changes in our thinking about preservation which will have to be part of our response to the preservation requirements of non-book formats and the increasing use of the creation of document surrogates through format conversion as a major instrument of preservation policy.[9] In a national survey of preservation policies in the United Kingdom, conducted in 1993-94, it was found that, although books, manuscripts and other paper documents, were still seen as the principal area of concern by preservation managers, non-book materials, and in particular digitally stored information, are increasingly identified as a major issue.[10] Although this area was not entirely neglected in the various studies in the late 1980s and early 1990s, it has become increasingly important during the last few years, and will continue to do so.

In a profession such as ours which is undergoing rapid change, much of it driven by external pressures in resourcing and by technological and social change, education is necessarily a life-long process. Initial professional education remains important in providing the fundamental knowledge and understanding which will underpin a career. Training in specific skills and competencies, however, continues throughout that career. It is here that the work of national library associations, *IFLA*, *UNESCO*, and our colleagues in other professions such as the archivists working through *International Council of Archives* (ICA), is essential.

Continuing professional development is a relatively new concept, and still unfamiliar in many countries. It can take many forms: conferences for the exchange of experience and opinions (such as this one); intensive short courses of instruction; workshops to develop specific skills; or more personal programmes of reading and study. There have been some such activities in our field, reflecting its increasing prominence in professional thinking. Many of these have been practical workshops at which conservation skills are disseminated and the results of research and development fed into the mainstream of practice. Many of the meetings and workshops for library managers, as opposed to conservators, have centred around comparatively conventional issues such as disaster planning, rather than exploring areas where new problems are emerging, and innovative techniques are being developed. On the other hand, some very valuable courses and programmes have been mounted, not least those sponsored by UNESCO through PAC in the early 1990s which provided opportunities for senior librarians from African countries to gain some insights into contemporary approaches to preservation issues. Workshops and similar activities have also been mounted on a regional basis in a number of parts of the world, including the United States,[11] and the Caribbean and Latin America.[12]

The task of education and training cannot be left to library schools alone. Quite apart from the role of international agencies, and training bodies in cognate fields such as art conservation,[13] the role of libraries themselves is crucial. The primary function of the library schools is to provide a sufficient number of well-qualified entrants to the profession. The precise form and content of the courses varies according to regional and national priorities and indeed the academic missions of individual schools, but the orientation towards initial professional education is a universal characteristic. Many library schools are, of course, actively involved in provision for continuing professional development by organising courses, conferences and workshops for practising librarians, but, as has been suggested, many other bodies have a role to play.

Libraries themselves, as employers of librarians, are key players. Some large libraries, especially national libraries, have significant preservation awareness and management training programmes for their own staff, some of which are also available to staff from other institutions. But all library managers need to be aware of the training needs of their staff, and to recognise that those needs will only be met if resources are made available. Training is costly; quite apart from the payment of fees, travel and expenses, staff have to be released from their duties. This makes the intensive short course a particularly attractive option. To be cost-effective, however, such courses need to attract an economically viable number of participants; in specialist fields such as preservation management, this almost inevitably means that much of this provision has to be international in scope. With a few exceptions - most obviously the USA, but also Britain, Australia, Russia and perhaps India - there are few countries where the demand is great enough to sustain activities at a national level. Regional co-operation is a vital element in effective training of this kind.

Another key role for libraries is in training their own non-professional staff. The literature of preservation management consistently emphasises the importance of non-professionals who are involved in such routine activities as shelving and circulation.[14] These members of staff need to understand the correct way to handle library materials, and how to identify possible problems. There are few countries in which there is well-developed training for such staff at national level. It is a responsibility of libraries themselves, and it is an area which needs urgent attention. There is some evidence from the United States that such programmes can be effective.[15] Recent work in the UK suggests that there is some activity in this field, but too little, and that the lack of appropriate training materials is a major obstacle. This issues has recently been addressed by the National Preservation Office, which has published Training Pack aimed at those responsible for training non-professionals.[16]

CURRENT NEEDS AND FUTURE STRATEGIES

Preservation must not be allowed to slip off the educational agenda. The key factor here is that there is sufficient pressure from the profession to ensure that at least one library school in each country can offer some real expertise in preservation management, and that all initial professional courses acknowledge the importance of preserving information media in order to provide access to the information which they contain. This is true whether curricula are determined by the schools themselves, by professional bodies or by government ministries or agencies. At the same time, however, we should recognise that preservation is now generally recognised as a significant element in the management of libraries, and that, as a consequence, the missionary tone which characterised some of the writing and teaching of the 1980s may no longer be appropriate. In our investigation of the current state of preservation management in Britain, we detected some signs of a reaction against the sometimes rather strident tones in which the preservation lobby has addressed the rest of the profession.[17]

Secondly, we need to address the whole issue of continuing professional development in the preservation field, especially in those parts of it where there have been major technological developments, such as digitisation, new techniques of paper repair and restoration and other applications of scientific research and technical innovation. IFLA and other international bodies have a key role to play here, especially, but not only, in the developing countries. The first task is to identify needs. The studies of the late 1980s,[18] like the IFLA Guidelines and other documents which were developed from them, concentrated principally on initial professional education courses in library schools. It is now becoming clear that there is a significant backlog of training, at all levels, which needs to be addressed. A study of the perceived training needs of practising professionals, especially those in management positions, would be an invaluable additional to our knowledge and understanding. We simply do not know to what extent senior managers are aware of preservation issues in most countries, and to what extent they would make use of training opportunities for themselves and their staff if these could be made available.

Thirdly, there is the question of the provision of such training when the need for it has been properly identified. PAC's unique network of Regional Centres could provide a framework for the organisation of such provision, building on the work which some of them have already done. This would be an even more valuable educational role for them than that which has been suggested by Cloonan.[19]

CONCLUDING COMMENTS

Much has been achieved, but much remains to be done. Persistent and knowledgeable lobbying, not least from the Section on Conservation, has put preservation management in its rightful place in the curricula of many library schools. Many of those basic needs identified ten years ago have been met. On the other hand, rapid technical advances, and the stringent financial and managerial regimes under which almost all libraries operate, have generated new questions to be answered and new issues to be addressed. This brief paper could do little more than skim the surface of such large issues, but it is hoped that it will provide the basis for further discussion of these important matters.

REFERENCES

1. See, *for example*, "Education for Conservation." *Journal of Librarianship* 17.2 (April 1985): 73-105; Cloonan, M.V., "Preservation Education in American Library Schools: Recounting the Ways." *Journal of Education for Librarianship and Information Science* 31.3 (Winter 1991): 187-203; Fang, J. R., and A. Russell, eds. *Education and Training for Preservation and Conservation.* (IFLA Publications 54) München: K.G. Saur, 1991.

2. Kathpalia, Y. P. *A Model Curriculum for the Training of Specialists in Document Preservation and Restoration: A Ramp study with Guidelines.* (PGI-84/WS/2) Paris: Unesco, 1984.

3. Forde, H., *The Education of Staff and Users for the Proper Handling and Care of Archival Materials. A Ramp study with Guidelines.* (PGI-91/WS/17) Paris: Unesco, 1991.

4. Clements, D.W.G., J.H. McIlwaine, A.C. Thurston and S.A. Rudd. *Review of Training Needs in Preservation and Conservation.* (PGI-89/WS/15) Paris: Unesco, 1989.

5. Feather, J., *Guidelines for the Teaching of Preservation to Librarians, Archivists and Documentalists from a Joint Working Party of IFLA's Sections on Conservation and Education and Training*. (IFLA Professional Reports, 18). The Hague: IFLA, 1990.

6. Cloonan, loc. cit. Feather, J., and A. Lusher. "Education for Conservation in British Library Schools: Current Practices and Future Prospects." *Journal of Librarianship* 21.2 (April 1989): 129-38.

7. Amodeo, A. J. "A Debt Unpaid: The Bibliographic Instruction Librarian and Library Conservation." *College and Research Libraries News* 49 (October 1988): 601-03. I am also indebted to my pupil Elizabeth Cooke who is currently conducting a study of in-house training for preservation in a number of UK libraries. We hope to publish the results of this work in due course.

8. Cloonan, M. V., *Global Perspectives on Preservation Education*. (IFLA Publications 69). München: K.G. Saur, 1994: 5, 25-26.

9. Ibid.: 39-40.

10. Feather, J., G. Matthews and P. Eden. *Preservation Management. Policies and Practices in British Libraries*. Aldershot: Gower, forthcoming (1995).

11. See, for example, Morris, P. A., "Educational Options for Preservation Administrators: An Afterword on the Preservation Management Institute." *American Archivist* 53.2 (Spring 1990): 244-55.

12. Sanchez, R., "Latin America and the Caribbean." *International Preservation News* 10 (July, 1994): 14.

13. Cloonan, *Global Perspectives*: 36-37; and Varlejs, J., "Preservation Education: A Call for Cooperation." *Art Documentation* 9:4 (Winter, 1990): 193-94.

14. Feather, J., "Staff Training for Preservation." *Library Management* 11:4 (Winter, 1990): 10-14; Intner, Sheila S. "Training Staff for Preservation." *Technicalities* 14:7 (July, 1994), 4-7.

15. See Buchanan S., and M. Esserman. "Preservation perspectives: notes on the care of collections." *Wilson Library Bulletin* 68:8 (October, 1994): 63. (speaker's note: I owe this reference to Elizabeth Cooke).

16. National Preservation Advisory Committee, Education Panel. *Preservation. A Training Pack for Library Staff.* London: The British Library, 1994; Feather, Matthews and Eden, *Preservation Management* (see note 10, above); and the work of Cooke (see note 6, above).

17. Feather, Matthews and Eden (see note 10, above).

18. See above, notes 2, 3, 4, 5.

19. Cloonan, *Global Perspectives*: 71, Recommendation B3.

WHICH KIND OF BOOK CONSERVATORS IN THE THIRD MILLENNIUM? THE STATE-OF-THE-ART IN ITALY AND SOME PROPOSALS FOR THE FUTURE

Carlo FEDERICI

Istituto Centrale per la Patologia del Libro (Italy)

The first aspect I wish to highlight concerns the, to my mind far from excellent, situation regarding the conservation of cultural property in general. The development of information technology for archives and libraries has brought about widespread undervaluing of conservation problems. Books and documents are increasingly identified as a series of bytes, and are becoming dematerialized as the book is seen purely in terms of its bibliographic information, and the book as an object in itself has become superfluous. However, it is to be noted that this *forma mentis* is far from having been formulated into a theory. (No library informatics expert would admit this.) It is nevertheless a fact, to which I will return later.

I, on the other hand, am convinced that conservation is one of the fundamental tasks of libraries, at least of those which are not entirely for public use. All the other functions (cataloguing, research, exhibitions, etc.) are in fact subordinate to this since, while it is possible to conserve - although imperfectly of course - without cataloguing, research and exhibitions, the contrary is not possible. This is because an object which is "not" conserved (*i.e.*, badly conserved) will, by definition, be lost; it will cease to exist. Yet it seems to me the idea of the eternity of the catalogued object is implicit in the cataloguer's *forma mentis*. Hence the aporia in which the archivists and librarians get entangled, taking great care of use, cataloguing, and so on, but considering conservation problems secondary.

Many schools in Italy are responsible for the training of restorers (although the methods used, as we shall see later, are often found wanting), but few, or none, concern themselves with the training of those who are to deal with the day-to-day conservation problems in libraries and archives. There has been a post-graduate school for archivists and librarians for thirty years at the University of Rome, to obtain the "librarians and keepers of manuscripts" diploma, but never has conservation been taught at this school.

At this stage, certain related questions have to be asked. Is it useful (and so important) to conserve our cultural heritage? If so, can conservation be taught? If so, how, where, and by whom, should it be taught?

The answer to the first question seems clear: all countries support the need to protect, through conservation, their own cultural heritage, even though they in fact do little to put these declarations of intent into practice. I mentioned first the problem of the spread of informatics and how this in practice surreptitiously obstructs the best way of conserving the book heritage, whereas it is often made out to be an aid to protection. To demonstrate that this situation is untenable, one has to start by saying that the "electronic library" is essentially of use in transmitting the information contained in the texts conserved in the actual library. It is not by chance that originally informatics was used above all for cataloguing and only lately for the transmission of texts. It is to be noted, however, that conceptually this form of transmission in no way differs from the distribution of old microfilm or Xerox copies which are a "simulacrum" of the original. Incidentally, the simulacrum is normally far more ephemeral, in terms of its life-span and conservability, than the original. I am not convinced that the library of the future will necessarily be a "virtual library" which can be consulted by connecting up to one of the large networks, even if it specializes in mediaeval manuscripts or daily newspapers. Of course, these services will very soon be available (are already so in part) and they will greatly aid research and documentation.

Yet there are two problems which cannot be ignored. The first concerns the durability of the material stored in computer memories. The question of physical durability should not be underestimated, but a more immediate problem is that of access to the information stored, given the fast rate of obsolescence characteristic of all software (an unavoidable fact relating to the commercial survival of the producers). The second problem regards the fate of the books now in libraries. Before accepting that these books can all be transferred on to an electronic support, I would voice some doubts. Even if someone can be found willing to take on the scanning of illuminated manuscripts, I doubt whether it will be so easy (?) to find a firm willing to transfer hundreds of thousands of philosophical, theological or juridical printed books of the 17th and 18th centuries of interest to only a few specialists (and therefore potential users) in the entire world.

At all events, as I said before, this process only involves the text of the objects we are dealing with. It is, I admit, the fundamental component, but it is not the only one. Should conservation of those originals which are transferred on to an electronic memory be neglected, they would eventually be destroyed (or at least their destruction would no longer be considered tragic). Fortunately, the material component of books and documents is beginning to take on importance for no other reason than the fact that it has become rarefied as a result of centuries of bad conservation, re-binding and badly-conceived restoration. And since preciousness is always linked to rarity, ancient books have now become precious and so important. This importance is, of course, still largely a fetish and mostly linked to the "aura" of the ancient book. Yet all this does not influence our goals. The essential fact is that public opinion will not easily accept the idea of destruction (or bad conservation, which amounts to the same thing) of the originals. Ergo, conservation is important and the physical protection of the cultural heritage cannot be neglected.

Given that everyone recognizes the need for conservation, I will try to answer the second question as to whether it is possible to teach (and so to learn) conservation. I would like to start by saying that the significance I give to this term is very wide and includes all the interventions carried out, directly or indirectly, on cultural property to safeguard as much historical information as possible (textual, aesthetic and material) of which cultural property is the vehicle and the evidence. This means that microfilming (provided that the book is not damaged during the process ...), dusting shelves (see the previous parenthesis) or restoration (*idem*, as above), can all be included in conservation. This sphere also covers the application of ultraviolet filters to windows or making protective enclosures for the books. (These steps are in all cases positive, as the absence of direct action on the object reduces the risks of damage.)

These few examples suffice to show that teaching conservation involves expanding a series of techniques and developing the capacity of selecting the best solution (or the least damaging) in each individual situation. The same goes for restoration, in which, however, the manual element plays an important role and conditions much of the teaching. This is the right moment to emphasize that manual dexterity in restoration must be placed at the service of the conservation of historical information, and that training in restoration must not separate history, the natural sciences, and manual skill, into isolated components. We need to remember that a good restorer is the one who fuses those components into a harmony. At all events, in order to avoid the risks taken in the past, manual dexterity should be learnt when the restorer-to-be is already in possession of the historical and scientific notions which are an indispensable requirement in mastering the knowledge of cultural property.

If the techniques of conservation can be taught and so learnt, only our third question remains to be answered: that is, how, where, and by whom, they should be taught.

In order to define the ideal training model I have to adopt a much-used comparison, even if it is conceptually inadequate: the medical schools. Moreover, it is not by chance that the Institute where I work is called the Institute of Book Pathology, precisely to indicate this paradigm. Actually, cultural property is not a living organism destined inevitably to conclude its existence at the end of a precise biological cycle. The doctor can try to prolong its existence as much as possible, but, in doing so, the organism must not be prevented from living, that is, from relating *lato sensu* with the surrounding world. Cultural property, which, I repeat, is a form of historical evidence whose "life in relation to the surrounding world" can change profoundly over the centuries, is a different case. A 14th century antiphonary is not used in the 20th century to sing the glory of God, just as the use made of the newspaper conserved in the Newspaper and Periodical Library is completely different from the use we all make of the paper we buy every morning. In short, it can at times be necessary to interrupt the life of a document in relation to its surroundings, limiting, or even temporarily discontinuing, consultation by scholars. In that case, not only will the document not be "dead" but this step may be the only one which guarantees its "life" (as a special case, of course, generalizations are very dangerous in this field).

Comparison with medicine may be theoretically erroneous, yet it works well in practice. The conservator's task is, in fact, to prevent "diseases" which the book can contract either from environmental causes or because of "genetic" problems (materials and manufacturing techniques). Once sick, the book can be given "pharmacological treatment" (disinfection, gaseous or spray deacidification) or "surgical treatment". The latter in turn may take the form of repair and may be aesthetic (non-invasive restoration) or total (restoration involving dismantling of the binding and its reconstruction).

As we can see, the parallel works, and it is no coincidence that the use made both in conservation and in medicine of the natural sciences is the same: biology, chemistry, and physics, are regularly used to find the solution to diagnostic and therapeutic problems.

Where lies the difference between medicine and conservation? In the object, obviously. On the one hand, we have a living organism, on the other, historical evidence. If it is impossible to treat a living organism taking it out of its social and environmental context - although how many times (in the past?) has this been done? - it is just as impossible to propose an intervention on a piece of cultural property before submitting it to historical analysis. That means understanding when, where, how, why, and by whom, it was made. It also means understanding what function it was made for, and analyzing the changes in that function up to the present day, and the use to which the object is now put. Only at this point will it become possible to begin thinking of any eventual "pathologies" or consequent "therapies" to be adopted.

Thus, studying the history of the cultural property which is to be conserved must precede any conservation intervention. In other words, the conservator must be *in primis* an historian of the category of cultural property he or she is working with. After which, however, the analogies with medicine are again relevant. The organization of teaching must be changed, following the model used for medicine if only for its centuries-old experience and which, despite many contradictions (but neither is conservation without these), seems to work fairly well.

So a book conservator must know the natural sciences (which medical students study from the very beginning of their degree); general biology (the main enemies of books are biological agents and most library materials are, in origin, living organisms); general chemistry (which is usually not taught well in secondary schools and yet a knowledge of which is necessary to understand the, essentially chemical, mechanisms of degradation of book materials); and organic chemistry (book materials are, as already mentioned, almost all organic in origin). In addition, I would not neglect physics (both environmental analysis and the knowledge of analytical and diagnostic instruments), and statistics, which play an increasingly important role in our field, most especially when allied with informatics (which is not "bad" in itself, of course).

But let us look at what we neglect today in the training of conservators, and we find it is the subjects which, in our medical analogy, relate to anatomy and physiology, *i.e.*, the study of the component materials of books and how these materials correlate to give life and function to the object/book. Those disciplines nearest to these topics are the archaeology of the book and the technique of bookbinding. Naturally, the archaeology of the book is related to the material culture which governs the manufacture of the book itself. The binding technique must be studied historically, following the evolutionary phyla which led to the different book typologies. In turn, this teaching should lead to the study of those techniques from which the main materials originate, differentiating them into the two main categories of celluloses (wood, paper, cloth) and proteins (skins, parchments, leathers). At this point, it becomes indispensable to know the "pathologies" and the methods to fight them: so biodeterioration, chemical degradation, and mechanical damage, which can all affect book materials. In addition, the conservator must know about restoration methods, since his or her work includes the important task of planning and supervision of interventions. Moreover, the restoration of paper is very different from that of parchment or hide, just as the knowledge of these techniques is a necessary condition, but still insufficient, to be able to restore bookbindings, which make up a group in their own right.

Finally, it is necessary to learn the administration of conservation, which means planning interventions within an institute as well as in the country as a whole, so as not to have a "flood" of money concentrated in some geographical areas, which sometimes do not even have the highest concentration of books at risk. This is also a sore point, because identifying risky conditions - which then means urgent intervention - is extremely complex, and too often a keeper is prone to define the restoration proposed as top-priority. Yet we are far from possessing reliable knowledge of the kinetics of degradation reactions. When we have in front of us a manuscript whose papers have been perforated by an acid ink, we do not know if most of the reaction occurred in the period immediately following the writing or whether it has advanced with a "uniformly accelerated" trend up to the present day. It is, however, true that the latter hypothesis - on the basis of what we know about the acid degradation of cellulose - is universally accepted, although I am personally beginning to have some doubts.

Let us turn to where this training should take place and, at the same time, to those responsible for it. I do not think there are any doubts that the training of the conservator should be the responsibility of the university, for no other reason than the need to ensure that the trainee conservator is already in possession of a number of notions normally taught in the secondary school.

In the last few years in Italy, 13 degree courses in conservation have been started up at 13 different universities, but none of these centers has really pursued the aim of creating an "interdisciplinary" setting such as to be able to provide a "roof" under which history and bookbinding, chemistry, and archaeology of the book, can all be taught. The failure of the degree courses in the conservation of cultural property has not lessened the need for them, but the conception of an organization of this kind is a complete antithesis to the present academic organization in Italy, which almost instinctively opposes institutions that are "too" interdisciplinary, and in which the demarcation of power becomes so blurred that it may no longer be clear who is in charge.

When we speak of place, it should be pointed out that the university bodies are necessary, but insufficient to the needs, since the institutes appointed to teach conservation of cultural property must carry out a primary role in training conservators. This role has so far been considered an optional, yet to learn conservation of cultural property you need to have contact with it and that is not possible outside the archives, libraries, and museums where it is kept.

To achieve these goals is extremely complex, most especially because, within these organizations, it is difficult to do specialized teaching, as they were started up and developed for different purposes, usually related to public use. On the other hand, just as it is impossible to learn medicine outside a hospital, so conservation must be learnt only in institutes where conservation is a daily activity. Bureaucratic and administrative shackles have played an extremely negative role, really obstructing the achievement of this goal. I do not know the situation in other countries in this field, and I am looking forward to hearing about their successes in an area where we are still far from "optimum". The last centuries of the millennium which is drawing to a close have brought an awareness of the importance of historical evidence, but this awareness is of a higher level than the quality of the methods and techniques adopted to safeguard them. It is time to fill this gap, and, in this, all the people involved in conservation will play a fundamental role. It will thus be essential to dedicate a significant part of our energy and imagination to the training of conservators.

PRESERVATION IN RUSSIAN LIBRARIES: CURRENT SITUATION, TENDENCIES, ASPIRATIONS FOR THE FUTURE

Galina KISLOVSKAYA

State Library for Foreign Literature (Russia)

Getting acquainted with preservation practices in other countries, a Russian librarian can easily pick up from an exquisite professional vocabulary key-words denoting leading dimensions in the field of preservation: public awareness, strategies, planning, standards, co-operation, bibliographic control, mass deacidification, permanent paper, digitization. This cluster of ultimately related terms when applied to a broad Russian reality will almost entirely turn into a cluster of their antonyms.

To justify this rather severe verdict, I will consider the above-mentioned terms one by one.

As is well-known, the core functions of a library are acquisition, storage and access.

Traditionally, Russian librarians ranging these basic functions according to their significance gave storage and, as a consequence, preservation, the last place. This most unfair neglect, not confined to a single library, stemmed from the prevailing opinion of the priority of acquisition among other basic library responsibilities.

Hence - the attitude resulting in irregular, scanty allocations for preservation programmes, ignoring of facts of inadmissible storage conditions, almost country-wide absence of trained specialists, primitive and low-productive equipment, *etc*.

I do not argue about priorities. The eternal question: what comes first: a chicken or an egg? is far more complicated than the issue of library functions priorities. Of course books (nowadays other formats) come first, giving way to storage and access.

What I want to underline is that the library should be treated as a very sophisticated system in which any imbalance of elements (or functions) will cause a break in the entire system.

In Russia an exceptional passion for acquisition led to creation of excellent collections. But many of these collections are currently in a very critical condition. Not surprisingly, access to quite a number of them is problematic. So it is restricted access to endangered collections that eventually is bringing back the role of preservation as one of the core library functions.

In the past, the state policy in the field of preservation was confined to a physical shift of rare and precious collections and separate publications of historic and artistic value to repositories in Moscow and St. Petersburg. It was assumed that centralization would create better conditions for preserving the national heritage. Consequently, major libraries like the Russian State Library (formerly the Lenin State Library), the Russian National Library, the Library of the Academy of Sciences, to some extent the Library for Foreign Literature, and the Scientific and Technical Library in Novosibirsk, became centres also for restoration and conservation and contributed greatly to the research in the field of permanent paper, deacidification, proper maintenance of collections, biological problems of conservation, restoration of leather and paper, application of different types of glue in restoration, restoration of fragile leaves by means of disintegration, lamination, leafcasting. But, alongside some obvious benefits, the centralized policy that governed all spheres of Russian life brought tangible negative results like impoverishment of collections of the provincial libraries, geographical distortions in the field of preservation, absence of trained specialists outside Moscow and St. Petersburg.

These sad conclusions have been made as a result of visits to different types of libraries all over Russia. Similar data were generated by a small-scale survey of 35 regional libraries which are the main information resources of huge territories - regions.

As I mentioned earlier, qualified experts have worked out standards for storage and accommodation of library materials. Library directors and senior staff working in the stacks are well aware of these standards, though, typically, reality is not what standards prescribe. And again, typically, it is the library buildings that are of key importance in success or failure of attempts to follow these standards.

The majority of library buildings in Russian provincial cities were built in the fifties and sixties. In contrast with the diversity of geographical and hence climatic characteristics, library buildings are almost like twins. Results of the questionnaire show that library buildings do not meet the requirements essential for preserving library materials. A variety of drawbacks, or a combination of them, is mentioned by respondents, among them: bad foundation, absence of compulsory ventilation, absence of hydro-isolation, bad heating or cooling systems, plumbing problems, incorrect position of fixed shelves, etc. Among the reasons reported as affecting the physical condition of collections is storage capacity of the buildings. As a rule, real needs have exceeded the projected capacities. Current collections in the majority of cases are twice as big as the projected figures. In the worst case (*e.g.*, Saratov), the collection is four times bigger than the space permits.

Similarly, federal libraries like two national libraries, LFL, Russian Historical Library, Arts Library, also suffer from the same disease. Lack of space more frequently affects newspapers, including pre-Revolutionary local titles. Dramatic shortage of allocations for the overall library activity, and for preservation in particular, results in poor handling of endangered materials. Dusting, blinding, and sometimes disinfection, are listed as the most common preservation techniques. Microfilming is not generally associated with preservation. It is just a means to solve space problems. The complexity of preservation microfilming and the necessity for bibliographic control are not recognized by both library administrators and staff despite the growing interest in reformatting.

Preservation of general collections is given much less attention in comparison with rare books. In general, preservation is traditionally associated with restoration of valuable materials.

Another area of concern is conservation and restoration supplies. In the former Soviet Union, a system of suppliers for preservation purposes did not exist. Separate libraries with strong restoration and conservation departments made enormous efforts to be able to support their services.
With *perestroika* and transformations in the economy, the situation became temporarily even worse. Fortunately, last year, in Moscow, stores appeared which specialize in selling preservation supplies and equipment. So, nowadays, shortage of supplies in libraries is no longer a case of their physical absence but rather a case of shortage of money or lack of information about vendors.

Summarized briefly, the results of my rather superficial survey look like this: preservation in Russia suffers from:-

- *lack* of resources;
- *lack* of expertise and training;
- *lack* of information.

There is yet another common feature that characterizes preservation, or better preservation mentality: it is still believed that preservation is a purely library matter. I know that there are other opinions on an individual level, but I want to highlight the prevailing views.

Raising public awareness, the goal which is stated as one of the major tasks of the PAC Core Programme and the IFLA Section on Conservation, is not yet understood as an objective by Russian librarians. Not surprisingly, books falling apart, disappearing collections, disintegrating newspapers, have still not become a matter of national concern. But this can only be achieved through persistency of committed librarians in stimulating public interest in the subject of preservation, stirring its emotions, awakening national pride and dignity, lobbying preservation projects. The fact that the general public is not aware of the magnitude of the preservation challenge and, in some cases, does not want to be, is explained by a number of social reasons, among which are the low social status of the profession, extremely low salaries leading to low self-esteem and, as a consequence, to a low level of initiative on the part of an average librarian. Russia badly needs figures like Patricia Battin or Hans Rütimann or Lisa Fox, whose daily activity has eventually changed the attitude towards preservation in the U.S.

I know only one Russian library director - Mrs. Pronina from Ryasan Regional Library - who has made local authorities show "Slow Fires" over the local TV net, thus starting a campaign for preservation.

Another attempt to raise preservation awareness through showing of this extremely emotional and impressive film, made during the preservation conference in Kiev, 1995, failed because TV authorities wanted money to be paid for the demonstration.

I know pretty well that it is not the best time for Russian librarians to get quick and impressive results in this campaign. But it is certainly worthwhile trying to change both yourself and the environment. Thus, convincing the public that preserving the national heritage for future generations is not only the responsibility of libraries is becoming one of the strategic goals in our professional activity.

Here I switch to a notion of a strategy which is interpreted as the display or exercise of skill and forethought in carrying out one's plans, schemes, etc.

In the context of preservation of the national heritage, this interpretation has acquired absolutely concrete content:

- assessment of the general situation, and evaluation of the physical condition of collections;
- setting priorities in actions and in treatment of the collections, based on the nature of these collections, staffing, funding, physical facilities;
- building a preservation organizational structure.

These leading strategies *have to be* applicable to both preservation programming on an individual library level and on a national level.

The modality that I used in the previous phrase - *obligation and necessity of fulfilling and action under the circumstances* - is, I am afraid, the only one option left. Otherwise, Russian society will be doomed to amnesia.

Strategic thinking on an individual library level, regrettably, has not become a working practice (with some exceptions).

It would be unfair, though, to say that there were no attempts to work out preservation strategies for the entire library community.

A report "The State Conservation Program (Concept Approach)" made at the Moscow IFLA Session (1991) by T. Burtseva and Z. Dvorjashina announced that, under the auspices of the All-Union Library Council, a state programme for preservation of documentary monuments had been set up. Four years which have passed have brought dramatic changes into Russian reality. All-Union structures like the above-mentioned All-Union Library Council have disappeared and the fate of the declared programme is not known by the library community.

However, nobody would deny that the defined strategies of the draft programme are more than valid at present, namely:

- proper maintenance of collections;
- research in the field of preservation;
- mass deacidification;
- restoration and conservation with focus on preventive conservation;
- training;
- preservation management.

I do share the view that preservation is an activity which cannot be carried out by a highly centralized programme at a national level. A national programme "must instead be built from the ground up, on a firm foundation of local, regional and network programmes".

As in the U.S. or Great Britain, where the initiatives of individual libraries or groups of libraries gave way to national programmes like the "Brittle books" project, or Newsplans, in Russia certain areas of preservation which can be considered as strategic on a national level started to evolve in the national libraries (RSL and RNL), Library of the Academy of Sciences, LFL.

The consolidating nature of these libraries is not at all surprising: the level of expertise, efficiency of staff, professional links with preservation centres abroad, are the factors that have to be taken into account while speculating on why these but not others have become centres of consolidation. As far as I know, the Russian State Library is working currently on a programme of preserving artefacts (a programme called "Memory of Russia"). The Russian National Library is extremely strong in research activity. The Library of the Academy of Sciences is a recognized centre for a phased conservation treatment. LFL has acquired a leading position in preservation microfilming.

Two years ago in Moscow there appeared a school for training restorators and conservators on the basis of the Russian State Library - a long, long awaited event that was possible due to the initiative of the former LFL staff member - Mrs. Nikolayeva, a member of the Standing Committee of the IFLA Section on Conservation.

Segments of the national preservation programme in which individual libraries or groups of libraries are especially strong will be united, hopefully, under the umbrella of the recently-created (October 1994) Russian Library Association.

I am not that naïve to believe that, given a centre, co-operation on a national level will just blossom. Again, it will take efforts and time on the part of recognized and respected librarians and libraries to pursue stubbornly the policy of eventual involving of the whole library community into well-co-ordinated projects.

The magic words "co-ordination" and "co-operation" as a spell were repeated before "*perestroika*" and are repeated now. What is happening in real life? Co-operation in Russia has seen more failures than successes.

I cannot mention more than two co-operative preservation projects that have been set up recently. (In the past they did not exist at all.) One is the Ural regional programme for 1995 - 2000 on preserving rare collections in the holdings of all the libraries and museums in the Ural Region. Another practical attempt to convert the familiar words "co-ordination" and "co-operation" from abstract notions into real tools of collaboration was made in November 1994 when the LFL initiated a pilot project on preservation of newspapers that currently unites ten regional and Moscow libraries, the most active being Tula, Ivanovo, Ryasan, Tver, Brjansk, Smolensk, Vladimir regional libraries. The co-ordinated initiative was supported by the Ministry of Culture (a parent body for all the mentioned institutions), though, of course, funding allocated for its implementation is evidently not sufficient even for the initial stage. Local fund-raising programmes have to be launched to implement the project.

These first two co-operative initiatives have brought to the surface deficiency of planning in preservation. This conclusion was confirmed by the respondents of the questionnaire. Nearly 60% of respondents stated absence of comprehensive preservation plans, 30% partial preservation plans, and only 10% have reported the existence of preservation plans incorporated into overall library plans. This situation needs to be commented on.

To my mind, this dangerous tendency is being provoked by traditional neglect of preservation. In other words, it is just lack of proper management. As a result of poor management stemming from lack of education, experience, information, there are single examples of overall library preservation plans covering different aspects like:

- shelving maintenance;
- climate control;
- collection security;
- disaster preparedness;
- book mending and restoration;
- reformatting;
- personnel training.

Of all the above-mentioned aspects, shelving maintenance, regulated by existing state standards, book mending, collection security, are generally understood as necessary components of plans.

However, library administrators have to understand that, unless they do not know in detail what they have to do, what their priorities are, even insufficient funding will be spent most inefficiently. Absence or lack of resources should not be a stumbling point for planning. On the contrary, well documented and justified plans are the basis for fund-raising to fulfil long-term and short-term plans. In the case of a zero funding, the first step is to educate staff and users, and establish low-cost preservation policies. Typically, there are no preservation administrators in libraries. The responsibilities for managing restoration and conservation departments, microfilming departments (if such exist), commercial binding, shelf maintenance, retention policies, library building, etc. are scattered among middle managers who report to different senior managers at the top level: either to a director or his deputies. Clearly, under current circumstances, a library cannot afford the introduction of a new position for working out a systematic approach to preservation. Hence, restructuring of job descriptions within the administration is an inevitable and an urgent step.

Another common drawback is that almost none of the institutions connects its mission statement with preservation. To be fair to my own Library, the LFL, I have to give credit to it for its adherence to the library mission statement in making preservation decisions, for the involvement of staff in making these decisions.

Staff problems are known as the most difficult managerial problems. One of the commandments of a committed professional is "read and educate yourself beyond what you already know".

In Russia, where institutes of culture that prepare professional librarians do not include in their curricula an in-depth course on preservation, the quoted commandment acquires special importance: training has to be integrated into library preservation plans. The question arises - where one can get such training?

First of all, RNL, RSL, LFL, are ready to accept librarians for practical training in their restoration and conservation laboratories.

Secondly, a school for restorators and conservators at the RSL admits trainees from all over the country.

These limited options, as you see, do not reflect any training in preservation administration or in preservation in the broad meaning of the word.

In my report, certain preservation areas were highlighted either as inadequate, like training, or as exceptionally new for Russia. Permanent paper is a concept that exists only in the consciousness of a very limited number of professionals: restorators and conservators. I suspect that librarians working in departments other than restoration and conservation simply never heard about it, which in itself is another illustration of a sort of isolation of restoration and conservation departments within the library structure. Similarly, Russian publishers have no idea of the mere existence of permanent paper, of the growing tendency of using it by European and American publishers. My assurance came from a test question on permanent paper which I asked at a conference of leading Russian publishers in May 1994 in the LFL. The question was met with an eloquent silence. All subsequent attempts to find out whether publishers ever heard about the production and usage of permanent paper had the same negative results.

I strongly doubt that the current economic situation in Russia would facilitate usage of permanent paper. But it does not mean that librarians should stop trying to promote this progressive practice, lobbying the idea in the legislative and executive branches, highlighting the ecological aspect of the production of permanent paper, direct and indirect financial implications of the introduction of permanent paper into paper production, publishing, and consequently into the life of libraries.

As was decided last year in Havana, I submitted the list of Russian publishing houses to the Standing Committee for further distribution of the information. In 1997, the LFL plans to organize a conference for publishers and librarians where the issue of permanent paper, alongside with other questions related to preservation, will be discussed.

I want to finish my critical revelations by an optimistic affirmation that, despite everything, I have witnessed so many signs of significant growth of interest in preservation that probably my next report will reflect some impressive landmarks in preservation in Russia.
My final remark: IFLA should enhance exchange of information, which to my mind is the key to many problems evolving in preservation.

MAIN STEPS TO IMPROVE THE CARE OF BOOK COLLECTIONS IN THE NATIONAL LIBRARY OF THE CZECH REPUBLIC

Jana ODVÁRKOVÁ

National Library of the Czech Republic

During the last five years after all the changes in our society, attention was also turned to the efforts aimed at improving the care of book collections kept in the National Library. These collections are considered to be a part of our national cultural heritage and testify to the history of the Czech nation. In this paper, I would like to mention some steps taken in this field in our library.

The Clementinum, a seat of the National Library of the Czech Republic, is a complex of historical buildings of the former Jesuit College, which originated in the second half of the 17th and the beginning of the 18th centuries. Its halls and rooms also serve up to the present as the main depository of the greater part of the National Library holdings. A considerable lack of storage space has been seen as early as the mid 20th century. In the course of time, it was therefore decided to store book collections in provisional depositories, *e.g.*, in deserted castles or in outside halls, etc., which were of course originally used for completely different purposes. This fact was later manifested with all negative consequences. It should be said that, in all the provisional depositories used, there are to be found all negative environmental characteristics improper for a long-time storage of library materials, namely impurity and too high humidity. In consequence, the materials are attacked by microorganisms, mainly mold. Some of the books have even been damaged by rodents. Other negative features are high temperature, great temperature differences, and the admission of unreduced sunlight. All these facts resulted in continuous damaging of the collections stored there.

However, at present, the Clementinum buildings do not meet the required climate quality needed for storing of library materials. That is to say that the Clementinum library buildings are situated in the heart of the city and the collections stored there are thus exposed to highly concentrated and aggressive pollution. Since the Clementinum is the national historical monument, the conservationists' reasons - which are understandable - do not allow reaching easily, and in all storage rooms, the acceptable microclimate parameters needed. In winter, during the heating period, the climate is very dry there, while in summer months the temperature in some of the rooms even climbs over 24°C. On the contrary, in the Clementinum basement there are rooms used for storing books which are characterized by constantly high humidity. The above-mentioned facts, together with a long-time lack of space, which is the reason for storing books in heaps or in plastic boxes (originally used for vegetables), have all contributed to either visible or hidden damage to the collections.

Activities realized to improve the state mentioned above can be summarized in the following three steps:-

1. to stop the deterioration of books already damaged;
2. to prevent further damaging of books (preventive methods);
3. to do away with the consequences of negative factors.

Each of the steps includes a complex of activities aimed at the same objective.

The first complex of activities is represented, above all, by the construction of a new library depository, which is both the most extensive and the most expensive project now being realized in the National Library. The depository building is seated in the outskirts of Prague and will be finished by the end of this year. In the first period, it will provide a high-quality storage space for more than 3 million volumes. However, its total capacity is about 4,5 million volumes. The depository will, at last, comply with microclimate parameters required for an optimal long-time storing of book collections, *i.e.*, it will be equipped with humidity and temperature control devices and with a device checking the purity of inside air. The depository will also be protected against sunlight. The first books should be moved there early in 1996.

There is also another extensive work of an emergency character, which should stop long-time damaging of book collections. It is a systematic mechanical cleaning, which started 3 years ago. The mechanical cleaning carefully removes impurities from all volumes and includes a complete cleaning of all storage rooms and their equipment. The volumes cleaned in this way are then shelved in proper order.

In my opinion, systematic controls of the inside microclimate conditions in depository rooms are the most important ones among the activities aiming at urgent removing of factors that cause inconspicuous damages to the book collections. The controls must be based on permanent taking of temperature and relative humidity values and light conditions, which must be followed with individual successful improvement of the characteristic parameters. This method is also one of the ways enabling fast preservation of a great part of the collected objects.

At the beginning, I have already mentioned the individual types of depositories which the National Library has at its disposal. In the past, the measuring of temperature and relative humidity was assured partly through the mediation of a system of single measuring instruments, *i.e.*, thermohydrographs, thermometers and hygrometers. However, they were not sited systematically, since their range did not cover all depository rooms and monitoring of microclimate conditions thus was not complete. Also the assuring of the run of all measuring instruments was very questionable. Some rooms with excessive humidity were furthermore equipped with dehumidifiers, the run of which, however, was not economical, so that they did not fulfill their function continuously.

Therefore, within the framework of the project of installing the high-quality measuring instruments in the National Library, we decided to start with the rare and unique collections that are, and in the future will be, kept in the Clementinum. In the beginning of 1995, the TESTODATA 02 system with the DATATAKER central control unit were installed to assure continuous recording and control of temperature and relative humidity values. For the time being, this system records data taken by six sensors. Records measured in this way cover the rooms in which the collections of manuscripts and rare printed books are kept, or delivered to and used by readers.

I would like to demonstrate the state of the inside microclimate of the storage space, as it follows from the graph of temperature and relative humidity values, recorded during the month of April in two of the so-called safe deposit rooms. In the first place, I will mention the Safe Deposit Room no.3 . This room is not heated. Its windows facing the North are constantly covered with metal shutters. The curve of relative humidity values gives evidence of its permanent shortage. In this part of the year, the values of relative humidity of this level are characteristic also for the most part of rooms in the Clementinum. To make a comparison, I present here records from the Safe Deposit

Room no.2, adjoining the Room no.3 and thus located in similar conditions. However, the Room no.2 has a humidifier installed. After some regulation, the relative humidity was successfully kept within the range of 55% (+ - 2%). We intend to assure similar conditions also in the other rooms in which the manuscripts, rare printed books, and other historical materials, are stored. Since the rooms are of quite different architectural design, there may be some problems with air circulation. In the future, we would also like to have installed the measuring unit working at the same time as a regulator of the run of the installed humidifiers.

We also measured the light conditions of the reading-room of the Department of Manuscripts and Rare Printed Books, the windows of which are situated to the South. The measured values of light intensity reached over the acceptable limit seven times, amounts of UV radiation were as much as four times higher. Still, in this year, the windows will be covered with films absorbing UV radiation and will be equipped with louvers.

Step-by-step, we intend to arrange also for the climate conditions as mentioned above in the other depository rooms in the Clementinum.

In principle, the resolving of problems concerning the inside microclimate in depositories is aimed not only at stopping further damaging of the individual materials of the collected objects but, if this question is managed successfully, it also represents one of the essential elements of prevention in the care of book collections. Also other activities of conservators in the National Library of the Czech Republic are to be reckoned among the methods of the preventive care.

The question related to microbiology of depositories and the volumes stored there is the first to be solved. For the purpose of control, series of microbiological samples are wiped off in the endangered rooms and then evaluated. On the basis of the results, individual volumes are consequently treated with disinfection agents, or the whole depository rooms are decontaminated.

The complex of preventive activities also includes long-time work in the field of conservation of leather bindings. Conservators in the National Library have been working on these problems since the seventies of this century. In cooperation with the Leather Research Institute, conservation mixtures for the vegetable tanned and the alum thawed leather bindings and parchments were developed and tested. These mixtures were then used for treating the selected sets of volumes. Further research and work in this field still continue. The Conservation Department of the National Library was even invited to participate in the international project STEP, within the framework of which, particularly, the questions dealing with degradation of leather bindings are solved together with the development of proper conservation mixtures to slow down the process of their aging.
Within the framework of a whole set of activities in the field of protection and care of book collections, a great deal of preventive treatments is represented with transfer of the selected originals to microfilms and other substituting carriers. Thus many of the early works and rare printed books or other historical documents damaged are preserved for the future and kept from further damaging. The most exacting form of the transfer, which is, however, of high quality, is represented by a transfer of the original on to a CD-ROM by means of digitization. There is the project of digitization of mediaeval illuminated manuscripts worked out in the National Library. Some of these manuscripts have already been transferred, some are under realization.

The third step is represented by doing away with the already existing damages of materials in the collection. Above all, it is the work for restorers and the staff of the bookbinding workshop.

Classical restoration methods are used for treating individual selected rare volumes or items. At the same time, a system of minor ambulant treatings of the damaged books has been prepared, as well as the so-called "boxing program". Within the framework of this program, volumes will be placed in protective boxes made of non-acidic paper-board, which will keep them from further damaging. At the same time, the authentic character of the volume will be preserved and its condition will be stabilized. The decision concerning the best way of treatment or protection of each individual volume for its preservation for the future should be made systematically, and a survey of conditions of the most precious and most endangered volumes in the National Library collections, which is in preparation, should also contribute towards this.

Briefly, this is all the problems and activities which have been recently, or are at present, realized in the National Library of the Czech Republic in the field of care of book collections. It is really positive that the efforts to improve the physical state of the collections are well supported. It must be said that all who are responsible for these collections have, in principle, a common work objective - to preserve the book collections for the future generations as historical objects of cultural as well as an artistic value, as an important source of information as a document. It is of no importance that a librarian is in charge of the book in terms of its content, while a conservator and restorer are responsible for its physical state and appearance, *i.e.*, for an object made of various materials, of different age and inner condition. Sometimes, much more time is spent with a permanent defending of a sense of the activity than with the work itself.

PERMANENT PAPER IN SLOVAKIA: ITS PRODUCTION, PROPERTIES AND USE

Jozef HANUS, Emília HANUSOVÁ, and Jarmila MINÁRIKOVÁ

National Archives of the Slovak Republic

University Library, Bratislava (Slovak Republic)

INTRODUCTION

"Time bomb" as it is usually called, the limited lifetime of machine-made paper with acid rosin sizing produced since the mid 19th century has been threatening the greater part of the cultural paper heritage of human civilization. Problems of acid paper degradation are well-known to the experts and have been well-documented by a large number of scientific, research and other publications, conferences, seminars, etc. Also, some commercial papers from the production of several paper mills in the Czech and Slovak Republics were thoroughly tested from this point of view.[1 2 3 4]

It is very obvious that the use of permanent paper for documents, books, etc., is the best way to preserve the cultural heritage of today for the future.

The North Slovakian Pulp and Paper Mills (Severoslovenské celulózky a papierne Ruomberok), the largest papermaker in the Slovak Republic, took its present form when two individual mills combined. These were the Solo mill, established in 1880, and the Supra mill, established in 1906. Both mills began modernization programmes in the late 1970s (Board Machine no. 2 and Paper Machines, no. 6, 7). All wood-free graphic papers produced by these paper machines are sized by AKD and filled with calcium carbonate at present.

At the beginning of the 1980s, both sulphite pulp mills (in Solo and Supra) and one obsolete sulphate pulp mill (Supra) were shut down. In 1981, a new kraft pulp mill was started up. It has a capacity of 200,000 tons per year of hardwood and softwood pulp, of which 156,000 tons are bleached. The pulp mill was supplied by the Canadian Company H.A. Simons (Overseas) Ltd., Vancouver.

In 1991, Paper Machine no. 8, supplied by Voith St. Pölten (Austria), was put into operation. It has a yearly capacity of 100,000 tons of wood-free printing and writing paper. The working width of the machine is 6,550 mm and maximum working speed is up to 1,000 metres/minute. PM no. 8 and the pulp mill form the third mill called Celpap. The entire production of PM no. 8 is sized with AKD and filled with calcium carbonate.

Most of Celpap papers were tested in laboratories of the National Archives of the Slovak Republic in Bratislava for their permanence and durability.[5]

The following paper provides some of our results from this point of view. In order to compare their permanence, some results of acid paper tests are shown as well.

MATERIAL AND METHODS

Paper samples

All alkaline samples - Xerox (XE), laser (LA), offset (OF) and writing paper (WP) - were produced on PM no. 8.

Writing paper was manufactured from softwood (32%) and hardwood (46%) sulphate pulps. It was sized by alkylketene dimer sizing agent Aquapel 127 (2.4%) and by starch (3.7%) on surface. It was filled by calcium carbonate (20%). Its basis weight was equal to 70 $g.m^{-2}$.

On the other hand, writing paper 1 (WP1) and book paper (BP) were manufactured from sulphate pulps, however, with acid sizing agent Furtin 3N and aluminium sulphate, filled with china clay in the same paper mill in 1985.

Composition of the papers used in tests is shown in *Table 1.*

Table 1 **Composition of tested papers**

[%]	WP	LA	OF	XE	WP1	BP
Softwood sulphate pulp	31.0	34.5	33.2	31.0	42.3	32.6
Hardwood sulphate pulp	42.9	43.0	43.1	46.3	25.3	32.6
$CaCO_3$	20.0	17.0	18.0	17.0	-	-
China clay	-	-	-	-	26.1	28.7
<u>Sizing agent</u>						
Aquapel	2.4	2.0	2.0	2.0	-	-
Starch	3.7	3.5	3.7	3.7	-	-
Furtin 3N	-	-	-	-	1.5	1.9
Aluminium sulphate	-	-	-	-	4.8	4.2
Basis weight [$g.m^{-2}$]	70	70	80	80	70	100

ISO 9706

Strength properties - Tearing resistance

Tearing resistance tests were performed on an Elmendorf Testing Machine according to ISO 1974 on samples cut in the machine and cross direction (MD, CD).

Alkali reserve

Alkali reserve of samples was determined as specified in Finnish Standard SFS 4465, as preparation of ISO 10716 for determination of alkali reserve has not been finished till the time of our investigation.

Resistance to oxidation

This was measured as Kappa number according to ISO 302 with the modification given in Annex A of ISO 9706.

pH measurements

pH was measured by cold extraction method according to ISO 6588.

Accelerated ageing

The accelerated ageing was studied at 103°C in accordance with the Czecho-Slovak Standard_SN 50 0375 in the laboratory drying oven WSU 100 (VEB MLW Labortechnik, Ilmenau) over the period of 24 days. Before testing, the samples were air-conditioned according to the _SN ISO 187.

Folding endurance

The folding endurance of paper defined by Schopper was determined in accordance with _SN 50 0345 on the equipment Doppelfalzgerät, DFP, WEB Werkstoffprüfmaschinen, Leipzig in machine and cross direction at a minimal tension of 7.7 N. It is expressed as number of double folds.

Ageing resistance

S was calculated, in compliance with _SN 50 0375, to be 100 . x_s / x_n; x_n being the value of a particular parameter before, and x_s after the 24-day accelerated ageing and given in %.

Evaluation of results

Results were evaluated by applying of mathematical statistical methods.[6]

RESULTS AND DISCUSSION

ISO 9706

Strength properties - Tearing resistance

For papers of grammage 70 g/m^2 or more, the tearing resistance in any direction (machine - MD and cross - CD) shall be at least 350 mN.

Table 2 **Initial tearing resistance of tested papers**

Tearing resistance [mN]	WP	LA	OF	XE	WP1	BP
MD	505	575	570	640	500	670
CD	645	790	715	720	510	730

No significant difference can be seen among the initial values of tearing resistance of both - alkaline and acid papers. From this point of view, all samples meet the requirements of ISO 9706.

In order to compare ageing resistance of tested papers, we followed their changes of tearing resistance during accelerated ageing at 103°C and at 70°C, 60% relative humidity.

High ageing resistance of alkaline paper to accelerated ageing at 70°C and 60% relative humidity was confirmed very clearly. The samples retained 88 - 98% of their original tearing resistance value after 24 days of ageing (*Table 3*).

Table 3 **Ageing resistance of permanent paper (70°C, 60%RH)**

		WP		LA		OF		XE	
		MD	CD	MD	CD	MD	CD	MD	CD
Tearing Resistance [mN]	[0 days]	505	645	575	790	570	715	640	720
	[24 days]	480	635	500	640	550	690	565	680
Ageing resistance	[%]	**95.0**	**98.4**	**87.0**	**81.0**	**96.5**	**96.5**	**88.3**	**94.4**

Alkaline papers produced on PM no. 8 also retained 77 - 95% of their original tearing resistance value after 24 days of dry ageing. On the other hand, acid samples, despite the similar initial values of tearing resistance to alkaline paper, retained only 37 - 41% of their original value (*Figure 1*). Also statistical evaluation showed significant difference between the course of alkaline samples tearing resistance and acid samples tearing resistance during accelerated ageing.

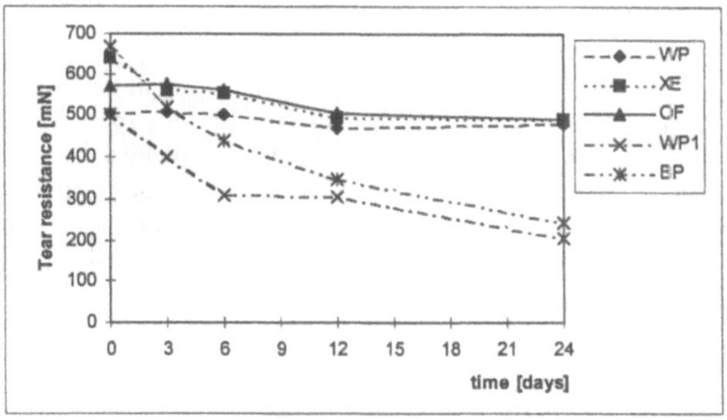

Figure 1 **Changes of tearing resistance during accelerated ageing at 103°C of the alkaline samples: writing paper (WP), laser (LA), offset (OF), and Xerox (XE).**

Alkali reserve

Despite the Note 3, ISO 9706 "when calcium carbonate is used to create the alkali reserve, the requirement is met if the paper contains about 20 g of $CaCO_3$ per kg of paper", we also determined alkali reserve according to Finnish Standard SFS 4465 as ISO 10716 had not been finished till the time of our measurements. The initial values, as well as changes of alkaline reserve for alkaline samples during accelerated ageing at 103°C and 70°C, 60% RH, together with ageing resistance values, are provided in *Table 4*.

In all samples, the values for alkaline reserve recommended by ISO 9706 are highly exceeded.

There is no alkaline reserve in acid samples of book and writing paper 1.

Table 4 **Changes of alkaline reserve [%] during accelerated ageing**

Accelerated ageing [days]	WP		LA		OF		XE	
	103°C	70°/60%	103°C	70°/60%	103°C	70°/60%	103°C	70°/60%
0	18.1	18.1	16.4	16.4	17.6	17.6	13.0	13.0
3	16.3	15.2	14.1	13.3	15.1	14.6	11.4	10.1
6	15.8	15.0	14.7	13.9	15.5	14.2	11.5	10.3
12	16.4	15.0	14.7	12.7	15.9	14.6	11.2	10.3
24	16.8	15.6	14.7	13.3	15.8	14.5	11.4	10.2
Ageing resist. [%]	**92.8**	**86.2**	**89.6**	**81.1**	**89.8**	**82.4**	**87.7**	**78.5**

pH values of aqueous extract

pH readings of tested samples are provided in *Table 5*. It can be seen from the results that the changes in acid papers differ only very slightly, however all the values are within a range which is very dangerous and unacceptable for long-life of paper. On the other hand, the decreased values in pH of alkaline paper could be explained by the influence of acid atmosphere which has been buffered by alkaline reserve of paper. Despite accelerated ageing over the period of 24 days, the final pH of alkaline paper is high enough to be considered as sufficient from the point of long-term storage of this paper and to meet the requirement of ISO 9706.

Table 5 **Changes of pH during accelerated ageing**

Accelerated ageing [days]	WP 103°C	LA 103°C	OF 103°C	XE 103°C	WP1 103°C	BP 103°C
0	9.3	9.3	9.3	9.3	4.8	4.7
3	9.0	9.1	9.0	9.0	4.7	4.7
6	9.0	9.0	9.0	9.0	4.7	4.6
12	8.9	9.1	9.1	9.0	4.6	4.6
24	8.4	8.3	8.3	8.2	4.6	4.6
Accelerated ageing at 70°C, 60% relative humidity						
0	9.3	9.3	9.3	9.3	4.8	4.7
3	8.9	8.9	8.8	8.7	4.6	4.6
6	9.1	9.1	9.0	8.9	4.6	4.6
12	9.2	9.2	9.1	9.1	4.5	4.5
24	9.3	9.3	9.3	9.3	4.5	4.5

Statement and symbol of compliance

As the quality of tested alkaline paper meets the requirements of ISO, it is also marked with the symbol of compliance with this standard. The symbol is one-side multiprinted by white Bianco Acquagem HSL/B, BASF and looks as follows:-

SCP Ruomberok

∞

ISO 9706

Folding endurance

Despite the fact that folding endurance has not been included in ISO 9706 as a property to be tested or recommended, its measuring is widespread in paper testing. The reason is the fact that folding endurance is very sensitive to paper ageing and is changed more rapidly during ageing process than other mechanical or chemical properties.[7]

The course of folding endurance changes during accelerated ageing at 103°C in MD and CD is shown in *Figures 2, 3*.

The difference between alkaline and acid papers is very significant and clearly demonstrates superiority of alkaline paper from this point of view.

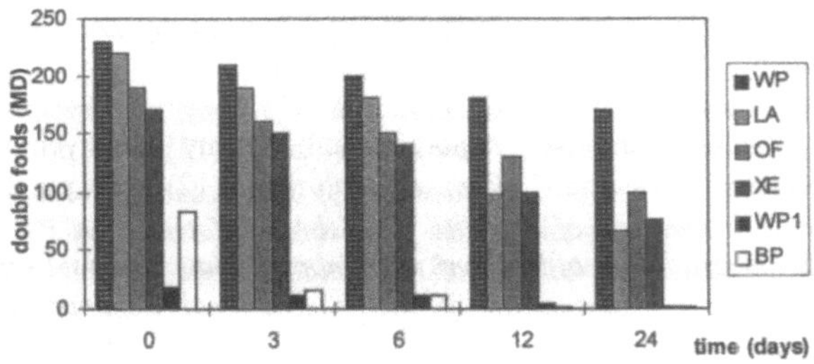

Figure 2 **Changes of folding endurance during accelerated ageing at 103°C (MD)**

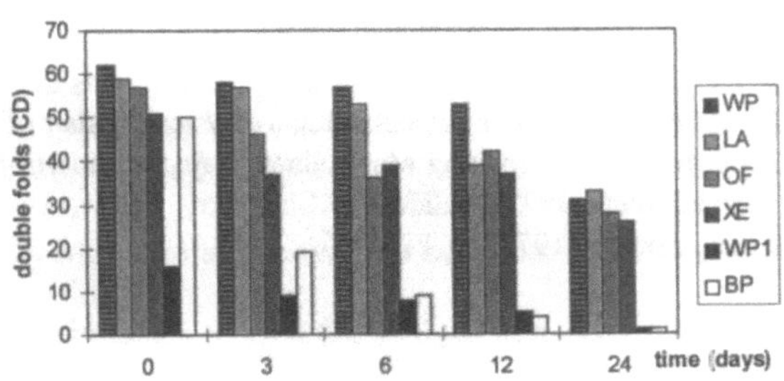

Figure 3 **Changes of folding endurance during accelerated ageing at 103°C (CD)**

Evaluation of alkaline paper ageing

Alkaline paper produced by the North Slovakian Pulp and Paper Mill in Ru_omberok was thoroughly tested in laboratories of the National Archives of the Slovak Republic in Bratislava for permanence and durability. On the basis of the results, it can be stated that this paper meets the requirements of ISO 9706 for permanence, its ageing resistance is very high, and its properties are suitable for documents destined for keeping and long-lasting storage.

REFERENCES

1. Hanus, J. *Stúdium starnutia papiera z h_adiska ochrany archívnych dokumentov. Kandidátska dizerta_ná práca.* CHTF SVST Bratislava 1987.

2. Krkoska, P. and J. Hanus. "Description of Paper Ageing by Zero-Span Tensile Strength", *Cellulose Chemistry and Technology*, 22 (6) 633 (1988).

3. Hanus, J., P.Krkoska and M. Komorníková. "Zmeny optických vlastností niektorých papierov pri urýchlenom starnutí", *Papir a Celulóza*, 43 (12) 1988, pp. 251-253.

4. Hanus, J., ed. *Degradation of Archives and Library Materials vs Permanent and Durable Paper for Archives. Proceedings of the International Seminar, SNA Bratislava 22.-23.4.1993.*

5. Hanus J. and J. Mináriková. *Stúdium stálosti a trvanlivosti niektorých druhov papiera z produkcie Severoslovenských celulózok a papierní v Ru_omberku. Záverecná výskumná práca.* SNA Bratislava 1993.

6. Hanus, J. and M. Komorníková. "The Application of Statistical Analysis in Evaluation of Changes in Some Properties of Aged Papers", *Archives et Bibliothèques de Belgique*, 1/2, 1987, pp. 161-182.

7. Browning, B.L. "The Application of Chemical and Physical Tests in Estimating the Potential Permanence of Paper and Papermaking Materials", in: *Preservation of Paper and Textiles of Historic and Artistic Value.* (Advances in Chemistry Series, 164) Washington, D.C.: American Chemical Society, 1977, pp. 275-285.

DEVELOPING OF A COMPUTERIZED INFORMATION SYSTEM ON CONSERVATION AND PRESERVATION

Victor ZAKHAROV

Library of the Russian Academy of Sciences (Russia)

Restoration and conservation of library collections is a new area of science and culture. It is a multi-disciplinary problem which has appeared on the cross-roads of chemistry, physics, microbiology, entomology, *etc*.

Informational support (IS) of this problem has its special features as follows:-
1) The problem of selecting the sources of information, its scarcity.
2) Unstable system of terminology.
3) Facts-based information plays a considerable role.
4) There are some specific tasks related with both IS and proper preservation problems (for example, the creating of electronic images of real pictures).

Two years ago we started development of a complex information system based on several interrelated databases. This system should provide informational support for investigations which are carried out at the Library of the Russian Academy of Sciences (BAN) in the field of conservation and preservation.

The database and system of knowledge on preventive conservation of library materials must be a system which includes at least three subsystems:-
- Documental bibliographical system of scientific and technical information on conservation and restoration;
- Factographical database on condition of the books and environment in the book storages;
- Expert system which should describe an intellectual retrieval system for specialists in conservation and restoration.

This work is currently being done according to the State programme "Federal Fund for Science and Technology". It is being carried out by a small team of specialists of the Department of Document Conservation, the Laboratory of Biological Protection, and the Automation Department.

I would like to list briefly what is being done and has been done at BAN at the moment.

1) The basic sources of information to form the database have been defined. The feature of these systems is that the sources of information are extremely dispersed.
   We are planning to include the research of bibliographical citations based on the electronic edition of *Science Citation Index*.

2) The bibliographical information retrieval system on conservation and preservation is being tested. This database includes the well-known bibliography written by G. Cunha and at the moment it consists of more than 10,000 bibliographical records.

3) The full-text documents of total volume of 2 Mbytes have been input. They include texts in Russian and English. The papers and developments published by the Library staff are an important part of these materials. The full-text database is being developed using a software package called "AGAMA". This system belongs to the new generation of the Information and Research facilities. At present, it seems to be the only system for these (full-text) documents on IBM-compatible computers which has the wide range of means for morphological analysis and grammar normalization both in Russian and English.

4) The model thesaurus for information retrieval has been developed and put in experimental operation. In compiling the thesaurus we are using the relationship "Coenus-kind" and some others relevant for this database and semantically relationships. We established the foundation for the descriptive information and searching thesaurus on conservation and preservation. At present, it includes about 2,5 thousand entries grouped in 897 descriptors. This model of thesaurus was used in the experimental operation of the bibliographical database in 1994.

5) The index method for the bibliographical database has been developed. The archive of typical requests is being collected. The requests were indexed on the basis of the subject classification which was developed for the system by an advanced specialist in restoration and conservation of documents, Dr. of Biology, Prof. Yu. P. Nyuksha. We were using the system and developing different linguistic tools for it almost simultaneously, and thus the system started to provide information virtually from the "Zero level".

6) To develop the selection methods for the vocabulary of terms, the frequency vocabularies in this subject area were created. Also the special software was developed to create and use these vocabularies.

7) Besides, some foreign sources of information have been studied. Since December 1993 BAN has connection by e-mail to the database on conservation and restoration at Stanford University Library (USA). Our specialists are involved in scientific discussions on conservation and preservation. The messages of the Conservation Distribution List provide considerable and diverse information to our specialists. They are accumulated in the AGAMA database.

At present, we have started work in another direction. Since all works in conservation and restoration at BAN are to be accounted for and planned, the factographical databases describing the condition of
books in storages have to be created. The first databases of such kind are databases describing the books of the damaged Baer Collection and books of the Collection of Peter the Great. A special computer form is being developed which includes both bibliographical description of rare books and manuscripts and description of an item from the point of view of conservation and restoration.

We can say in conclusion that the system developed at BAN will soon be available for specialists in this field of conservation in St. Petersburg and Russia. At the same time BAN is going to publish an informational bulletin on this topic.

TRAINING OF BOOK CONSERVATORS IN HUNGARY

Beatrix KASTALY

National Széchényi Library (Hungary)

HISTORICAL BACKGROUND AND GENERAL CHARACTERISTICS OF TRAINING

Archives and library conservation in Hungary has been going on since the late fifties at the National Archives and the early sixties at the National Széchényi Library. At present, about 25-30 conservators work in five workshops at archives, some 50 conservators in ten workshops at libraries, and there are about fifteen museums where there are 30 or so conservators having a qualification in paper and book conservation. Besides the public collections, 10-15 freelance book and paper conservators work in Hungary.

Until now, there has not been any full-time training in this field in Hungary. In the late fifties, a course was held at the National Archives providing some basic theoretical knowledge. From the late seventies, some 15-20 conservators have graduated specializing in paper conservation, including book conservation, in the part-time training for object conservation at the Academy of Fine Arts. This was a four-year part-time programme for conservators who had already gained considerable experience during their 5-10 years' work in museums. In 1991, the part-time academic training was increased to five years. In this training programme, there is a three-year general training and a two-year specialization. One of the five fields of specialization is the conservation of paper and leather objects. Besides the museums, there have been about 15 students from libraries and archives who have attended this training programme and have received or will receive M.A. degrees.

The regular training exclusively for book and paper conservation was launched in 1981. By this time, a definite demand was realized for an intermediate professional course in book and paper conservation. At the National Library, the book conservators worked with a bookbinder qualification, and paper conservators at the National Archives and in many museums worked without any professional qualification at that tune. They all had some practical training gained from the older colleagues in their own workshop and as interns in other workshops. It was equally important, however, to train them in both the theoretical and practical fields and to provide them with a professional qualification.

Between 1981 and 1987, five evening courses were launched at the vocational school of applied arts on the initiation of the National Library. The professional training was directed by the conservators of the National Library and the practical lessons were held at its conservation workshops. Drawing and history of art were taught in the school. The exams were organized and the final certification was given by the school as well. In 1990, the National Library gained the right to give examinations and issue certificates, which is why the courses went completely to the Library. By 1993, there were 95 book and paper conservators qualified in six courses. The first three courses lasted two years (660 lessons) and the second three lasted two-and-a-half years (820 lessons). In the first six courses the conservation of paper and books was taught in parallel. The foundation of training was the logical and appropriate arrangement of the theoretical knowledge and that the practical operations were taught in a progression from simple to more difficult ones.

The duration, the number of lessons, and the structure of the seventh course which started in September 1994, have considerably changed. This course will last three years with 1,120 lessons, and will be a higher grade professional course with nation-wide acceptance by the Ministry of Culture and Education. It is divided into two parts, each lasting one-and-a-half years. In the first part the students learn the conservation of flat paper and parchment documents and that of prints and drawings. In the second half they will learn the conservation of books. On the basis of previous experience it was necessary to increase the number of practical lessons. Those who have no bookbinding knowledge have to learn the necessary basic bookbinding in the first half of the course, but outside of it.

In the current course there are 18 participants. II of them work in libraries, 4 in archives, and 3 in museums. 14 students have a qualification in bookbinding and 17 work in a conservation studio or a hand bindery.

PREREQUISITES FOR APPLICATION TO THE PROGRAMME AND THE ENTRANCE EXAMINATIONS

For applying to the Academy of Fine Arts, one must have either a basic qualification in museum conservation or an intermediate one in book and paper conservation, or have had three years of conservation practice. Applicants for the book and paper conservation course must be employed in the conservation or bookbinding department of a collection, and it is preferable to have several years in conservation or hand bookbinding practice. As there are generally two or three times as many applicants as places, entrance examinations are held. In the Academy, this examination includes practical sessions in technology and conservation, drawing and sculpting, a paper on chemistry, and an oral examination on the knowledge of arts and the collections. For entering the book and paper conservation course, the applicants have to write papers on chemistry and the history of the book, there is a practical session on manual abilities in working with paper, and an oral examination on their interest and general knowledge in arts.

COMPOSITION OF THE LESSONS AND THE CONTENT OF TRAINING

In the academic training, the students spend one week monthly at the university and have a two-week practical period every summer devoted to drawing, sculpting, archaeological excavation, and to conservation in their specific area. During the first three years, they have a lot of theoretical subjects both from the humanities, history and the sciences, such as history of civilization, art history, introduction to archaeology and to ethnography, care of monuments, museology, the history and ethics of conservation, chemistry, physics and biology. In connection with conservation and restoration, the students learn about the different technologies of materials, craft methods, and they replicate original objects and technology to get acquainted with the ancient techniques. The programme focuses on the conservation of ceramic and glass objects in the first year and metal objects in the second. The third year is dedicated to the basic conservation of objects made of wood, paper, textile and leather. They also have lessons on the museum environment and the care of objects while handling, storing, exhibiting and transporting them. After this general training, the students can specialize in one of five fields, among them conservation of paper and leather objects. During their specialization in the fourth and fifth years, the students attend lectures on the history of art and technology in their special field and learn ancient techniques of making and decorating paper and leather objects. They learn the basic methods of paper and leather investigation and the examination of the objects. More than one year is dedicated to practicing the conservation methods of paper and leather objects, including both flat and three-dimensional works of art made of paper and parchment, and books in leather- and parchment-bindings.

In the *book and paper conservation course* of the National Library, there are 11 lessons a week divided into two days. Each week there are 4 practical lessons, and the other day there are 4 lessons in professional theory or drawing and 3 lessons in history of art.

Professional theory contains the basic knowledge of general, inorganic and organic chemistry; the science and technology of papers, inks and colors, adhesives, seals, parchment, photographic materials, leather, wood and metals; the testing methods of paper, adhesives, inks and leather. The students learn about physical, chemical and biological deterioration, and the methods of preventive conservation of flat paper, parchment and photographic documents as well as the different types of books. The subjects related to history play a very important role in their training: the lessons in the history of writing, printing and bookmaking techniques; the history of book decoration styles; the history and practice of printmaking and old photographic techniques, and basic knowledge of museums, archives and libraries, together with lessons on the general history of art, amount to about 30% of the total number. The third major area of the professional lessons is conservation theory, which consists of the ethics, the methods and techniques of the conservation and restoration of flat paper and parchment manuscripts, printed paper documents, and books with wooden and paper boards and bound in leather, parchment, paper or cloth.

Most of the practical lessons are held in the three conservation workshops and classrooms of the National Library in one, two or three groups depending on the nature of the actual practical lesson. Outside the Library, a hand paper mill, a paper factory, a leather factory, a museum conservation studio for prints and drawings, and the store-rooms of public collections, can be mentioned where the students can see or practice the manufacturing processes and the techniques of printmaking or can make preservation surveys.

In the conservation laboratories and workshops practical lessons are held on the following fields:-

- chemistry and material testing;
- dyeing and mixing cellulose fibers and the techniques of leafcasting;
- traditional and newer methods of mending and strengthening of paper and making enclosures;
- taking photographs of the objects to be conserved;
- writing documentation;
- the techniques of simpler paper-marbling;
- the possibilities and limits of fixing inks and colors;
- cleaning and disinfection of paper and parchment the removal of old adhesives and stains, and the processes of bleaching, deacidification and drying of paper;
- basic operations and techniques of the conservation of parchment manuscripts;
- preparing models of historical endpapers, sewing types, headbands and board attaching to the textblocks;
- making a half-leather binding;

- techniques of the different types of parchment bindings.

Besides these practical lessons, which aim first of all at the learning of the different techniques, the students have to accomplish conservation tasks based on the techniques they have already learned. These tasks are progressively more and more difficult and complex.

The sequence of these conservation tasks is as follows:-
- flat, printed paper documents such as placards, maps, newspapers, thin booklets, mourning cards, playbills, charters of guilds, *etc.*;
- paper manuscripts, manuscript maps and archival plans; simpler cases of prints and drawings;
- fragments of vellum/parchment manuscripts;
- the conservation repair of damaged cloth-, paper-, leather- and parchment-bindings;
- the complete conservation/restoration of a book in either leather- or parchment-binding.

At first they test the materials, take photographs, and make a description for documentation on all types of documents to be conserved.

The aims of the *drawing lessons* at the book and paper conservation course are to make the conservators able, among other things, to:-
- bring out the characteristic forms of the objects in connection with the functions; distinguish the different colors regarding their shades, tones and intensity, and produce the shades of colors needed;
- recognize the connection between the forms and colors in order to use the colors for presenting the objects;
- bring out the materiality of different surfaces;
- recognize and apply various drawing and painting techniques in making replicas and retouching.

WAYS OF ASSESSMENT AND THE EXAMINATIONS

At the Academy of Fine Arts, students are asked to prepare essays on a subject and deliver a lecture during the semester. At the end of each semester, there are oral examinations. The individual conservation work done in each semester is accompanied by an essay and a written documentation report, as well as an illustrated oral report. The conservation works are evaluated by a group of conservators. The training ends with a diploma project. Objects representing serious conservation problems are chosen from a collection, preferably where the student works. The documentation of their conservation work is a detailed M.A. thesis. At the end of their training, students hold an exhibition of their M.A. project works and give lectures on them to an invited audience. On the same day, they are examined in the field of art history, history of technology, material science and investigation, as well as in conservation-restoration in their specially fields.

In the book and paper conservation course, there are also different ways of assessment: papers on chemistry, material science, and conservation processes, written during the terms; oral examinations on the history of art and the book and on certain parts of conservation theory; the assessment of technical and conservation works and the drawings at the end of each term. The assessment of the technical and conservation works is done by a group of conservators and the results are discussed with the students.

For the final examination, the students have to prepare a diploma work in flat paper or parchment and book conservation. While preparing these works, they have to solve at least five conservation problems on each object and have to make a detailed written documentation with drawings and photographs. They have to present the conservation of their diploma work in a public lecture and have to defend it. There is a final written examination on material and conservation sciences, and oral examinations on the history of art and on the history of the book in its every aspect (writing, printing, binding, styles of decoration). We generally hold exhibitions of the works of the students made during the course and for the final examination.

Bei Fragen zur Produktsicherheit wenden Sie sich bitte an:
If you have any questions regarding product safety,
please contact:

Walter de Gruyter GmbH
Genthiner Straße 13
10785 Berlin
productsafety@degruyterbrill.com